Contemporary Fiction and Climate Uncertainty

Environmental Cultures Series

Series Editors:
Greg Garrard, University of British Columbia, Canada
Richard Kerridge, Bath Spa University

Editorial Board:
Franca Bellarsi, Université Libre de Bruxelles, Belgium
Mandy Bloomfield, Plymouth University, UK
Lily Chen, Shanghai Normal University, China
Christa Grewe-Volpp, University of Mannheim, Germany
Stephanie LeMenager, University of Oregon, USA
Timothy Morton, Rice University, USA
Pablo Mukherjee, University of Warwick, UK

Bloomsbury's *Environmental Cultures* series makes available to students and scholars at all levels the latest cutting-edge research on the diverse ways in which culture has responded to the age of environmental crisis. Publishing ambitious and innovative literary ecocriticism that crosses disciplines, national boundaries, and media, books in the series explore and test the challenges of ecocriticism to conventional forms of cultural study.

Titles Available:
Bodies of Water, Astrida Neimanis
Cities and Wetlands, Rod Giblett
Civil Rights and the Environment in African-American Literature, 1895–1941, John Claborn
Climate Change Scepticism, Greg Garrard, George Handley, Axel Goodbody, Stephanie Posthumus
Climate Crisis and the 21st-Century British Novel, Astrid Bracke
Colonialism, Culture, Whales, Graham Huggan
Ecocriticism and Italy, Serenella Iovino
Fuel, Heidi C. M. Scott

Literature as Cultural Ecology, Hubert Zapf
Nerd Ecology, Anthony Lioi
The New Nature Writing, Jos Smith
The New Poetics of Climate Change, Matthew Griffiths
This Contentious Storm, Jennifer Mae Hamilton
Ecospectrality, Laura A. White
Teaching Environmental Writing, Isabel Galleymore
Radical Animism, Jemma Deer
Cognitive Ecopoetics, Sharon Lattig
Digital Vision and Ecological Aesthetic, Lisa FitzGerald
Weathering Shakespeare, Evelyn O'Malley
Imagining the Plains of Latin America, Axel Pérez Trujillo Diniz
The Living World, Samantha Walton
Reclaiming Romanticism, Kate Rigby
Ecocollapse Fiction and Cultures of Human Extinction, Sarah E. McFarland
Environmental Cultures in Soviet East Europe, Anna Barcz

Forthcoming Titles:
Ecocriticism and Turkey, Meliz Ergin
New Forms of Environmental Writing, Timothy C. Baker
Reading Underwater Wreckage, Killian Quigley
Climate Fiction, John Thieme

Contemporary Fiction and Climate Uncertainty

Narrating Unstable Futures

Marco Caracciolo

BLOOMSBURY ACADEMIC
LONDON • NEW YORK • OXFORD • NEW DELHI • SYDNEY

BLOOMSBURY ACADEMIC
Bloomsbury Publishing Plc
50 Bedford Square, London, WC1B 3DP, UK
1385 Broadway, New York, NY 10018, USA
29 Earlsfort Terrace, Dublin 2, Ireland

BLOOMSBURY, BLOOMSBURY ACADEMIC and the Diana logo are
trademarks of Bloomsbury Publishing Plc

First published in Great Britain 2022
This paperback edition published 2023

Copyright © Marco Caracciolo, 2022

Marco Caracciolo has asserted his right under the Copyright, Designs and
Patents Act, 1988, to be identified as the Author of this work.

Cover design: Rebecca Heselton
Cover image © Paolino Massimiliano Manuel / Alamy Stock Photo

The Preface on pp. ix–x constitutes an extension of this copyright page.

This work is published open access subject to a Creative Commons Attribution
Non-Commercial-No Derivatives 3.0 licence (CC BY-NC-ND 3.0,
https://creativecommons.org/ licenses/by-nc-nd/3.0/).
You may re-use, distribute, and reproduce this work in any medium for
non-commercial purposes, provided you give attribution to the copyright
holder and the publisher and provide a link to the Creative Commons licence.

This book is available as open access through the Bloomsbury Open programme and
is available on www.bloomsburycollections.com.

This project has received funding from the European Research Council (ERC)
under the European Union's Horizon 2020 research and innovation programme
(grant agreement n° 714166).

Bloomsbury Publishing Plc does not have any control over, or responsibility for, any
third-party websites referred to or in this book. All internet addresses given in this
book were correct at the time of going to press. The author and publisher regret any
inconvenience caused if addresses have changed or sites have ceased to exist, but
can accept no responsibility for any such changes.

A catalogue record for this book is available from the British Library.

A catalog record for this book is available from the Library of Congress.

ISBN: HB: 978-1-3502-3389-8
PB: 978-1-3502-3393-5
ePDF: 978-1-3502-3390-4
eBook: 978-1-3502-3391-1

Series: Environmental Cultures

Typeset by Newgen KnowledgeWorks Pvt. Ltd., Chennai, India

To find out more about our authors and books visit www.bloomsbury.com
and sign up for our newsletters.

Contents

List of Figures	viii
Preface	ix
Introduction	1
1 Uncertainty in the Future Tense	25
2 Pathways to Unstable Worlds	59
3 Strange Animals and Metonymic Mysteries	89
4 The Meta and the Uncertain	107
5 Deus Ex Algorithmo	133
6 Ecologies of Interactive Narrative	155
Coda: Weathering Uncertainty, with Jenny Offill	183
References	191
Index	207

Figures

2.1 Two pages from Richard McGuire's *Here* (2014). Copyright © 2014, Richard McGuire, used by permission of The Wylie Agency (UK) Limited   62
2.2 The Shimmer in Alex Garland's *Annihilation* (2018)   70
4.1 The reader's relocation from the real world to a storyworld. Adapted from Dannenberg (2008: 24). Reproduced by permission of the University of Nebraska Press. Copyright 2008 by the Board of Regents of the University of Nebraska   111
4.2 A visualization of the structure of Mitchell's *Cloud Atlas* (Mitchell 2004). Author's creation   115
4.3 Two pages from *Diary of a Bad Year* (Coetzee 2008), showing the typographical subdivision into three levels   122
6.1 A key moment of ontological interactivity at the end of season 1 of *The Walking Dead* (Telltale Games 2012)   160
6.2 The layout of the grove scene in Act IV of *Kentucky Route Zero* (Cardboard Computer 2020), with two columns of text unfolding in parallel and reflecting the perspectives of Cate (left-hand column) and Ezra (right-hand column)   168
6.3 The game's characters commemorate the death of two horses in the flood, in the final act of *Kentucky Route Zero* (Cardboard Computer 2020)   171
6.4 Decoding the Ancient language in *Heaven's Vault* (Inkle 2019)   173
6.5 Aliya chooses between vaulting and staying in the nebula, in the final scene of *Heaven's Vault* (Inkle 2019)   176

Preface

A simple Google Ngram Viewer search shows that the use of the word "uncertainty" in English-language publications remained relatively stable from 1800 to the late 1950s but has since then increased to roughly double the frequency of 1950. The Ngram search coverage only goes up until 2019 (as of October 2021), but one can be reasonably sure that 2020 and 2021 will see another bump in frequency. With the Covid-19 pandemic raging in much of the world (and its economic impact felt even where it doesn't rage), uncertainty has become a household word and daily experience for many. This book is about how literary narrative may play a role in making uncertainty more tangible and more manageable in psychological and ethical terms. The form of uncertainty I write about stems from today's ecological crisis. More precisely, it concerns the way in which our collective imagination of the future is destabilized by climate change, ocean acidification, and many other environmental threats that are the result of capitalist exploitation of the nonhuman world. Humanity hangs in the balance between what scientists refer to as "pessimistic" and "optimistic" scenarios, generating unprecedented uncertainty. In that respect, this book has a great deal in common with my *Narrating the Mesh* (2021) and *Slow Narrative and Nonhuman Materialities* (2022). This "trilogy" grows out of a project known by the acronym NARMESH and funded by the European Research Council. While *Narrating the Mesh* foregrounds the formal dimension of narrative's engagement with climate change, *Slow Narrative* explores the ecological and ecocritical value of a particular experience of narrative form—namely, the deceleration of readers' attention.

This book builds on both formal and experiential questions but ultimately places the emphasis on the existential: how reading narrative (or engaging with narrative in other media) may train audiences in the *acceptance* or *embrace* of ecological uncertainty as a fundamental dimension of the experience of the present. I use these terms interchangeably despite being aware of their different connotations: acceptance can suggest resignation, while embrace is both more active and more joyful. The exact meaning I have in mind hovers between these conceptual poles: it involves a psychological shift from a negative understanding of uncertainty, in which uncertainty is to be avoided or reduced at all costs, to a more sophisticated, multifaceted understanding, in which uncertainty is shaped by a complex mixture of negative emotions, hopefulness, and critical distance. This argument is pursued through a series of close readings that seek to approach multiple dimensions of the experience of uncertainty.

Like all my recent works, this book would not have existed without regular conversations and exchanges with the core members of the NARMESH team, Susannah Crockford, Kristin Ferebee, Shannon Lambert, Heidi Toivonen, and Gry Ulstein. Our dialogue is truly the soul of the book—the rest, as they say, is narratology. I would also like to thank the many colleagues, in Ghent and around the world, who have contributed to the NARMESH project over the years. As always, I am grateful to Wibke Schniedermann for abiding me and my numerous uncertainties.

I have presented chapters from this book at the following gatherings, most of which took place online due to the pandemic: the 2019 American Comparative Literature Association conference (Georgetown University), the 2020 SLSAeu conference on "Anthropocenes" (University of Silesia in Katowice), a workshop on "Narratives and Climate Change" (Open Universiteit, Utrecht, 2020), a panel on "Narrative beyond Story" at the 2021 MLA conference, and a guest lecture hosted by the "Sustainability and the New Human" research group at the University of California, Santa Barbara, in 2021. I would like to thank the organizers of these events (among them Melba Cuddy-Keane and Sowon Park) and my audiences for their insightful feedback. Along with Shannon Lambert, three anonymous reviewers for Bloomsbury provided helpful comments on the manuscript. A version of Chapter 3 first appeared in *Green Letters* in 2020. Chapter 5 is based on my article "Deus Ex Algorithmo: Narrative Form, Computation, and the Fate of the World in David Mitchell's *Ghostwritten* and Richard Powers's *The Overstory*," *Contemporary Literature* 60, no. 1 (2019): 47–71 (© 2019 by the Board of Regents of the University of Wisconsin System. Reprinted in this book by permission of the University of Wisconsin Press. All reprint rights belong to the University of Wisconsin Press). The European Research Council made Open Access publication possible under the European Union's Horizon 2020 research and innovation program (grant agreement no. 714166).

Introduction

In recent memory, there was never a better time to write about uncertainty. As of October 2021, much of the world remains in the throes of the Covid-19 pandemic. While the vaccination campaign provides much-needed respite from the worst effects of the virus, the rise of increasingly contagious variants of SARS-CoV-2 and the unevenness of the vaccines' global distribution suggest that the end of the pandemic may still be far away. Around the world, the pandemic has profoundly undermined what sociologist Anthony Giddens discusses under the heading of "ontological security": "the confidence that most human beings have in the continuity of their self-identity and in the constancy of the surrounding social and material environments of action" (1990: 92). This is particularly true in the Global North, whose faith in the "business as usual"—based on consolidated wealth and privilege—was dramatically shaken by the virus, tearing the fabric of societies' day-to-day existence. These are, then, deeply uncertain times.

But there is another outbreak taking place alongside the viral one: a far less deadly outbreak, to be sure, but one that still holds considerable significance for social animals like us. It is an explosion of narratives—in the news or social media, on videoconferencing platforms, or on the phone, soon enough in books of fiction and nonfiction. These narratives are in their own way circulating, spreading, and mutating, some of them becoming "viral," to use a clichéd metaphor that smacks of insensitivity at this juncture. And of course these narratives do not come from nowhere: our cultural imagination has been carefully tilled by countless postapocalyptic films, novels, comic books, and video games that offer now eerily resonant images of deserted streets and empty shelves in grocery stores. Any individual instance of narrative is always positioned vis-à-vis other narratives. Whether they do so consciously or not, storytellers tap into a vast cultural repertoire whenever they start narrating. These narratives are being circulated to come to terms with the uncertainty that the pandemic creates: to confront our most nightmarish fears of societal collapse or laugh them away, to make sense of a destabilizing present and imagine a post-Covid-19 future.

The uncertainty I want to address in this book doesn't stem from the virus directly, but narrative is just as central to its negotiation. As the world battens down the hatches to control a deadly pandemic, the ecological crisis may easily slip into the back of one's mind, even for those of us who just a few months ago were keenly aware of the dramatic repercussions of climate change on the Earth's ecosystems. Yet climate change is not going away, and despite frequent talk in the media of nature "taking back" our cities during the lockdowns of 2020, the estimated impact of these public health measures on global warming is startlingly small (see Forster et al. 2020). "Climate change" denotes a number of processes—melting ice caps, rising sea levels, widespread desertification and acidification of the oceans, species extinction—that are bound to have devastating consequences for human communities and nonhuman ecosystems around the globe, if humanity doesn't change its course drastically. The future, from this environmental perspective, looks like a time of enormous upheaval—a projected instability that is only compounded by the shifting nature of our *knowledge* of the possible effects of climate change.

It cannot be stressed enough that, despite the reluctance to act upon current scientific knowledge in some areas of society and policymaking, the anthropogenic nature of climate change is a scientific certainty. Yet the complexity of human societies' entanglement with the climate makes it impossible to predict the consequences of climate change with absolute certainty, a fact that is often used strategically by climate change deniers: differences across scientific models are leveraged, misleadingly, to cast doubt on the existing consensus around the basic science of climate change (Dunlap and McCright 2016). Possible climate futures vary dramatically: they range from local disruptions to species-threatening catastrophe in the most pessimistic scenarios. Even when it does *not* lead to downright denial, the lack of clarity surrounding the consequences of climate change has been shown to be detrimental to climate change mitigation (Lewandowsky et al. 2014): the more uncertainty there is, the more unlikely people are to take action spontaneously; therefore, Lewandowsky et al. argue, the more uncertainty there is, the more we should be worried about the future. From that perspective, uncertainty is a source of deep concern, because it can obstruct action and fuel indifference and even fatalism about the future. But uncertainty can also be difficult (or indeed impossible) to dispel, particularly when the phenomenon we are facing is as complex and multifaceted as climate change. Perhaps, rather than attempting (and failing) to *eliminate* uncertainty, we should learn to coexist with it and make the most of it intellectually and ethically. *Contemporary Fiction and Climate Uncertainty* argues that there are benefits to reframing uncertainty from a lamentable state of not knowing to an existential stance that promotes resilience and critical thinking. The trajectory I have in mind goes from avoidance of uncertainty to accepting and even embracing it as an opportunity for a fundamental reappraisal of society as we know it in the Global North. This book's central argument is that narrative practices have an important part to play in fostering that psychological trajectory.

To understand how, let us take a step back and think about the parallels between the Covid-19 pandemic and climate change. Compared to, say, 9/11, Covid-19 is a slow-moving crisis: it doesn't come in the media-friendly package of a single day's tragic events, but it involves a gradual and abstract crescendo of cases, victims, and vaccination rates over the course of months or even years. This is not quite as slow as the ecological crisis, of course, but it is significantly slower than most other crises that have rocked the Western world since the Second World War.[1] More importantly perhaps, the Covid-19 crisis *feels* slower because it has such a significant impact on the daily lives of millions of individuals: routines and civil liberties are disrupted, our cherished museums, libraries, and cafés are periodically shut down, we are legally and morally obliged to shelter in place and unable to visit friends and relatives. In the locked-down Global North, as we live secluded (and still, by the standards of the developing world, very comfortable) lives at home, time seems to drag on, particularly because there are no certainties as to when—or if—"normalcy" as we have known it before the pandemic will return.

But the virus has even more in common with climate change than its perceived slow pace: it is largely invisible, abstract, and yet pervasive and globally distributed. Covid-19 started in the Chinese city of Wuhan as a result of transspecies crossing (although the exact circumstances of that crossing are still contested). On March 11, 2020, when the World Health Organization declared it a pandemic, the virus had spread to four continents and 114 countries. The outbreak is a result of interconnectedness at multiple levels. The virus itself is a nonhuman agent that replicates by colonizing human and animal bodies. Further, the current outbreak is probably linked to the unethical treatment of animals in China's so-called "wet markets," where multiple species—including wildlife—are kept in captivity, creating ideal conditions for the transspecies leap of viruses (see Myers 2020). Finally, the virus was able to travel so quickly thanks to our hyperconnected, globalized world, where China is merely hours away from Europe and North America. "Patient Zero coughed in China, and this week, California and New York are on lockdown," writes John Thatamanil (2020) in a blog post.

In a very literal sense, there is a vast network of viral transmission that connects all Covid-19 cases, and it is a global network that crisscrosses the human–nonhuman divide both in its origin and in its mechanism of propagation. This too is reminiscent of climate change. As Timothy Morton argues, the "ecological crisis makes us aware of how interdependent everything is" (2010: 30); it reveals, in particular, the inextricable entanglement of human society and nonhuman phenomena that Morton captures by way of the metaphor of the "mesh." Just as the virus, climate change is mostly perceivable in its dramatic effects; it is abstract and geographically distributed: North America's carbon emissions, for instance, contribute to coral bleaching in Australia and the melting of our planet's ice caps. Climate change, like the virus, knows no borders, although developing countries are much more vulnerable to an unstable climate. Again, the comparison is imperfect: there is a great deal we don't know about Covid-19, but its effects are much better understood than those of climate change, because we have extensive evidence from past pandemics and because the outbreak itself is a far more linear affair than the staggeringly complex processes (physical, meteorological, but also sociocultural) that underlie climate change.

All of this is to say that the uncertainty of the outbreak and the uncertainty of our climate future have more in common than one may assume at first, even as the former vastly overshadowed the latter in recent debates. In fact, convincing arguments have been proposed that climate change makes outbreaks like the Covid-19 pandemic more likely through habitat loss and the rapidly decreasing distance between human populations and wildlife (Vidal 2020). One can only hope that the acceptance with which highly restrictive and economically impactful measures have been met in many Western countries as a response to the outbreak may pave the way for more decisive climate change action in the near future.

In this book, however, it is a different kind of acceptance that interests me. Narrative can help us come to grips with an unknowable future, especially when the "ontological security" of our lives (to use again Giddens's phrase) is fundamentally threatened. Climate change raises an unprecedented challenge to our way of life—and to that of all human societies and nonhuman species. I argue that narrative is capable of negotiating the uncertainty of the climate crisis, and part of my agenda in this introduction is to unpack the idea of narrative's "negotiation" of uncertainty by drawing on contemporary theories of narrative. As a literary scholar, I will turn my attention to current narrative practices that use the tools of literary fiction to negotiate uncertainty. Why focus on literature? If many narratives attempt to come to grips with uncertainty, not all of them are equally incisive in doing so. As Hubert Zapf (2001, 2017) has shown, literary texts are an ecological force that can intervene in cultural debates and assumptions surrounding human–nonhuman interconnection. Largely, the effectiveness of this intervention has to do with *form*: a successful negotiation of uncertainty is one that breaks with convention and received ideas, one that hits us with new insight—and this, as I argue in this book, is only possible if the storyteller can find a form that is adequate to channel the crisis at hand.

How does contemporary narrative negotiate uncertainty through form? I approach this question in two steps: in the next section, I discuss what it means for narrative to negotiate cultural topics (including, but not limited to, ecological issues) through form; in the section that follows, I examine uncertainty as a key dimension of the present moment and bring into focus the specific contribution that narrative form makes to our cultural engagement with uncertainty. *Contemporary Fiction and Climate Uncertainty* suggests that literary narrative offers formal tools to cultivate readers' acceptance of uncertainty. This acceptance can, in turn, help steer our collective anxieties toward an embrace of today's ecological predicament and its high ethical stakes. While laying out these ideas in the next pages, I also sketch out the main scholarly debates that this book aims to enter. The final section of the introduction offers a bird's-eye view of the formal devices and interpretive concerns examined by this book's six chapters.

From Narrative Negotiation to Form

The functions of narrative are legion. Sharing stories creates interpersonal bonds, much like grooming in primates. (Think about campfire storytelling and how that ancestral situation can build a sense of community even among strangers.) Stories allow us to make sense of our experiences and memories in both individual and collective terms. (Think about your life and how it is accessible through narratives that you either tell yourself or you have told others.) Stories encode information about our physical environment that is relevant to human communities; they model and regulate social behavior; they affirm and disseminate cultural values; they reinforce or critique widely circulating ideas.[2] In order to understand these functions, we need a robust theory of narrative negotiation—the process, that is, whereby story responds to a certain issue of personal or cultural relevance. Luc Herman and Bart Vervaeck (2017) have formulated such a theory by cross-fertilizing the work of French sociologist Pierre Bourdieu (1990) and Stephen Greenblatt's (1988) New Historicist account of cultural dynamics. The most important takeaway is that storytelling—in general, not just in artistic practices like literary fiction or cinema—involves a double process of circulation and negotiation.

Circulation is fundamentally an act of transmission, something like a children's game of telephone on a cultural scale: someone tells a story, which is then retold a number of times, evolving with each iteration. But circulation is not merely about *complete* stories: schematic forms of story—what Herman and Vervaeck call "templates"—also spread and change over time.[3] Templates include genres (the joke, tragedy, the short story), subgenres such as postapocalyptic fiction or the castaway narrative, various familiar tropes and motifs (the haunted house, the road trip, and so on), and more particularized formal devices (e.g., first-person narration or an evaluative comment addressed to the audience). These narrative elements circulate within the broader context of what Herman and Vervaeck, using Bourdieu's (1990) terminology, call the field of culture. Thus, circulation is both a process of physical transmission through a medium (voice, print, film, a digital platform, etc.) and a more abstract dynamic whereby stories, and their constituent elements, bump into one another within a certain cultural context. Not all of these stories and templates exist on an equal footing, of course: some tend to be more significant or widespread, others have extremely limited currency.

Narrative circulation is inextricable from negotiation, because stories are never disseminated in a value-neutral way: as they circulate, they become entangled with a wide range of cultural issues. To quote from Herman and Vervaeck's article, "This process involves a negotiation in two senses of the word. First, negotiation means coming to terms with cultural topics, some of which may be quite thorny, as a driver might negotiate a (sharp) curve. Second, negotiation indicates that the form, range, and freedom of the circulation is open to a continuous give-and-take" (2017: 613). Negotiation thus involves the imaginative transformation of cultural issues—more often than not, in affective terms, through the emotional effects elicited by story (which range from horror to humor, from compassion to contempt).

As Herman and Vervaeck point out, not all instances of narrative negotiation are equally effective. In effect, the question "Does narrative x constitute a successful negotiation of cultural topic y?" cannot be adjudicated a priori but only through the practice of interpretation. I define interpretation as an attempt to extract the relevance of a story vis-à-vis a background of shared cultural issues.[4] Interpretation may involve any combination of implicit evaluation as we engage with a story, retrospective reflection, and explicit commentary (e.g., in practices like literary criticism). Although the emotional evaluations bound up with the audience's real-time experience of story tend to be less elaborate than post hoc reflections or critical commentary, all these activities are interpretive in nature in that they bring out the relevance of narrative: why it matters and why it is worth engaging with. There is interpretation whenever audience members work out the "stakes" of a story in emotional terms—even if they don't end up discussing them in a scholarly book. Interpretation is an activity that seeks to disclose *what* cultural topics are negotiated by narrative, *in what way*, and also *how effectively*; hence, all of this book's chapters feature interpretation as a cornerstone of my approach to narrative and uncertain futures.

Equally central to understanding narrative negotiation is form. Every narrative has a form that reflects the storyteller's choices, from the macro-level (such as genre) to the microcosm of—for instance—strategies of spatial description or characterization. The field of narrative theory (also known as narratology) has developed a sophisticated metalanguage to describe these formal choices.[5] Nor is "form" merely accessory, like a shell to be discarded to reveal the "content" of narrative. This form–content dualism is a serious misunderstanding of formalist approaches. The kind of formalism I practice in this book, inspired by Caroline Levine's (2015) work, does not operate by erecting barriers between formal strategies, ideological agenda, and cultural context; rather, the aim of my formalist approach is to bring into focus the specific contribution that form makes to narrative meaning and experience. Paying close attention to form steers the audience's interpretation productively and expands the emotional resonance of narrative—its capacity to speak to the ecological crisis and negotiate its profound uncertainty.

As Herman and Vervaeck also argue, form is directly implicated in narrative negotiation: it is only through the intervention of forms, in the broadest sense, that narrative can fruitfully engage with cultural issues and initiate the "give-and-take" theorized by Herman and Vervaeck. This does not mean that a given form will *determine* the result of a negotiation, however, because that process relies on the audience's interpretive input and predispositions.[6] But form is nevertheless an important part of the equation, and my analyses in the following chapters focus on formal features that enable contemporary fictional narrative to negotiate the many unknowns of the ecological crisis: the disruption of temporal linearity and retrospectivity (Chapter 1), spatial devices (Chapter 2), the use of unreadable animal minds (Chapter 3), metalepsis or the blurring of ontological boundaries (Chapter 4), the intervention of a computational "deus ex machina" in a narrative's ending (Chapter 5), and the distinctive possibilities created by interactive storytelling in digital media (Chapter 6).

Throughout the book, the preference will go to forms that experiment with existing templates, based on the assumption that formal innovation (of the kind we find in literature and other artistic narrative practices) is a precondition for the impactful negotiation of cultural topics. Negotiation is, after all, a transformation of existing ideas and tensions within the cultural system—a gesture that calls for a highly sophisticated and self-conscious use of narrative's formal resources. My turning to *literary* narrative in this book reflects an investment in formal experimentation as a source of culturally meaningful and pointed negotiations of uncertainty—an investment that will be shared by many (albeit perhaps not all) literary scholars, and that I hope will be shared by all readers by the end of the book.

Narrative form has particular relevance vis-à-vis the negotiation of ecological issues, as I have argued in *Narrating the Mesh* (Caracciolo 2021). The human relationship with the environment is defined by formal templates. In the medieval doctrine of the "great chain of being" or "scala naturae," for example, humankind's position vis-à-vis the natural world involves a linear hierarchy: human beings are situated at the top of the "chain," second only to God and His angels (Lovejoy 2001). This setup is thought to reflect humanity's intellectual and moral superiority over animals and plants and our right to leverage the Earth's resources; as historian Lynn White puts it in a famous article on the Christian roots of the ecological crisis, "it is God's will that man exploit nature for his proper ends" (1967: 1205). The spatial form of the vertical line ("scala" means "ladder" in Latin) encodes this stance toward the natural world. Equally linear ideas of unrestricted technological progress and economic growth also affirm human mastery, even as they reject the religious metaphysics of the great chain of being.

Importantly, there are other forms that compete with linear models of human–nonhuman relation: circular forms, as for example in the closed cycle of Buddhist rebirth, but also more decentralized forms such as the "mesh" discussed by Morton, which denotes an intricate network of nonhierarchical connections. These spatial forms coexist with linear models in Western culture, but the latter have arguably become dominant with the emergence of modernity. Non-Western cultures often assign a different priority to these forms of human–nonhuman connection; however, it would be an oversimplification to say that linear models are an exclusive feature of Western thinking. (The traditional Buddhist doctrine of reincarnation, for instance, assumes that being reborn as a human being is more desirable than being reborn as an animal, so there is a linear hierarchy within this circular system.) The takeaway is that narrative forms do not exist in a vacuum but are always positioned vis-à-vis the ideological forms that circulate in the field of culture at large, including the forms that regulate human societies' understanding of their place within ecological processes.[7] This consideration begins to explain why narrative form is a helpful tool in negotiating the uncertainty brought into view by climate change.

My approach to narrative form follows in the footsteps of narrative scholars Alexa Weik von Mossner (2017), Erin James (2015), and the other authors whose essays are collected in *Environment and Narrative: New Directions in Econarratology*, coedited by James and Eric Morel (2020).[8] Historically speaking, the field of environmentally oriented literary criticism (or "ecocriticism") has tended to busy itself with literature that stages environmental issues in a fairly straightforward fashion, particularly nature writing à la Annie Dillard and Barry Lopez.[9] Form was not a major concern in this strand of literary scholarship, at least not in any systematic way: ecocritics were attracted to works that resonated directly with their environmental agenda. Early ecocritical work has been followed by what Lawrence Buell (2005: 18–21) calls "second-wave" ecocriticism, which looks beyond nature writing and focuses on the entanglement of nature and human culture within a wider range of literary genres. This second wave is more theoretically informed and builds on fields such as Bruno Latour's (2005) Actor-Network Theory, artificial intelligence, and Ulrich Beck's (1992) sociology, in an attempt to question dualistic conceptions of the nonhuman environment. Buell mentions Katherine Hayles (1999) and Ursula Heise (2008) as influential scholars working within this second-wave paradigm. Despite the stronger theoretical grounding of these ecocritical contributions, however, subject-matter still eclipses form when it comes to the discussion of literary works. The "econarratology" advocated by James seeks to address that gap: it puts form on the agenda of ecocriticism and shows—as I also argue in *Narrating the Mesh*—that formal issues are of prime importance in literature's engagement with human–nonhuman relations.

In many ways, this book can be read as a companion piece to *Narrating the Mesh*, which explores narratological strategies for figuring the entanglement of human societies and the nonhuman world in the age of climate change. Here, I focus on the distinct—but certainly related—problem of how formal strategies may help audiences negotiate the uncertainty of the climate crisis. The emphasis shifts, then, from how narrative models the complexity of the ecological crisis per se to how it may model readers' existential and psychological *stance* on this crisis.

Literature Faces up to the Climate Crisis

A subgenre that has attracted increasing attention in ecocriticism is that of climate fiction—"cli-fi" in short.[10] Coined by journalist Dan Bloom, the term denotes a strand of the contemporary novel that engages with climate change by imagining its catastrophic consequences (the dystopian mode of cli-fi) or by centering on characters who become involved in political or scientific debates surrounding the climate (the realist mode of cli-fi).[11] An example of the former mode is Margaret Atwood's *Oryx and Crake*, while *Flight Behavior* by Barbara Kingsolver and *Solar* by Ian McEwan typify the latter. Most scholars understand cli-fi as fiction that features climate change as an explicit plot element. In that respect, the term "cli-fi" is different from Adam Trexler's (2015) label "Anthropocene fictions." Trexler focuses on literary narrative's engagement with the proposed geological epoch of the "Anthropocene" (Crutzen 2002), which is defined by humanity's lasting impact on the geological record, not only through climate change but also through phenomena such as plastic pollution and large-scale urbanization.[12] The term "Anthropocene fictions" thus casts a broader net than "climate fiction," in that a novel doesn't need to refer to climate change explicitly to address Anthropocene-related issues.

The genre of climate fiction has received a great deal of attention in both ecocriticism and media discourse, with various commentators—especially in environmentally conscious media outlets—arguing that reading fictional narratives promises to raise readers' awareness of the severity of our environmental crisis and inspire pro-environmental action.[13] Climate change, as I argued above, is highly elusive and abstract: perhaps fictional representation can indeed help concretize it. There are, however, reasons to remain skeptical about this direct link between fiction and readers' environmental attitudes. In *Ecocriticism on the Edge*, Timothy Clark (2015: 18–19) offers an incisive critique of this belief in the power of literature. For Clark, the argument that literary reading can play a role in developing solutions to the climate crisis is based on misguided faith in the power of the literary imagination. Certainly, the climate crisis raises important cultural challenges and literature can create awareness of the scale and profound societal implications of climate change. However, Clark asks, "How far does a change in knowledge and imagination entail a change in environmentally destructive modes of life?" (2015: 18). Put otherwise, how does increased awareness of the crisis translate into material and behavioral changes that would overturn the West's consumerist and individualistic way of life? That process of translating the literary imagination into concrete choices and policies is nonlinear at best. Keeping in mind Clark's challenge, I will not assume a straightforward connection between the narrative negotiation of climate change and pro-environmental behavior. My focus is not on how narrative practices can prevent or remedy the ecological crisis per se but on how they may be able to prepare us—ethically and psychologically—to *coexist* with the crisis and the uncertainty it brings in its wake.

Another significant caveat is that representing climate change through plot and character and negotiating climate change through narrative (in the sense of negotiation I articulated above) are entirely different things: merely building a plot around the consequences of climate change does not guarantee a successful or transformative negotiation of climate change as a cultural issue. For that productive negotiation to take place, one needs a sufficiently well-disposed reader—that is, a reader who is already aware of climate change as a disruptive force—and one also needs innovative narrative forms that are able to recast or reimagine the contemporary debate surrounding the ecological crisis.[14] Importantly, neither of those conditions is dependent on climate change being foregrounded or even mentioned by the narrative: following Trexler's example in *Anthropocene Fictions*, the ecological crisis can be brought to bear on narratives that do not qualify as cli-fi in the standard sense. For instance, Cormac McCarthy's postapocalyptic novel *The Road* has been widely read in an ecocritical vein (De Bruyn 2010; Johns-Putra 2019: chap. 2), but the devastation witnessed by the protagonists is never explicitly linked to climate change. Interpretation can bridge the gap between narratives like *The Road* and the ecological crisis, pointing to the significance of their formal devices and exploring their affective relevance to our times.

Ultimately, while contemporary ecocriticism has mostly focused on the representation of the climate crisis, it is through interpretation, and not through mere narrative representation, that cultural meanings are negotiated. This point inspires all of my close readings in the following chapters. Some of my case studies, like Jesse Kellerman's *Controller* and Alexis Wright's *The Swan Book*, are straightforward instances of cli-fi; others (e.g., Ali Smith's *How to Be Both* and J. M. Coetzee's *Diary of a Bad Year*) do not mention climate change at all. Nevertheless, my interpretations seek to show that all these narratives offer insight into the stakes of the climate crisis. It is one particular aspect of the crisis that interests me here, of course: namely, the future uncertainty that it discloses. So-called weird fiction, to which some of my textual examples belong, is particularly well positioned to stage climate-related uncertainty because of how it builds on ontological hesitations and paradoxes (see, e.g., Hegglund 2020).[15] The weird is a hybrid literary mode arising at the intersection of science fiction, horror fiction, and the fantastic (see Luckhurst 2017). David Mitchell's multilinear storytelling on a global stage is similarly attuned to catastrophic gaps in our imagination of the future. This explains why Jeff VanderMeer's weird oeuvre makes regular appearances throughout this book, and why two chapters deal with Mitchell's novels, *Cloud Atlas* (Chapter 4) and *Ghostwritten* (Chapter 5). Both VanderMeer's weird and Mitchell's fantastical plots represent effective negotiations of climate uncertainty, as my close readings detail.

The topic of uncertainty has surfaced in ecocritical discussions of contemporary literature along multiple routes. In *Climate Change and the Contemporary Novel*, Adeline Johns-Putra (2019) addresses the question of posterity in climate fiction, tying it to an ethics of reading inspired mainly by Martha Nussbaum's (2001) work. As Johns-Putra suggests, climate fiction stages the uncertainties of the future by interrogating "parental care as an ethical position" (2019: 9)—the idea, that is, that environmental responsibility involves preserving the world for posterity. Although parenthood is a culturally salient way of thinking about posterity, it frequently dovetails with an anthropocentric, gendered, and heteronormative worldview. Johns-Putra argues that, at its best, climate fiction interrogates this understanding of posterity while developing a biocentric alternative. The uncertainty of climate change is thus cast primarily as an ethical problem, rather than an ontological or epistemological one, with literature becoming a privileged site for ethical reflection (Johns-Putra 2019: 53–5). In *Literature and the Anthropocene* (2020), Pieter Vermeulen takes a different tack. Although Vermeulen's formalist method—convergent with the one I adopt in this book—does not foreground uncertainty per se, his attention to false starts and ruptures in literary engagements with the climate crisis does begin to show that uncertainty may become bound up with formal devices. This is evident, for instance, in Vermeulen's claim that "the self-interrupting dynamic of literary world-making makes it possible to adumbrate the world-without-us in the gaps and cracks between generic and formal templates" (2020: 77). As conventional genres break down, "literary world-making" reaches toward the "world-without-us"—that is, a climate future defined by human extinction.

Vermeulen's world talk introduces an ontological dimension: uncertainty derives from the collapse of fundamental assumptions about the future as the seamless continuation of the world of today, reflecting also, in part, the crisis of parenthood-based notions of posterity discussed by Johns-Putra. These are highly suggestive insights; my engagement with uncertainty draws inspiration from both Johns-Putra's ethics of reading and Vermeulen's exploration of the ontology of literature. Different from both scholars, though, I conceptualize uncertainty as arising from the encounter of formal devices and readers' experience (including, of course, their extratextual experience of the climate crisis). To that experiential dimension of uncertainty—and its multiple dimensions—I turn in the next section.

Probing Uncertainty

The uncertainty of the climate crisis stems from the unprecedented complexity of the current geopolitical moment. While the basic physics of climate change is well understood, the interactions between various planetary parameters and subsystems in a warming climate are difficult to predict with absolute certainty. Here is a quick example: we know that methane is a potent greenhouse gas (more powerful than carbon dioxide, in fact), and that vast amounts of methane are trapped within the Earth's permanently frozen ground or "permafrost." Scientists call these subterranean deposits of methane in solid form a "gas hydrate." Will the thawing of permafrost result in the release of these deposits, which might represent a point of no return for the Earth's climate due to the greenhouse effects of methane? Scientists are still debating that question: a "challenge for the future is determining the contribution of global gas hydrate dissociation to contemporary and future atmospheric CH_4 [i.e., methane] concentrations," concludes a survey article by Carolyn Ruppel (2011). That is just one of the myriad factors that one needs to consider when predicting the consequences of a certain degree of warming.

Moreover, the physical complexity of the Earth system is compounded by the deep uncertainty that surrounds governments' responses to climate change.[16] So far, several rounds of climate change talks have made important steps toward a legally binding agreement to limit greenhouse gas emissions, but the current targets are widely regarded as too low and ineffectual in keeping global warming under control in the long run (see, e.g., Kemp 2018). The US government's decision to withdraw from the Paris Agreement in 2017 is an example of how the political process behind climate change negotiations is fundamentally nonlinear and difficult to forecast with precision. The result of these overlapping complex systems—the Earth's geophysical setup and climate, political decision-making on a local and global stage—is the near-impossibility of knowing what the future will look like. Scientific predictions fail, as Chapter 1 will detail, and that failure risks undermining our ontological security, much like the current Covid-19 crisis, but with even more devastating consequences: while we know that the pandemic will fizzle out eventually, either by itself or thanks to vaccines, climate change is here to stay. The resulting uncertainty is a source of anxiety for at least those of us who are listening to climate scientists. We may wonder whether having children is ethically responsible in the face of an unstable climate and what skills we should be teaching our children—a common concern in the environmental movement.[17] Our way of life in the affluent West is in question: our consumption patterns, our globe-trotting habits, the faith in the ascending trajectories of economic growth and technological development. Crucially, the uncertainty that derives from the collapse or at least the destabilization of these assumptions is ripe for narrative negotiation.

It is time to be more concrete about the narrative negotiation of uncertainty. How can narrative tackle the challenges of an opaque and unstable future? The concern over uncertainty has made its way into contemporary literary studies through Anahid Nersessian's (2013) discussion of "nescience," or not knowing.[18] Nersessian calls for literary-critical practices "capable of moving between what can and what cannot be seen, tracked, or measured" (2013: 308) in the anticipation of environmental catastrophe. For Nersessian, nescience emerges in poetry of the Romantic period in formal terms—it gives rise to a "calamity form," or "an operation performed on language, syntax, and image that may stage a very particular kind of intellectual crisis. This crisis concerns, above all, the unknowability of the future and the uncertain impacts of our actions on it" (2013: 324). Nersessian acknowledges that form has an important part to play in literature's negotiation of uncertainty. However, Nersessian's essay largely avoids engagement with *narrative* form, and for good reason: as the etymological link between the words "narrative" and "knowledge" suggests, narrative as a practice is historically and conceptually complicit in the *reduction* of uncertainty. Story, after all, constitutes one of the most basic means of explaining the world, by creating causal linkage between physical events or by ascribing beliefs and intentions to other human subjects.[19] These narrative practices help create the certainties upon which human communities have long been built: a mythology, a shared language to talk about mental life, and so on.

Yet narrative also has the formal resources to engage with uncertainty.[20] Two scholars in recent times have offered a persuasive case for this. The first is Porter Abbott, whose book *Real Mysteries* (2013) argues that the unknowable can become an engine of narrative, and particularly of readers' *experience* of narrative. I will discuss Abbott's work more extensively in Chapter 3, where I explore narratives in which the unknowability of animal minds takes center stage and becomes—in my reading—a metonymic stand-in for the uncertainty of climate futures. The second scholar is Namwali Serpell, whose *Seven Modes of Uncertainty* (2014) foregrounds the ethical dimension of what cannot be known, again with a focus on the reading experience. For Serpell, the experience of uncertainty builds on the tension between readerly estrangement and identification, for example, with the shockingly murderous narrator of Bret Easton Ellis's *American Psycho*. Abbott and Serpell develop useful tools to complement Nersessian's account of nescience, but (unlike Nersessian) they do not address the ecological dimension of uncertainty. For both, uncertainty is an ethical and experiential gap located within the domain of human intersubjectivity. The formal devices they discuss are not calamity forms in Nersessian's sense.

Studying the narrative negotiation of uncertainty in the context of human-nonhuman relations requires a new framework. According to philosophers Richard Bradley and Mareile Drechsler (2014), uncertainty comes in four different flavors. The most elementary one is "empirical uncertainty": what we simply do not know about the world. Are rising global temperatures going to release massive amounts of permafrost methane into the Earth's atmosphere? That is a factual question that we cannot answer yet—hence the empirical uncertainty. "Ethical uncertainty" comes closer to Serpell's discussion. It arises when the desirability of a certain course of action remains unclear, either because we don't have the necessary information at our disposal or because there are conflicting values at play. For instance, in determining a climate change mitigation strategy, one is likely to encounter a tension between anthropocentric and biocentric ways of thinking about the future—that is, respectively, measures that maximize the well-being of human communities and measures that prioritize more-than-human ecologies.[21] That tension may give rise to ethical uncertainty. What Bradley and Drechsler call "option uncertainty" pertains to the link between actions and consequences: sometimes we find ourselves in a situation in which we do not fully understand (or cannot always predict) the consequences of our actions. That is almost always the case with a system as complex as the Earth's climate. Finally, we have "state space uncertainty," which Bradley and Drechsler describe as awareness "of the possibility that [one] may not be aware of all relevant contingencies" (2014: 1245). Again, that is a common experience when dealing with the climate: the factors shaping our climate future are far too numerous for a single person or organization to grasp. This complexity can make us uncomfortably aware of our intellectual and practical limitations.

While Bradley and Drechsler's arguments are mainly directed at the uncertainty faced by policymakers, rather than readers of narrative, their account can help us unpack the idea that climate change destabilizes our thinking about the future: When confronting the climate crisis, empirical and ethical difficulties are compounded by inadequate knowledge of how our choices today can impact future generations—and by the awareness that there are actions that are not being considered (because of short-term thinking in government, corporate greed, sheer force of habit, or for other reasons).

In sum, the uncertainty of climate futures is multilayered and cannot be reduced to lack of empirical knowledge. This point explains why the narrative negotiation of uncertainty, as the close readings in this book will illustrate, can follow multiple trajectories. I suggest breaking down this process of negotiation into four levels, which bridge the gap between textual strategies and narrative's overall imaginative impact on readers. This is what I call the "spectrum of negotiation," the assumption being that a fruitful negotiation will span the full spectrum, from narrative representation to its psychological effects on the audience.

As a first step, climate-related uncertainty can affect the characters that inhabit a narrative's "storyworld" (a metaphor discussed in more detail in Chapter 2). This is a direct mapping of real-world uncertainty onto the dynamics of the characters' minds. While common in climate fiction and present in some of my case studies, this strategy operates at the level of narrative representation rather than form or effect on readers.[22] Moving now to the level of form, real-world uncertainty can be captured through a range of devices that translate structural aspects of the *experience* of uncertainty: the anxious projection into an unknown future (as discussed in Chapter 1), a persistent gap or instability that defines the spatial setup of a storyworld (Chapter 2) or the characters' mental processes (Chapter 3), the blurring of ontological boundaries between what is considered real and what is purely imaginary or fictional (Chapter 4), a desire for emotional closure that only a nonhuman agent can provide (Chapter 5), the foregrounding of state space uncertainty—that is, the uncertainty surrounding the consequences of our choices—in video games that deliberately obfuscate the player's decision-making (Chapter 6). In all of these cases, narrative implements concrete formal strategies that convey features of the *phenomenology* of uncertainty.

However, this formal evocation of uncertainty may only register conceptually and not experientially in the audience. As a third, experiential level of negotiation, uncertainty can be directly elicited in the reader. Narrative, as I will argue in the next chapter, is an inherently "gappy" practice: our emotional investment in stories is driven by facts that we don't know *yet*—typically (but not exclusively) about how the story will end. Yet narrative can also maximize that uncertainty, pushing it to the foreground of the reader's experience through ambiguities and instabilities left unaddressed by the ending. The experience of engaging with narrative thus mirrors, and blends with, the extrinsic (i.e., real-world) opacity of climate change futurity.

Finally, the fourth level falls squarely within the domain of narrative's psychological impact on readers. Creating an experience of uncertainty through characters and formal devices can help the audience *manage* real-world uncertainty: it can put it into perspective and offer affective distance or intellectual insight. The result is an affective reframing of uncertainty: despite being typically seen as undesirable and detrimental to one's well-being, uncertainty is not rejected but cautiously embraced. Clearly, whether readers respond in this way depends on a highly nonlinear interaction of text, context, and individual personality. Many of my readings presuppose an audience that is susceptible to narrative's invitation to embrace uncertainty (instead of dismissing or turning a blind eye to it). This effect is often accompanied by an acceptance of the more-than-human scale of the current ecological crisis, which not only fosters human responsibility toward the nonhuman but also evokes a sense of sharing uncertainty with an entire planetary system.

Ultimately, the fourth level is the endpoint of my discussion—what I think the narrative negotiation of uncertainty can achieve, and the reason narrative form holds particular value in the present moment. In some respects, this embrace of uncertainty ties in with the mental skill that psychologists discuss under the rubric of "resilience." Commonly described as "bouncing back" after a traumatic event (Zolli and Healy 2012), resilience has been widely hailed in policymaking as a desirable response to a crisis—one that should guide behavior on the scale of entire communities. In combination with sustainability, resilience has become one of the key words—some would say buzzwords—of environmental science. The discourse of resilience is not entirely unproblematic, however: two commentators, Brad Evans and Julian Reid (2014), see it as complicit in a neoliberal mindset, particularly as it favors individual over collective action.

While my notion of embracing uncertainty also has its roots in individual psychology through the act of engaging with narrative, it acknowledges that interpreting stories and negotiating uncertainty through them are necessarily collective gestures. Interpretation and negotiation are shaped by social practices, including the media and the educational institutions to which—no doubt—most of this book's readers belong. Embracing uncertainty through narrative involves engagement with collectivity at two levels: it means opening oneself to dialogue within these institutions and facing up to the communal dimension of the ecological crisis itself, where the word "communal" encompasses both human societies and nonhuman life. This embrace of uncertainty can certainly pave the way for resilience in the pragmatic sense of adaptation to changing material conditions.[23] But my emphasis here is on the existential stance that *enables* resilience—the mental and affective resources that are required to transform anxiety at an unstable future into a nuanced appreciation of instability.

To understand how narrative can foster this mental shift we need to take into account the full spectrum of narrative negotiation. Rather than positing a direct link between literary representation and pro-environmental beliefs, as much ecocriticism does, this book argues that the value of literary responses to the ecological crisis lies in their affective impact. By implementing formal devices that channel the experience of uncertainty, literary narrative can model the instability of our climate future in affective terms and potentially deepen the reader's acceptance of its fundamental ambivalence. However, that effect presupposes a reader who is able and willing to pick up on the right cues, paying attention to formal devices and to their significance vis-à-vis the culturally shared horizon of an unstable future.

Put otherwise, I am not claiming that *all* readers of the narratives discussed in this book will come to a stoic acceptance of uncertainty. That construal of my argument downplays the role of interpretation in mediating (or negotiating) the impact of narrative. Storied negotiations are a multilayered process: to prompt an embrace of instability—what Donna Haraway (2016) memorably calls "staying with the trouble"—narratives need to be read and culturally framed in an apposite fashion. That framing is something that requires a concerted effort in contexts like schools, reading groups, the media, and of course literary scholarship. Narratives do not and cannot work miracles: at best, reading a single story can have short-term effects on individual readers, while the kind of negotiation of uncertainty I am interested in requires attention, focused debate, and minds receptive to the affective and material instabilities of the contemporary moment.[24] Those skills and predispositions cannot be imparted by an individual narrative, but they may be gradually shaped by long-term exposure to formally sophisticated stories. The readings offered in the following chapters aim to open up space for considering what stories might be most effective in attuning the audience to the challenges of unstable futurity, and what aspects of those stories we should foreground—in practices like literature education—to cultivate an embrace of uncertainty.

Outline of Chapters

Time, as we know from Paul Ricoeur (1984, 1985, 1988) and many others, is the fundamental dimension of narrative, a practice that works by establishing causal and psychological linkage within temporal experience. It is therefore no coincidence that this book's engagement with uncertainty in Chapter 1 begins with temporality. How can narrative accommodate the specific futurity of what is not known (and its affective experience)? My argument adopts a two-pronged approach to this question: First, I show that climate change unsettles our personal and societal projection into the future; second, I discuss how storytellers can adopt formal devices that mirror that temporal destabilization. I focus on two such devices, each typified by two texts: the future-tense narrative that emerges at the end of Jennifer Egan's short story "Black Box" and Ali Smith's *How to Be Both*; and the implementation of multiple versions of reality (or "parallel storyworlds," as I call them) in Jesse Kellerman's *Controller* and Jeff VanderMeer's *Dead Astronauts*. In developing this argument, I explore how such formal strategies in twenty-first-century fiction differ from those adopted by postmodernist authors, despite some broad similarities.

Chapter 2 shifts from time to the other fundamental parameter of (narrative) experience, spatiality. After a discussion of the narratological concept of "storyworlds," this chapter investigates four motifs through which narrative can figure uncertainty in spatial terms: oscillation, erasure, fragmentation, and floating. These motifs undermine the coherence that is at the core of the world concept, and therefore present readers with an imaginative stand-in for today's climate-related instability. My examples come from a broad range of contemporary novels: the "weird" fiction of China Miéville (*The City & the City*) and Jeff VanderMeer (*Annihilation*), but also Emily St. John Mandel's *Station Eleven*, Mark Danielewski's *House of Leaves*, Jonathan Lethem's *Amnesia Moon*, Dale Pendell's *The Great Bay*, Hanya Yanagihara's *The People in the Trees*, and Michel Faber's *The Book of Strange New Things*. The chapter traces the four tropes of spatial instability within these narratives and examines their affective ramifications for readers' negotiation of the ecological crisis.

After time and space, a storyworld is bound to contain a set of inhabitants—more commonly known as characters. Chapter 3 focuses on the narrative significance of nonhuman characters whose minds remain opaque and impervious to both psychological and symbolic readings. My argument is that these animals—the mischievous foxes of VanderMeer's *The Strange Bird* and the black swans of Alexis Wright's *The Swan Book*—model the unreadability of the future in times of climate change. Further, by integrating these nonhuman figures in their progression, the narratives by VanderMeer and Wright encourage a shift from metaphorical construals of the nonhuman to a metonymic acknowledgment of how the fate of humanity is causally and materially bound up with nonhuman species. As a formal figure of unknowability, these elusive animal minds disrupt empathetic perspective-taking (with its promise of transspecies understanding) in order to cultivate acceptance of ecosystemic processes beyond human control.

One of the central features of the experience of uncertainty is that it troubles the ontological boundary between what is real, what is possible, and what is a mere projection of one's anxieties. This blurring finds a narrative equivalent in metafictional devices, which operate by questioning ontological divides (between the storyworld and everyday reality, or among subdomains of a storyworld). That role of metafiction in contemporary narrative negotiations of uncertainty is the topic of Chapter 4, which draws on debates on ontology in anthropology and narrative theory. The chapter explores two works—*Cloud Atlas* by David Mitchell and *Diary of a Bad Year* by J. M. Coetzee—where the ontological structure of a storyworld breaks down in order to make space for broader questions concerning the default ontology of Western thinking (which rests on binaries such as nature vs. culture, human vs. animal, subject vs. object). Mitchell's playful style is geared toward a postapocalyptic future in which the scientific ontology of the West has been replaced by faith in the transmigration of souls; Coetzee's hybrid essay-novel creates uncertainty by blending the real author with a flawed protagonist who confronts the limitations of his own thinking on the human–animal divide. In both works, metafiction does not lead to inward-looking self-referentiality but encapsulates the hesitations and instabilities generated by the ecological crisis.

Chapter 5 looks at how narrative may attempt to address those hesitations through nonhuman intervention. While the uncertainty of our climate future seems to resist any possibility of closure in human terms, contemporary fiction can create formal closure by invoking the quasi-magical power of algorithms, in a reinterpretation of the classical trope of the "deus ex machina."

This is particularly evident in the endings of my two case studies—Mitchell's first novel, *Ghostwritten*, and Richard Powers's *The Overstory*. The former introduces a supercomputer—the Zookeeper—which determines that the only way of saving the planet is to let go of its human inhabitants; the latter deploys a set of machine-learning algorithms, known as "learners," to bridge the plot and a fundamentally posthuman and deeply ambivalent future. Of course, the resolution brought by these works' computational denouements is partial and colored by uneasiness about the fate of humanity. The affective instability of these endings reveals, like the opaque minds of Chapter 3, the metonymic proximity of human and nonhuman realities, while at the same time shedding light on the utopian valence of computational intelligence in contemporary culture.

That same computational intelligence occupies the foreground of Chapter 6, but in a more literal way. My case studies are two recent interactive fictions in the video game medium: Cardboard Computer's *Kentucky Route Zero* and Inkle's *Heaven's Vault*. Literary language is here deployed in conjunction with a striking audiovisual vocabulary and with the focus on decision-making that defines the game medium. Via a dialogue with different literary genres (respectively, magical realism and science fiction), these story-rich games face players with choices so as to, paradoxically, highlight their lack of control over the unfolding narrative—a formal constraint that serves as the main engine of uncertainty. Both games foreground ecological issues through catastrophic scenarios: a devastating flood in the last act of *Kentucky Route Zero*, an elusive "darkness" that is about to ravage the universe in *Heaven's Vault*. The uncertainty of human–nonhuman entanglement fuses with a pervasive sense of mystery that players are asked to embrace rather than penetrate. Ultimately, the games read (or "play") as experiments in the ethics of decision-making in the midst of an unstable and enigmatic world that eludes human grasp.

Finally, in the coda I return to the intersection between the Covid-19 pandemic and the ecological crisis. I examine a number of internet commentaries on Jenny Offill's climate change–focused novel *Weather* to disclose the affective resonances between climate uncertainty and the outbreak. This discussion allows me to explore empirically what I call "embrace" of uncertainty in this book, also as a way of the pointing to the significant challenges it involves. The successful negotiation of uncertainty through narrative requires a predisposed audience, and educational institutions—I suggest in the coda—have a key role to play in fostering this mindset.

Notes

1. On slowness and the climate crisis, see Rob Nixon's (2011) influential treatment (from a postcolonial perspective).
2. See Scalise Sugiyama (2001) on the evolutionary underpinnings of narrative, Herman (2003) on stories as a tool for sensemaking, Mar and Oatley (2008) on their function in modeling and regulating social behavior.
3. The term "template" comes from Anne Harrington (2008), as Herman and Vervaeck (2017: 609) point out.
4. In a similar vein, Richard Walsh (2007) discusses narrative meaning-making as a process guided by relevance. See also Caracciolo (2016b).
5. Useful introductions to narratology are Herman and Vervaeck (2005) and Fludernik (2009).
6. In narrative theory, this relative independence of formal choices and ideological meanings is known as the "Proteus principle." See Sternberg (1982).
7. This is a central insight in the field of so-called New Formalism, which aims to open up literary form to the extratextual forms of the social world; see Levine (2015) and my own discussion in *Narrating the Mesh* (2021: introduction).
8. See a special issue of *English Studies*, also coedited by James and Morel (2018).
9. For an introduction to ecocriticism, see also Garrard (2004).
10. For a survey of cli-fi, see Trexler and Johns-Putra (2011).
11. In the words of the editors of a recent companion to cli-fi, the term denotes "a distinctive body of cultural work which engages with anthropogenic climate change, exploring the phenomenon not just in terms of setting, but with regard to psychological and social issues, combining fictional plots with meteorological facts, speculation on the future and reflection on the human-nature relationship" (Goodbody and Johns-Putra 2019: 2). See also Bloom's website, http://cli-fi.net/.
12. I will return to the Anthropocene concept, which is the subject of considerable debate in the environmental humanities, in the next chapter.
13. See J. K. Ullrich's (2015) article in *The Atlantic* for an example of this rhetoric: "Stories can never be a solution in themselves, but they have the capacity to inspire action, which is perhaps why cli-fi's appeal among young adult readers holds such promise." For an empirical appraisal of these claims on the influence of climate fiction, see Schneider-Mayerson (2018).
14. The first idea—namely, that climate change fiction is more likely to resonate with readers who are already attuned to the ecological crisis—is supported by Schneider-Mayerson's (2018) empirical study.
15. It is customary to distinguish between the "old weird" à la H. P. Lovecraft and a "new weird" typified by contemporary authors such as Jeff VanderMeer, China Miéville, and Caitlín Rebekah Kiernan. The latter writers avoid Lovecraft's racism

and problematic gender politics and instead confront a number of contemporary issues, including (but not limited to) the ecological crisis. For more on weird fiction's engagement with ecological themes, see Ulstein (2017) and Robertson (2018) as well as the following chapters.

16 The complexity of the ecological crisis is a central focus of *Narrating the Mesh* (Caracciolo 2021), which cross-fertilizes narrative theory and the framework of complexity science.

17 See, for example, David Wallace-Wells's (2018) discussion in the *New York* magazine.

18 For another perspective on literature's confrontation with uncertain futures, see Horn (2018).

19 Philosopher David Velleman (2003) offers a nuanced discussion of narrative explanation. For more on narrative and the ascription of mental states, see Hutto (2008).

20 See also a special issue of *Style* I coedited with Lieven Ameel (Ameel and Caracciolo 2021) for more on ontological uncertainty as a central dimension of literature's engagement with the contemporary moment. The articles in the issue address the climate crisis as one of the many concerns through which the destabilization of ontological security enters contemporary fiction.

21 For more on the distinction between biocentric and anthropocentric reasoning, see Kahn (1999).

22 It is important to acknowledge, though, that form and representation are deeply bound up in narrative. This is part of what Meir Sternberg (1982) dubbed the "Proteus principle": the effects of a particular formal strategy in narrative are always contingent on the representational and ideological subject-matter of a story.

23 See also Bendell: "The initiatives under the resilience banner [in climate science] are nearly all focused on physical adaptation to climate change, rather than considering a wider perspective on psychological resilience" (2018: 22).

24 Building on a series of experimental studies, psychologists Kidd and Castano (2013) have argued that reading literary fiction is beneficial to readers' "theory of mind" skills—their ability to engage with other people's mental states. Kidd and Castano acknowledge that literature's psychological impact may depend on prolonged exposure rather than the reading of a single text: for instance, the authors administered an Author Recognition test to establish the participants' familiarity with literary authors, as an indication of literary competence in general. A more theoretical argument for literature's power to gradually "train" readers can be found in Landy (2012). I will return to this point in this book's coda.

1

Uncertainty in the Future Tense

"Ecological thinking ... remains inseparable from some form of thinking about the future," write Brent Bellamy and Imre Szeman (2014: 192). Exactly what form of future-oriented thinking is called for by the uncertainty of the climate crisis, though? To begin answering this question, we can find some perhaps unlikely inspiration in the financial markets. Weather derivatives are a financial instrument introduced in the 1990s to hedge against the unpredictability of weather conditions (rainfall, temperature, wind, etc.) that might impact a company's operations. If, for example, you own a solar power plant, there might be an advantage in buying weather derivatives as insurance against long stretches of cloudy weather. Discussing the trading of derivatives on global markets, social scientist Melinda Cooper presents the local unpredictability of the weather as an aspect of the much more dramatic fluctuations introduced by climate change. Both weather derivatives and climate change "[demand] a particular kind of relationship to the future, one that might be characterized as speculative, as opposed to predictive, expectation" (Cooper 2010: 178). The shift from prediction to speculation signals a breakdown of statistical probability vis-à-vis a phenomenon that is as nonlinear and multifaceted as climate change: because we cannot predict very far into the future, we start speculating—that is, for Cooper, we start comparing possible scenarios and models rather than focusing on the most probable outcome.[1]

Earth scientists are already struggling with the uncertainty of the planet's future understood at a purely physical level, in terms of rising sea levels, melting ice caps, and acidification of the Earth's oceans. The available models differ vastly, an uncertainty that plays into the hands of climate change skeptics and indirectly contributes to the severity of climate change itself (Lewandowsky et al. 2014). The climate is changing and will continue doing so, that much is certain: but the exact degree to which it will change, and how dramatically those changes will impact human communities, is far harder to forecast, because those processes depend on a staggering number of factors. Further, as discussed in the introduction, the scientific uncertainty increases by several orders of magnitude when we consider the variability of political responses to climate change at both the local and the global level, how climate change–related catastrophes may reshape the world economy, the possible consequences of regional conflicts and migration patterns, and so on and so forth.[2]

In short, climate change faces us with a failure of probability, mirroring the lack of empirical data that could support predictions, the spatiotemporal scale of the ecological crisis, and its complexity as it straddles the divide between human cultures and decision-making and the history of the Earth system. To understand the radical ramifications of this failure of probability, consider the close alignment between the history of Western science and the rise of statistics in the early modern period—a link consolidated in the course of the nineteenth century (Porter 1986; Hacking 2006). If statistical models cannot come to grips with the uncertainty of our climate future, then a whole worldview based on confidence in science's capacity to model (in the sense of both predict and shape) the future is challenged at a fundamental level.

This is, in broad strokes, the cultural backdrop to Cooper's distinction between prediction and speculation, with the latter being a more viable response to the uncertainty of climate change. For Cooper, the concrete tool of speculation is scenario planning, a mode of future-oriented thinking adopted by think tanks and governments worldwide. Scenario planning is not based on statistical probabilities and remains a strictly speculative endeavor. It bears a resemblance to the philosophy of possible worlds, as Cooper notes, in that it entertains

> a semantics of counterfactual propositions. … If x were to occur, what world would we be living in? If x had occurred (or had not), what world would we be living in? As these discontinuous ramifications unfold, the spectrum of alternative futures is expanded beyond the logical possibilities of simple prediction, affording us a glimpse not only into the possible futures of the actual world but also into the proliferating pasts and futures of counterfactual worlds. (2010: 173)

In a sense, this language of speculation, counterfactuals, and possible worlds brings us remarkably close to the literary imagination: as suggested by the popularity of so-called SF or "speculative fiction" (which includes, but is not limited to, science fiction), literary narrative is at ease with what-if scenarios.[3] In this chapter, I explore how contemporary narrative practices are integrating speculative scenarios and their "discontinuous ramifications" as a means of coming to terms with the unstable futurity of climate change. Put otherwise, negotiating the uncertainty of climate change involves developing narrative forms that are able to capture the clash between multiple scenarios of what the future will look like.

My investigation thus starts with temporality, a primary dimension of experience with which narrative enjoys a close relationship. Narrative, writes Richard Walsh, is "the semiotic articulation of linear temporal sequence" (2017: 473), but the results of this articulation of time need not be linear in themselves. In this chapter I will be discussing two highly nonlinear devices through which contemporary fiction seeks to integrate the unpredictability of our climate future. This formal operation provides us with conceptual tools for negotiating uncertainty when existing cultural models—especially those derived from science and technology—fall short. The devices in question are future-tense narration and parallel storyworlds, and they are formally innovative ways of generating uncertainty by disrupting the expectation of closure that comes with narrative (and with endings more specifically). In the terminology I outlined in the introduction, narrative form recreates a structural feature of the experience of uncertainty, the fragmentation of the future into multiple scenarios (the second level of the spectrum of negotiation), often through the mediation of characters who are themselves struggling with uncertainty (the first, representational level). This strategy gives rise to an experience of uncertainty in the audience and promises to shape their affective outlook on the ecological crisis (the third and fourth levels of the spectrum).

Future-tense narration starts by reversing the prototypical retrospectivity of storytelling. As I will argue, this future orientation leads to a sense of mystery and ethical puzzlement in which the boundaries of the human are, potentially, renegotiated. The strategy of parallel storyworlds baffles the reader through the multiplication of timelines, worlds, versions of the same character: but the result of this proliferation of future uncertainty is, paradoxically, an expanded, affective sense of both the stakes of the present and the concrete possibility of a future shaped by nonhuman vitality. I will comment on two contemporary fictions for each category, using them to illustrate both different formal options and nuances of affect and meaning: Jennifer Egan's "Black Box" and Ali Smith's *How to Be Both* for future-tense narration, Jesse Kellerman's *Controller* and Jeff VanderMeer's *Dead Astronauts* for parallel storyworlds.

Bringing into focus the significance of these formal devices requires an understanding of four distinct but interrelated discussions: the cultural challenges raised by climate change vis-à-vis temporality and, in particular, futurity; the complex position of narrative as a practice mediating, in individual and collective terms, our temporal experience; the narratological question of what it means to tell a future-oriented story; and, finally, how postmodernist literature has paved the way for both future-tense narration and parallel storyworlds while deploying such narrative devices in significantly different ways from contemporary fiction.

Destabilizing the Future

The future has, of course, always been uncertain. Collectively, however, Western modernity has built itself on the possibility of managing the risks—including the environmental risks—that come with technological advances, as Ulrich Beck (1992) has influentially shown at the end of the 1980s. Notions of technological progress and unlimited economic growth provide a safety net that reduces the perceived uncertainty of the future by projecting into it the kind of linear development that Western societies have by and large experienced since the end of the Second World War. This means that, while the future can never be known with absolute confidence, the West has long tended to conceptualize it as a linear extrapolation from the present, which is in itself a way of constructing certainty.

Even before climate change entered public debates in the 1980s and 1990s, this model of futurity was coming under growing suspicion. Jean-François Lyotard (1984: xxiv) famously argued that the defining feature of the postmodern condition is "incredulity" toward the "metanarratives" of science and religion: these practices, which have long steered Western societies, have started to lose traction. Climate change arrives at a time when distrust in institutions is on the rise and deepens that feeling by shaking the very foundations of Western modernity: science (with the crisis of predictability mentioned in the previous section), technology, and economic growth (both of which are causally linked to the ecological crisis). We will return to postmodernism later in this chapter; for now, it is crucial to examine the multiple ways in which climate change unsettles ideas of futurity that have become established in Western culture, and in all cultures that have embraced Western models of scientific progress and advanced capitalism.

Since the pioneering work of geologists like James Hutton and Charles Lyell in the late eighteenth and nineteenth centuries, scientists have known that the temporal scale of geological processes surpasses the history of human civilizations by several orders of magnitude.[4] The concept of "deep time" paved the way for Charles Darwin's discoveries and met with considerable resistance in the Victorian period through its clash with the creationist views held by Christian thinkers. But while most individuals in the West have come to recognize the validity of scientific insights into geological history, the gap between everyday experience and scientific models of temporality lingers. Precisely because of the scalar difference between human and geological time, these temporalities have been perceived as operating in parallel and largely independently, without ever converging outside of the arcane world of science. It is only with discussions on climate change that we begin to see how these timelines may not be as impervious to each other as previously assumed. Through industrial and military activities from plastic production to nuclear experiments, human societies are leaving physical traces whose impact on the Earth can be measured in geological eons, not in human years. This "signature" of humanity in the geological record is the premise for Paul Crutzen's (2002) proposal to name our geological epoch "Anthropocene," or the human age.[5] In an influential article, Dipesh Chakrabarty describes this convergence of human and geological time as a "collision" of three histories, including also the history of natural evolution: for Chakrabarty, humans "now unintentionally straddle these three histories that operate on different scales and at different speeds" (2014: 1). Chakrabarty's collision is a far more violent metaphor than convergence, and there is no doubt that seeing human actions as operating across multiple temporalities calls for a dramatic reconsideration of experienced time and, more specifically, futurity. We live surrounded by "hyperobjects," in Timothy Morton's terminology: "products such as Styrofoam and plutonium that exist on almost unthinkable timescales" (2010: 19). In a very real sense, the plastic bowl that contained my takeout lunch today will outlive me. This strange realization underlies the discourse of sustainability and is bound to inflect understanding of both the present and the future as the site of increasingly deep and dramatic entanglements between human decision-making and the fate of entire ecosystems.

But this clash of timelines is not the only reason we have come to a turning point for conceptions of futurity. Scientific predictions, as we have seen, falter in the face of the material and sociopolitical complexity of the ecological crisis, which prompts a political shift from statistics (the backbone of Western science) to speculative scenarios. Because speculation is not bound to statistical regularities, it offers not only more freedom but also fewer epistemic comforts than the stringent predictive logic of science. Put more simply, speculation feeds uncertainty instead of reducing it. Meanwhile, despite the periodic resurfacing of discussions on carbon capture and geoengineering, technological solutions are proving insufficient to deal with the full extent of the climate crisis—another way in which faith in technological progress is being shaken.

Ultimately, the seemingly neutral concept of future is revealed to be the product of a highly specific, and controversial, cultural history rooted in the Western world. In the introduction to a special issue of the journal *Resilience*, Susie O'Brien and Cheryl Lousley (2017) offer a useful overview of the factors that have shaped Western conceptions of futurity. As a first factor, O'Brien and Lousley point to the colonial history of European nations, arguing that it was in the colonial context that "science began to raise concerns about the long-term impacts of practices of deforestation on soil and water on 'future generations'" (2017: 4). The inspiration of these colonial ideologies was "explicitly biopolitical" (2017: 6), as O'Brien and Lousley put it, in that Indigenous notions of time and futurity were deliberately stamped out in favor of chronological, linear, and "objective" Western time, with its upward curve of capitalist production and technological advancement.[6] O'Brien and Lousley add that the Cold War was the second defining moment in the history of contemporary conceptions of futurity: anxieties of nuclear Holocaust and contamination became bound up, after the fall of the Soviet Union, with the looming uncertainty of climate change.

Caught between the specter of colonial violence and geopolitical clashes, any linear projection of the present into future becomes even cloudier and more uncertain.[7] A further challenge to entrenched conceptions of futurity comes from queer theory, as Nicole Seymour discusses in *Strange Natures* (2013).[8] For Seymour, Western views of futurity are bound up with a heteronormative framework whereby emotional investment in the future derives from the obligation to reproduce and care for one's children.[9] Seymour argues that this assumption is a problematic extrapolation from a European, middle-class, and fundamentally heterosexual model of family. This critique extends to the environmental movement, which has frequently appealed to childhood and future generations in its campaigns. Instead, Seymour proposes a concept of "queer time" that troubles standard accounts of futurity via the link between the boundary-crossing experience of the queer subject and the inherent unruliness of the natural world. Put otherwise, queer individuals have an intrinsic, empathetic affinity with the nonhuman, which supersedes kinship-based models of environmental responsibility.[10] Futurity is thus uncoupled from sexual reproduction, a particularly provocative move as humanity's dramatic environmental impact is compounded by the risks of overpopulation.

Whether through colliding temporal scales, the limitations of scientific predictions, the traumatic legacies of colonialism and the Cold War, or the critique of heteronormative reproduction, the model of futurity that defines Western modernity is fundamentally questioned by the environmental crisis.

One possible response to this unstable futurity is a call for alternative models of temporality, such as those advanced (to name two significant trends that share cultural space with environmentalism) by "slow philosophy" and the "degrowth" movement: slowness and degrowth overturn ideas of productivity and progress that are at the core of modern notions of futurity.[11] Literary narrative, as I will show in the next section, has its own means of responding to this crisis of futurity. These are formal means, as we know from the introduction, but they resonate with broader cultural tendencies to disrupt and decelerate the mad rush of modernity.

Narrative between Extrinsic and Intrinsic Futures

There are few narratological works to which the adjective "monumental" is applied as consistently as it is to Paul Ricoeur's three-volume *Time and Narrative* (Ricoeur 1984, 1985, 1988). This study is an inevitable starting point for any discussion of narrative's entanglement with temporality. The conceptual centerpiece is Ricoeur's account of "mimesis" as a threefold process that captures how story taps into our intuitive understanding of action ("prefiguration" in Ricoeur's terminology) to arrange events in a certain temporal pattern ("configuration"). This gesture of arrangement may, in turn, enter day-to-day experience and disclose new ways of making sense of life through narrative ("refiguration"). Temporality is central to all of these dimensions of mimesis: stories are woven out of temporal experience, through concepts that allow us to, first, break the world down into people, intentions, and actions and, subsequently, string them in a temporal sequence.[12] The experience of narrative configurations—that is, concrete stories—is also temporally extended, an act of reading (listening, viewing, etc.) that unfolds over time and has a certain internal dynamic. Finally, culturally circulating stories provide us with templates to place a meaningful order on our own experience of time as it is filtered by consciousness in both memory and anticipation.

However, as Mark Currie argues in *About Time* (2007), narrative theory has been more concerned with the retrospective dimension of narrative's engagement with time (memory) than with its prospective dimension (anticipation). This privileging of retrospectivity goes hand in hand with the prototypical use of the past tense in narrative, a preference that has been the subject of much narratological work.[13] The past tense indicates a retrospective relation to what is being told: the end point of a narrative seeps into and shapes its moment-by-moment progression (a dynamic perhaps best illustrated by first-person narrative, with the narrating self imposing a retrospective viewpoint on the events experienced by his or her earlier self).[14] After all, experiences tend to be told after the fact: we need to take distance from an event to be able to arrive at what Ricoeur calls a narrative "configuration." Peter Brooks puts this point rather dramatically in *Reading for the Plot*: "All narrative may be in essence obituary in that ... the retrospective knowledge that it seeks, the knowledge that comes after, stands on the far side of the end, in human terms on the far side of death" (1984: 95). For Currie, this exclusive interest in narrative as "retrospective knowledge" is limiting: *futurity* is an equally salient dimension of storytelling and should thus be given more consideration in narrative theory. Currie offers important guidance in exploring narrative's confrontation with the uncertain temporality of climate change, even though—as we will see—some aspects of his account will need reworking to pursue this chapter's goals.

Currie's argument works on two levels. On the one hand, drawing on phenomenology and poststructuralist philosophy (particularly Jacques Derrida), Currie shows that the experience of the present is always already structured by prospection, through a process of "continuous anticipation in which we attach significance to the present moment" (2007: 6). This is true of both everyday experience and narrative fiction. However, in the former the future remains open and uncertain, whereas in the latter the future is already given and can be determined simply by reading on or skipping forward (Currie 2007: 19). This is the narratological and philosophical dimension of Currie's argument. On another level, Currie is working toward an account of the contemporary novel and argues that future orientation is one of the distinctive features of post–Second World War fiction. That orientation manifests itself in the widespread use of flashforwards or prolepses, in Gérard Genette's (1980) terminology, textual instances of anticipation in which the chronological order of the telling is suspended to reveal a future outcome. This prospective device serves a "performative function which produces in the world a generalised future orientation such that the understanding of the present becomes increasingly focused on the question of what it will come to mean" (2007: 22). Of particular interest in Currie's discussion is how the future orientation of the telling— evoked through prolepsis—inflects the present, how it reveals the potentialities inherent in the present moment. This is the effect created by the future-tense passages I will analyze below, which tie in closely with Currie's discussion of prolepsis: these sections infuse the present (of the story, and of the reading experience) with new significance by destabilizing the retrospective stance that is generally associated with narrative.

Currie presents storytelling as a practice that, by configuring events in a temporal sequence, invites *both* retrospection and prospection. While part and parcel of all narrative forms (and of everyday temporal experience), the evocation of futurity through prospection becomes particularly significant in the contemporary novel for reasons that reflect, in complex ways, the material possibilities of digital technologies as well as today's collective practices of temporal organization. Currie (2007: 9–11) points to time–space compression in a globalized world, the accelerated circulation of stories and ideas, and obsession with archiving ("archival fever") as phenomena that mark the present cultural juncture and inspire its future orientation.

There is a clear link between the "continuous anticipation" theorized by Currie and the crisis of futurity brought about by climate change: when confidence in a culturally given model of futurity wanes, the experienced present fills with anticipation; we keep prospecting because of our inability to fix a coherent image of the future that could guide, unconsciously and unproblematically, our actions. The result is a darker, more restless version of Currie's "continuous anticipation." But other aspects of Currie's discussion of contemporary narrative's future orientation call for further scrutiny. Particularly controversial is the claim that in "written text, the future lies there to the right, awaiting its actualization by the reading, so that written text can be said to offer a block view of time which is never offered to us in lived experience" (2007: 18). This idea downplays the temporally extended, processual nature of the reading experience, in which "a block view of time" never truly presents itself, not even when the ending comes into sight: the retrospective recollection of a story is just as partial as its moment-by-moment (prospective) apprehension. Of course, the future of the reading experience is predetermined in a way that the future of real experience is not, but this conceptual difference does not always register in the act of reading. The so-called paradox of anomalous suspense supports this analogy between real and fictional futurity: consider the common experience of feeling suspense despite knowing the outcome of a story (either through previous exposure to the story or through cultural knowledge of its subject-matter).[15] Why would we reexperience suspense if we have already attained a "block view of time"? The reality is that suspense emerges affectively within the dynamics of the reading experience, which are both prospective and retrospective (as Currie shows), and which remain relatively impervious to abstract knowledge of the text's future.

Equally important for our purposes is to trace a distinction between intrinsic and extrinsic narrative futures. The models of futurity we have examined in the previous section belong to what Ricoeur discussed under the heading of prefiguration: how knowledge structures and cultural practices surrounding the future serve as a backdrop to narrative mimesis. This is the extrinsic meaning of the word futurity. By contrast, the intrinsic futurity *of* the narrative is fully a matter of textual *con*figuration: of how characters' interactions fall into a pattern that has a certain internal dynamic oriented toward the story's future (i.e., eventual outcome). When Currie discusses the future orientation of the contemporary novel, he runs the risk of conflating the intrinsic and the extrinsic meaning of futurity—a duality that plays an essential role in the reading experience.[16] Readers' expectations concerning future states of the narrative (intrinsic futurity) are governed by a logic of prediction, as Karin Kukkonen (2014) has argued by building on an approach to cognition known as "predictive processing." From that perspective, readers' engagement with narrative involves forming predictions based on previous experiences (including both real-world interactions and familiarity with narrative conventions). These predictions are then adjusted dynamically to track the textual configuration. Suspense, curiosity, and surprise—Meir Sternberg's (2001) triad of "narrative universals"—are the affective expression of these underlying predictions, and they define the moment-by-moment experience of stories.

In parallel with this predictive dynamic driven by the narrative's internal configuration, readers interrogate the extrinsic relevance of the narrative, how it brings into play and renegotiates values they are familiar with through everyday experience.[17] Thus, when we talk about narrative's future orientation, we can mean two things: how it places unusual pressure on the reader's work of anticipating the story's future states and updating those anticipations to match new textual data, for instance, by challenging established narrative patterns; or, alternatively (and more broadly), how it engages with culturally circulating ideas of futurity and thus makes an intervention in debates on the stakes of the present and the shape that the future will (should, could) take. After all, this is the kind of cultural work that science fiction—an intrinsically speculative narrative practice—performs: it surveys possible futures and brings them, more or less implicitly, into dialogue with the reader's everyday reality.[18] By manipulating a configuration that is future-oriented in the intrinsic sense, narrative may be able to stage the breakdown of established notions of extrinsic futurity (e.g., the metanarratives of progress and economic growth discussed above). In this process, the experience and possibility of *closure* will come under question, and a sense of *mystery* will be generated as a result of narrative's grappling with a radically uncertain future. The mystery not only mirrors our extrinsic stance toward climate change but also creates an opportunity for an affectively rewarding negotiation of uncertainty, as we will see.

Lack of Closure, Rise of Uncertainty

Where do extrinsic and intrinsic futurity converge in narrative? Clearly, the ending is a good place to look for that convergence. The ending's function is quite literally to reveal the story's future, bringing together (more or less satisfyingly) the affective strands of the reader's predictions. Extrinsically, the ending is also where the narrative opens onto extratextual reality, prompting the reader to consider the story's bearing on the world of everyday experience in both personal and collective terms. The breakdown of cultural models of futurity is thus likely to become salient in the ending, where it emerges through the problematization of closure (and thus the production of uncertainty). This effect should be kept distinct from its concrete narrative realization through future-tense narrative and parallel worlds, which will be the topic of the second half of this chapter.[19] Indeed, it is perfectly possible to problematize closure and evoke uncertainty *without* adopting formally innovative or experimental techniques. To illustrate this point, I will take as example Lauren Groff's novella *Boca Raton* (2018), which explicitly thematizes climate change by focusing on Ange, a single mother struggling with mental health issues. In the course of the story, Ange becomes obsessed with how the rising sea will reshape her coastal town in Florida and impact her young daughter's life. *Boca Raton* is future-oriented both intrinsically and extrinsically, but it stages a crisis of futurity in a more conventional way than the case studies offered below. Nevertheless, the ending of Groff's narrative can be said to both resist closure and generate uncertainty; thus, it will help me introduce these narrative dynamics before turning to more formally innovative examples.

Closure is a familiar concept that is curiously undertheorized in scholarly work on narrative.[20] As a concept, closure has had circulation in psychoanalysis and Gestalt psychology, which explains perhaps why the term straddles artistic practices and everyday life: the Oxford Dictionary of English defines closure as both "a sense of resolution or conclusion at the end of an artistic work" and "a feeling that an emotional or traumatic experience has been resolved" (Stevenson 2010: 329). The experience of formal completion afforded by the arts thus becomes a model of emotional resolution, and this is of course one of the ways in which exposure to narrative "configurations" can "refigure" (to go back to Ricoeur's terminology) our understanding of everyday events. But it should be uncontroversial to say that artistic works, including narratives, are equally adept at *resisting* closure. Plots are typically set in motion by an instability that challenges the status quo. Herman (2009: 19–21) calls this process "world disruption": two characters fall in love, or someone becomes seriously ill, or a city's prosperity is threatened by an invader—these are all standard examples of world disruption.[21] Readers come to expect that such tensions will be resolved by the ending, so that the storyworld can return to a state of relative equilibrium (albeit, in most cases, an equilibrium significantly different from the starting point). This expectation serves as the engine of both the reader's cognitive-level predictions and the patterning of suspense, curiosity, and surprise that (as discussed in the previous section) accompanies them. Yet storytellers can leave certain plot instabilities open at the end of a narrative or introduce new, unexpected instabilities while resolving previous ones.

If this is too abstract, let us take a closer look at *Boca Raton*. The story begins with Ange's insomnia and follows her dwindling mental health as she is unable to sleep for several nights, with visions of ecological catastrophe gradually becoming more insistent; this is the main instability behind the novella's plot. In the final scene, Ange, still sleepless, decides to leave her beachfront house and take a nighttime walk, during which she has an epiphany of the ocean, "chewing darkly at the sand. Only the ocean was awake. Ange and the ocean. Ange being eaten, the ocean that will eat everything" (Groff 2018: Kindle Location 349). Suddenly, Ange hears the voice of her daughter, Lily, calling her from the porch of their house. Ange starts making her way back, thinking glumly that "she could not save her daughter, that there would be no saving, that she would be left behind among the disappointed" (2018: Kindle Location 365). The final line reads, "as she walked, either the [streetlights] went out together all at once, or the dread that had followed her down here on the run gathered itself thickly there in the street, and the darkness fell across the way out; the darkness sealed the gap" (2018: Kindle Location 368). There is little here in the way of resolution: not only is the plot's main instability—Ange's insomnia—still present, but it does not result in any recognizable outcome or endpoint, whether negative (e.g., Ange commits suicide) or positive (e.g., Ange regains control of her life). Instead, a sense of ambivalence pervades the final episode: closure is denied, and the intrinsic futurity of the novella (Ange's life, but especially what the future has in store for Ange's daughter) blends with extrinsic futurity through the real-world threat posed by climate change.

In the ending of Groff's novella, the darkness is also a straightforward image for what readers do not and cannot know about the two characters' future. The novella's lack of closure ties in with a deep sense of uncertainty in which the failure of readers' predictions overlaps, through a mechanism of identification, with Ange's own inability to imagine a future for her daughter. It is plainly ironic that the text ends with a gap being *sealed*, given the impossibility of closure; in effect, the novella's ending advances an epistemic gap that cannot be closed, and yet will stimulate the reader's predictive work beyond the end of the text. Porter Abbott develops a comprehensive narratological account of these gaps in *Real Mysteries*, where he calls them "egregious gaps." For Abbott, egregious gaps need not occur at the end of a story; they aim to "immerse the reader in a state of unknowing, robbed not only of cognitive mastery but of its resources" (2013: 17). Abbott argues that there is value in lingering within this experiential state instead of trying to shake it off by way of interpretation: sensing such fundamental limitations of our knowledge is a humbling experience that can productively destabilize readers' sense of mastery.

If we approach Groff's novella in this way, the impossibility of closure and thus the unreadability of intrinsic futurity bring into view the extrinsic uncertainty of our climate future. Through the configuration of narrative, readers can contemplate the broader stakes of the ecological crisis—and while this process may not offer resolution, it holds great existential payoffs in that it may teach readers to let go of the need for control and mastery (values that, by guiding the relationship with nature of Western societies, have paved the way for climate change). However, as I pointed out above, the way in which Groff's narrative explores a crisis of futurity remains relatively conventional, particularly because of the character-driven nature of the reader's engagement: the uncertainty here reflects, in a relatively linear fashion, the character's mental breakdown, which makes it possible for readers to dismiss Ange's predicament as the product of mental illness. Recall the spectrum of negotiation discussed in the introduction: *Boca Raton* foregrounds the first level of the spectrum (the evocation of uncertainty through characters' minds) and doesn't fully use the resources of form (level 2) to model the challenges of the climate crisis. The story falls short of creating a sustained experience of uncertainty for the reader (level 3), other than of course the open ending. That privileging of representation over form limits the ability of Groff's narrative to trigger the affective shift that I discussed as an embrace of uncertainty (level 4 of the spectrum of negotiation)—even if that effect cannot be completely ruled out, since it is deeply reader-dependent. By contrast, the strategies examined in the second part of this chapter involve a significant leap from the level of representation (in Groff's case, of the protagonist's mental processes) to the formal level of narrative techniques: the result is that radical uncertainty is uncoupled from individual psychology and presented as a structural feature of our collective predicament. In order to fully understand this formal operation, however, we need to consider the continuities and discontinuities between experimental techniques of uncertain futurity in my contemporary examples and in postmodern literature.

Beyond Postmodernist Time

The future, as I said above, has always been uncertain, but the value systems that made that uncertainty more tolerable (such as religion, technological progress, and economic growth) started collapsing well before climate change came into view at the turn of the twenty-first century. Thus, it is essential to place the crisis of futurity that this chapter is exploring within this longer history. In part, I have done so by drawing on O'Brien and Lousley's (2017) discussion of how Western notions of futurity are entangled with the histories of European colonialism and the Cold War. But, as we move toward questions of literary form, there is another important history that should be put on the map—namely, the way in which both the discourse of postmodernism and postmodern *literature* more specifically have anticipated the crisis of futurity. The strategies of future-tense narration and parallel storyworld-building I examine in the following sections have a good deal in common with the experimentations of postmodernist authors such as John Barth, J. G. Ballard, and Robert Coover. Yet they also differ from the work of these earlier authors in ways that will be worth discussing in detail.

A useful starting point is *Chronoschisms* (1997), a study of narrative and time in postmodern literature by Ursula Heise. *Chronoschisms* focuses on how technological and cultural innovations in the decades following the end of the Second World War led to a radical problematization of temporality as metaphysical concept capable of harmonizing individual time consciousness, the sociopolitical history of modernity, and scientific knowledge. Put otherwise, it has become impossible to think about time as a coherent, unified phenomenon. Instead, what prevails in the postmodern moment is a sense of deep fragmentation in which temporality appears to swim in what Heise calls, borrowing a phrase from Helga Nowotny (1989), "extended present." Together with the incredulity toward metanarratives posited by Lyotard, this negation of temporal distinctions creates sweeping uncertainty: the "paradox in the postmodern sense of time scale, then, is that although we know more about the overall functioning of time in our universe than ever before, our own operation within it has become more uncertain, so that temporal coherence increasingly eludes us" (Heise 1997: 46). Postmodern fiction engages with these cultural developments by introducing a number of formal innovations that, according to Heise (1997: 55), resonate with Jorge Luis Borges's prescient metaphor of the "garden of forking paths" (from the title of a 1941 short story). In particular, Heise draws attention to two formal strategies that define postmodernist experimentations with time: the first is the disorienting use of temporal anachronies—especially flashbacks—that, unlike their modernist antecedents, remain unmoored from the consciousness of an experiencing character (1997: 53); the second is that postmodernist authors "tell event sequences in contradictory and mutually exclusive versions that do not allow the reader to infer a coherent story and reality" (1997: 53).

It should be evident that these postmodernist techniques for channeling temporal disorientation pave the way for the two strategies I discuss in this chapter. Yet their differences are as important as their similarities. At a purely formal level, Heise's discussion focuses on flashbacks, not flashforwards; as she acknowledges explicitly, the "postmodernist novel confronts the more radically contingent future of Western societies in the late 20th century by projecting the temporal mode of the future into the narrative present and past" (1997: 67). This point marks a significant difference from the "future orientation" of contemporary fiction theorized by Currie: Heise argues that postmodernist writers do not confront the uncertainty of the future on its own terms but rather map it onto the present and (especially) the past, in well-known modes of postmodernist literature such as Linda Hutcheon's (1988) "historiographic metafiction." As contingency becomes projected into the past, its origin in a breakdown of personal and collective futurity may easily take a back seat. This displacement is not a luxury that contemporary fiction can afford: with the impact of climate change and similarly destabilizing global processes becoming more and more tangible, the question of futurity can no longer be eluded.

Postmodernist writing is sometimes understood as a self-referential practice characterized by deep distrust in narrative and severed from the demands and crises of the real world. This is, of course, an oversimplification that does not do justice to the depth and breadth of postmodernist works by the likes of Italo Calvino or Thomas Pynchon. Nevertheless, Robert McLaughlin has argued persuasively that, as postmodernist techniques entered the mainstream through the mass media (and particularly, for McLaughlin, television), they were largely uncoupled from their social and political relevance. Writers working in the wake of postmodernism sought to distance themselves from this shallow reading of postmodernist literature by finding "a way beyond self-referential irony to offer the possibility of construction" (McLaughlin 2004: 65). The comeback of social engagement in contemporary fiction testifies to that desire for a more constructive role of the writer in society. This renewed confidence in the relevance of narrative also underlies what Nancy Armstrong (2014) terms the "affective turn" in twenty-first-century fiction: how contemporary authors (Armstrong's main example is Kazuo Ishiguro) strive to expand the circle of readers' sympathies in order to challenge a conventional, anthropocentric notion of personhood and thus express a broader range of biopolitical realities.[22]

Indeed, the affective takes center stage in contemporary fictions that engage with human–nonhuman entanglements in times of climate change. Future-tense narration and parallel storyworlds face readers with the uncertainty of the future and, in the same breath, with the affective significance of the present, where that significance reflects the immense moral and material stakes of humanity's predicament. While postmodernist irony tended toward a dematerialization of the world and a retreat into the intellectualized prison house of language of Jamesonian fame (Jameson 1972), the materiality of human impact of the planet is adopted by contemporary fiction as an inevitable starting point for staging a crisis of futurity. Further, this focus on materiality correlates closely with the broad range of affective responses that the climate crisis can elicit, from paralyzing anxiety (as typified by Groff's protagonist) to grief and indignation.[23] If, according to Heise, postmodernist literature presented us with a completely disjointed experience of temporality, that sense of fragmentation persists in the contemporary moment but enters into a tension with an affective interest in materiality that is fundamentally unifying: the materiality of human and animal embodiment becomes interwoven with biological and geological processes that are in themselves material.

By building on this notion of materiality that crisscrosses the human–nonhuman divide, contemporary fiction revives confidence in the possibility of forging a link between the ethical responsibilities of the present, the traumatic histories of colonialism and twentieth-century conflicts, and a stubbornly uncertain futurity. The ruptures of temporality in contemporary fiction extend an invitation to muster the affective resources needed to embrace uncertainty as an existential condition and, at the same time, recover the experiential thickness of the present. Let us return for a moment to Cooper's claim that, as "discontinuous ramifications unfold, the spectrum of alternative futures is expanded beyond the logical possibilities of simple prediction" (2010: 173). In fiction as in the world economy, the failure of scientific forecasts calls for new methods of scenario building whose value is primarily strategic: rather than perpetuating a logic of "discontinuous ramifications" for its own sake (as postmodernist literature tended to do), these narratives discern the most desirable scenarios from the least desirable ones, bringing them back into the fold of the present and showing how we could act to achieve the best possible outcomes. But fiction, of course, has its own criteria of desirability, which—unlike those of global finance—sit squarely within the domain of ethics and affect.

Cyborgs and Fifteenth-Century Painters: Future-Tense Narration

"Among the odd tenses of narration, the future tense is perhaps the most striking. After all, one lives first and tells about it later, and to tell the future—except in prophetic passages—seems more than counterintuitive," writes Monika Fludernik (2012b: 90) in a book chapter on verbal tense and narrative. Fludernik names a few examples of future-tense narration by authors such as Christine Brooke-Rose (*Amalgamemnon*, 1984) and Carlos Fuentes (*The Death of Artemio Cruz*, 1962), but she also notes that future-tense narratives are extremely rare: even in the few texts that do use this tense, it is typically deployed in conjunction with another tense, such as the present tense. She also adds that it can be extremely difficult to tease apart the "*will* of hypothetical speculation" and the "*will* of future reference" (2012b: 90), because any event presented in future-tense narration is likely to be interpreted by readers as less certain than in present-tense or past-tense narrative.

This oscillation between future reference and speculation is part of the reason why the future tense is so effective at evoking uncertainty. Not all instances of the future tense in narrative are meant to produce uncertainty, of course: the future tense may be used rhetorically in sentences like "As for Professor Cottard, we shall meet him again" (from Marcel Proust's *In Search of Lost Time*; discussed in Genette 1980: 74). Genette calls this type of prolepsis an "advance notice." In these instances, the authorial narrator's voice has, to lift Lubomír Doležel's (1998) terminology, an "authenticating" function, reducing the uncertainty associated with the future tense. Such uses of the future tense are justified by a narrator who has retrospective control over the events being related. However, other factors may contribute to *maximizing* the uncertainty of future-tense passages and thus generate a unique tension between the futurity inherent in the narrative and its orientation toward an extrinsic future shared by the readers. I will focus on two uncertainty-enhancing devices: the clash between narration and a nonnarrative text type that warrants the use of the future tense (e.g., the instruction manual); and the counterintuitive positioning of the future tense at the *end* of a narrative (the place where we would normally expect retrospection).

My example of the first category is a short story by Jennifer Egan, "Black Box" (2012: n.p.).[24] The story was published in *The New Yorker* after being initially released as a series of tweets, which explains the brevity of Egan's sentences. The narrative situation emerges gradually in the course of the first few pages: a 33-year-old woman is addressed, in the second person, by an anonymous narrator working for a US government agency. The woman is part of a training program for "citizen agents"—nonprofessional spies whose mission is to obtain information on powerful men who are suspected of involvement in criminal activities. An overblown rhetoric of "national security" justifies this endeavor: "Some citizen agents have chosen not to return. / They have left their bodies behind, and now they shimmer sublimely in the heavens. / In the new heroism, the goal is to transcend individual life, with its petty pains and loves, in favor of the dazzling collective," we read toward the end of the text.[25] In an early passage, the protagonist recalls her training, with instructions cast in a generic (and fully conventional) future tense: "You will be infiltrating the lives of criminals. / You will be in constant danger." But elsewhere in the text the future tense is *not* justified in the same way: effectively, these future references tell a highly particularized story in which the protagonist meets and seduces her "Designated Mate" in the South of France in order to gain his confidence and acquire intel on his involvement in the criminal underworld. The two travel to an unnamed island in the Mediterranean, where the protagonist's lover meets another rich man to strike an illegal deal. We also discover that the protagonist is a cyborg, and that her body has been modified to serve as a recording device. The situation goes awry when the protagonist attempts to obtain evidence of the deal: despite a serious gunshot wound, she manages to reach a secret location or "Hotspot" where she is rescued by a helicopter dispatched by the government agency she works for. The story's ending denies closure by withholding information as to whether the woman survives this harrowing experience; the final sentence reads "You won't know for sure [if there are human beings inside the helicopter] until you see them crouching above you, their faces taut with hope, ready to jump," which directly stages both lack of knowledge ("You won't know") and the suspenseful openness of the ending (through the "tautness" of the agents' face and readiness to spring from the helicopter).

The future tense alternates with the imperative mood of the instructions. Consider, for instance, this passage:

> When you reach the approximate location of a Hotspot, cut the engine.
>
> You will be in total darkness, in total silence.
>
> If you wish, you may lie down at the bottom of the boat.
>
> The fact that you feel like you're dying doesn't mean that you will die.
>
> Remember that, should you die, your body will yield a crucial trove of information.

Because these sentences occur near the end of the story, after a detailed account of the woman's actions, instructions such as "cut the engine" are not credible as literal advance instructions, and the future-tense spatial description ("You will be in total darkness") is likely to be read as a statement of fact rather than as a prediction: the situation is far too specific for anyone to have foreseen it. The oddity of this passage, and indeed of the whole short story, reflects the clash between the choice of verb tense and mood, which suggest the distance of anticipation, and the immediacy of the woman's immersion in a high-stakes situation. One way to read this tension is as an internalization of the training program's instructions, as if the protagonist was trying to distance herself from danger by imagining, in as much detail as possible, someone telling her what to do in advance.[26] This approach ties in with the "Dissociation Technique" that the protagonist has been taught to mentally extricate herself from the challenges of her mission: "The Dissociation Technique is like a parachute—you must pull the cord at the correct time." Perhaps the whole narrative situation is one of such defensive techniques, and the narrative unfolds entirely within the woman's consciousness, as if she was deliberately adopting a prospective stance on events that are actually unfolding in the present.

To some extent, this conflation of immediate experience and anticipatory instructions is thematized by the text, which states that these "Field Instructions, stored in a chip beneath your hairline, will serve as both a mission log and a guide for others undertaking this work." The suggestion is that, even if the protagonist dies at the end, the instructions could be retrieved from the woman's technologically augmented body, forming the basis for the text we are reading. However, this interpretive strategy does not completely eliminate the strange indirectness of the narrative, along with the deep uncertainty created by future-tense narration in combination with the open ending. At a relatively superficial level, "Black Box" focuses on how initiatives such as the "war on terror" have infiltrated the lives and even the minds of private citizens, who become unwittingly implicated in state surveillance and violence on a global stage. The protagonist's own body turns into a technological instrument in the hands of an unnamed government agency. The body and its affects thus become the site of a conflict between individuality and the anonymizing perspective of technological control, invoked by the rhetoric of sentences such as "For millennia, engineers have empowered human beings to accomplish mythical feats." Naturally, it is difficult not to read such pronouncements ironically. At stake here is the extrinsic future of humanity and whether the liberal human subject, with its cherished values, will survive the onslaught of technological innovation and pervasive state surveillance in the face of global threats. Thus, when the narrator remarks confidently that "Human beings are fiercely, primordially resilient," we are invited to read this statement ironically, as exposing the fragility of a conception of the human that is exclusively based on individual rights and aspirations.

Whether we interpret the future-tense narration psychologically or thematically, the verb tense amplifies these future-oriented anxieties by introducing a persistent gap between the traumatic affects of the present and a future payoff that is dubious at best. "Black Box" thus places future uncertainty at the heart of the very definition of the human: it confronts readers with a human (or at least human-like) character caught in a system that dehumanizes her; and while this system is powerfully undermined by Egan's irony, no alternative set of values comes to the protagonist's rescue. The uncertainty surrounding the woman's intrinsic future (i.e., whether she survives or not) is thus compounded by a sense of ethical disorientation as well as by broader questions on the fate of the human in a world increasingly governed by technologies. Even though climate change is not an explicit thematic element in the story, the natural world does play a role, in that its beauty is the only source of comfort as the protagonist struggles to stay afloat: "Looking up at the sky from below can feel like floating, suspended, and looking down. The universe will seem to hang beneath you in its milky glittering mystery." Perhaps that illusion of being "suspended" and "looking down" is the spatial equivalent of the baffling temporal operation attempted by the text, with its conversion of narrative retrospectivity into uneasy anticipation.

The same sense of mystery occupies the foreground of Ali Smith's novel *How to Be Both* (2015), my second example of future-tense narration (illustrating the second category, narratives in which the future tense only emerges in the ending). This novel is divided into two parts, one set in modern-day Britain, the other in the Italian city of Ferrara in the second half of the fifteenth century. The protagonist of the former is George (short for Georgia), a teenager traumatized by the sudden death of her mother, while the latter is narrated by Francesco del Cossa, a painter active in the Renaissance court of Borso d'Este. After visiting Ferrara and admiring Francesco's frescoes in the Palazzo Schifanoia, George develops an obsessive interest in his paintings; in parallel, Smith imagines that Francesco's consciousness is transported to twenty-first-century London, where he meets George and starts following her.

The use of the future tense in the final section of George's half of the novel can be understood in light of one of the text's central thematic preoccupations: in today's world, mainstream narrative practices are invested in stories in which, eventually, everything "adds up," leaving no room for mystery and ambiguity. Thematically, this idea is spelled out by George's counselor at school: "now we live in a time and in a culture when mystery tends to mean something more answerable, it means a crime novel, a thriller, a drama on TV, usually one where we'll probably find out—and where the whole point of reading it or watching it will be that we *will* find out—what happened" (2015: 72). Mystery, in this sense, denotes a short-lived gap destined to be filled by an ending that is satisfying only to the extent that it brings perfect closure. Because she builds on this understanding of narrative, George faces a deep personal crisis as she fails to integrate the mystery of her mother's death into a meaningful, future-facing life narrative. This breakdown of narrative meaning-making is symptomatic of our culture's broader inability to deal with uncertain futurity. It is only through George's strange relationship with Francesco that she learns to end this impasse, coming to an acceptance of mystery and instability as underlying dimensions of both narrative and life—the same experiential stance that the novel seeks to foster in readers.

How to Be Both presents this lesson as an expression of the painter's early modern and prescientific worldview. "In hell there is no mystery cause in mystery there is always hope," declares Francesco (2015: 227), and his section of the novel creates a fascinating portrait of a fifteenth-century mind for which the human world is closely entangled with nonhuman realities. Here "one thing meets another" (2015: 370) and a sense of creative potentiality emerges as "the root in the dark makes its / way under the ground / before there's / any sign of the tree / the seed still unbroken / the star still unburnt / the curve of the eyebone / of the not yet born," to quote from the long, typographically spiraling poem that concludes Francesco's half of the novel (2015: 371–2). From this vitalistic standpoint, the human is part of a higher mystery that cannot be rationally solved or captured through the closed grid of conventional narrative, only distantly sensed in affective and material terms. This metaphysics seeps into George's half of the novel, enabling her final embrace of an uncertain future.

How to Be Both channels this insight along two formal routes, both of which enrich and deepen the thematic dimension of the novel I have teased out so far. The first is the physical interchangeability of the two halves. My edition has George's half before Francesco's, but other copies of the book reverse that order, and the digital edition even allows readers to pick which of the two halves they would prefer to read first. The variability of the two parts' sequence evokes indeterminacy and unwillingness to contain the novel's central mystery through linear teleology, consistently with what George learns in the course of her relationship with Francesco. This openness of structural organization is translated into the use of the future tense at the end of George's half of the novel. George composes an email to a friend and realizes "that she'd used, in its first sentence, the future tense, like there might be such a thing as a future" (2015: 173). This disclosure of the character's intrinsic futurity is directly enacted by the narrator a few pages later, when George is at the National Gallery, contemplating a painting by Francesco del Cossa. An old friend of George's mother suddenly enters the scene, and we see George following her in order to find out more about the woman's enigmatic identity and connection to her mother. The sequence is relayed in the future tense: "She will track the woman, staying behind her and aping the ordinary disaffected teenage girl all the way across London" (2015: 184). But the mystery that surrounds that character is never dispelled. Instead, the chapter ends with a return to the present tense: "But none of the above has happened. Not yet, anyway. For now, in the present tense, George sits in the gallery and looks at one of the old paintings on the wall. It's definitely something to do. For the foreseeable" (2015: 185–6).

The elision of the word "future" in this final sentence is indicative of the novel's sophisticated play with futurity: the holding out of the creative *possibility* of a future that is, nevertheless, enfolded by mystery and uncertainty. The back-and-forth in verb tense suggests as much: as explicit closure is denied, accepting the openness of the future is presented as a necessary condition for a hopeful ending (for George and for the reader). Through this indeterminacy the character's intrinsic future converges with the extrinsic future of a society that faces, like

George, a profound epistemic crisis. Living with that crisis, as George discovers by joining forces imaginatively with Francesco, requires embracing mystery as a response to the collapse of the linear narratives of modernity. In different ways, then, Egan and Smith adopt future-tense narration to explore the existential limits of the human both internally (through the dehumanizing psychology of Egan's cyborg) and externally (through the material entanglements with the nonhuman foregrounded by Francesco's premodern worldview).

"Tiny Fractures in Reality": Parallel Storyworlds

Neither of the two narratives examined so far addresses climate change directly; rather, their strategic use of the future tense engages with a sense of uncertain futurity that *resonates* with the ecological crisis without staging it at the level of plot. Nevertheless, Egan's story and Smith's novel offer formal and affective resources to understand how the contemporary moment destabilizes conceptions of the human derived from Western modernity—conceptions that are, arguably, at the forefront of the climate crisis. My case studies in this section—Jesse Kellerman's *Controller* and Jeff VanderMeer's *Dead Astronauts*—evoke climate catastrophe much more straightforwardly. I turn to another unconventional narrative strategy, the juxtaposition of mutually exclusive scenarios that do not fit into an overarching plot; I call them "parallel storyworlds." Relevant in this context is Marie-Laure Ryan's (2006b) discussion of "ontological pluralism" in physics, possible worlds theory, and narrative: Ryan explores the puzzles of parallel universes as they are conceptualized by contemporary physics, and how narrative may capture such many-worlds universes. Ryan's final example—a well-known postmodernist short story by Robert Coover, "The Babysitter"—is particularly pertinent to our discussion, in that it presents a large number of variations on a simple premise, a babysitter looking after three children.[27] The narratives by Kellerman and VanderMeer also work with multiple "versions" of the same storyworld, a device that creates uncertainty directed specifically at the ecological crisis and its catastrophic consequences: Will humanity have a future? And is there still time to avoid the worst-case scenarios? These are the anxieties surrounding extrinsic futurity probed by both Kellerman's novella and VanderMeer's novel. The main difference between them is that Kellerman juxtaposes three mutually exclusive scenarios in a relatively straightforward fashion, while VanderMeer's experimentation with multiple timelines remains much more puzzling and disjointed. VanderMeer's work not only develops themes of the new weird—a literary trend with which the American writer is frequently aligned (see introduction)—but also complicates them through formal innovation.[28]

Kellerman's *Controller* was published digitally by Amazon as part of the climate change-themed "Warmer" series in which Groff's *Boca Raton* also appeared. Already at a paratextual level, then, there can be little doubt that the novella centers on climate change. The text is divided into three parts, the first two of which contain five numbered chapters each. Part one starts with a date ("Tuesday, January 8. 3:37 pm") accompanied by a temperature reading (87.8° F). Parts two and three carry the *same* date along with a temperature that is significantly higher in the former (96.9° F) and lower in the latter (78.7° F). In both parts one and two, chapter 5 is set on the following day, but again the temperatures differ (respectively 99.3° F and 108.8° F). Plainly, Kellerman places side-by-side versions of the same situation at different levels of warming, as in a scientific study of the psychological consequences of climate change: formal experimentation thus meets a narrative method that draws inspiration from *scientific* experimentation (e.g., randomized controlled trials with multiple groups of participants).

The protagonist of *Controller* is a man, Raymond, who lives with his bedridden mother. The setting is a relatively familiar suburban environment, except that the streets tend to be deserted during the day owing to the unforgiving temperatures. The three alternative scenarios present variations on a mundane conflict: Raymond's mother is in charge of the titular "controller" (a remote) to adjust the indoor temperature. She tends to set the thermostat at a level that Raymond finds exceedingly warm. This everyday situation plays out in vastly different ways across the three scenarios. The subtle resentments and verbal clashes of part one become a much more violent confrontation in part two, which also presents a rich portrayal of how the extreme heat disrupts Raymond's mental processes: "He could not muster a reply, his thoughts went runny before he could take hold of them" (2018: Kindle Location 219). Part three, by sharp contrast, shows mother–son relations in a much more positive light and ends on a hopeful note: "Raymond mounted the stairs. A walk was definitely in order. You couldn't take such a beautiful day for granted, though most everyone did" (2018: Kindle Location 397). The basic takeaway of the narrative couldn't be clearer: the higher the temperature, the more strained personal relationships are likely to become. The story thus explores how climate change has an indirect but dramatic impact on family ties. At this level, the parallel storyworlds map the extrinsic uncertainty of our climate future onto a sequence marked by a dramatic crescendo (part two intensifies the frictions hinted by part one) and what comes close to a happy ending (part three). If *Controller* is an exercise in speculative "scenario planning," the more moderate warming of part three is certainly the scenario we should be aiming for in real life.

However, this linear mapping between the parallel storyworlds and extrinsic futurity is complicated by an allegorical device that greatly expands the reach of the uncertainty at the heart of the narrative. In essence, there are numerous echoes between Raymond's fight over lower temperatures at home and the current framing of the climate crisis. Consider the emphasis on "negotiation" as Raymond and his mother squabble over the thermostat (with the mother firmly in control of the remote), recalling the enormous diplomatic efforts required to produce a climate agreement: "His mother was ringing the bell, crying out in her need. She sounded grateful, and she sounded afraid. Soon enough he would rouse himself and go to her, while the terms remained up for negotiation" (2018: Kindle Location 187). As the temperature rises, Raymond can feel, with a pang of pain, his beloved "ice cream going irretrievably soft" (2018: Kindle Location 298), with a possible foreshadowing of the Earth's melting ice caps. In part two, with the temperature far above Raymond's comfort zone, he comes close to humanity's reluctance to engage in long-term thinking by imagining "every future foreclosed on the pretext that it was a notion to be entertained later" (2018: Kindle Location 155). Could it be that these characters are participating in a human-scale, allegorical reenactment of the Anthropocene? In that reading, Raymond would stand in for humanity, and particularly younger generations who are dramatically running out of time and options as warming reaches a point of no return.[29] Raymond's intractable and demanding mother, by contrast, would serve as an embodiment of older generations, who have been "controlling" the climate far too long. The basis of that analogy is, of course, the mother's determination to keep the indoor temperature abnormally high despite Raymond's best efforts to "control" her. Taken together, the two characters would illustrate the intergenerational drama of a society that fails to adopt a coherent strategy to mitigate climate change.

Without pushing this allegorical reading too far, we can certainly say that the language in which the mother–son conflict is couched—the language of "climate control" and "negotiation," in particular—resonates suggestively with the climate change debate. The juxtaposition of the three scenarios mirrors the broader crisis unfolding on a planetary scale, but because the story is not *blatantly* allegorical the gap between the local conflict and the planetary crisis remains tangible. This gap reflects what Derek Woods (2014: 133) calls "scale variance": how moving from one scalar level to another involves "real discontinuities," rather than a smooth, continuous progression. For instance, an experiential gulf separates our abstract concept of global warming from everyday life (driving to work, flying to a conference, etc.), despite the latent awareness that these mundane actions contribute to global warming. The two scales—the quotidian and the planetary—are causally connected but in a highly nonlinear, discontinuous way (hence the variance).[30]

In *Controller*, this scale variance is introduced by the way in which the allegorical reading of the characters' conflict fails to account for its lifelike affectivity, which Kellerman's style reconstructs painstakingly through its close focus on Raymond's embodied experience. If the three parts of the novella present us with more or less desirable extrinsic futures for humanity, the text never completely bridges the divide between the vividness of the human conflict that triggers these scenarios and its more abstract or allegorical takeaways. The presentation of mutually exclusive scenarios channels the sense of scalar disjunction and cognitive disorientation that underlies our experience of the present as humanity hovers, indecisively, between multiple courses of action, with the least desirable scenario becoming increasingly likely as the window of opportunity closes. As a result, uncertainty is not merely projected into a future that is by definition unknowable, it is appropriated as a structural feature of the present crisis, reflecting the ambivalence and hypocrisy of climate debates that often pursue petty squabbles while the ice caps, like Raymond's ice cream, keep melting. Put otherwise, we *know* what the best future scenario is, and Kellerman's novella leaves little room for doubt as it implicitly compares the domestic ramifications of three trends of global warming. However, we fail to translate that knowledge into concerted action. This failure is an aspect of what Clark (2015: 54) calls "Anthropocene disorder," "a sense of the destructive incongruity of given norms of behaviours and thinking, without, as yet, any clear sense of an alternative." That cognitive dissonance between knowing and acting derives from the scalar leaps involved in climate change. It is an integral part of the uncertain futurity experienced by those of us who are heeding the warnings of climate scientists and environmentalists.[31] Kellerman's parallel storyworld-building, with its probing of intergenerational conflict (via Raymond's troubled relationship with his climate-controlling mother), succeeds in conveying to the reader that affective dimension of uncertainty as well. The key to that operation, as I argued here, is a doubly experimental narrative form: it is experimental because it departs from the novel's conventional focus on a single, teleological arc, and also because it is modeled on scientific experimentation via the juxtaposition of three "controlled" scenarios.

VanderMeer's foregrounding of multiple "versions" in *Dead Astronauts* also seeks to render that complexity of the climate crisis but does so without a direct comparison of situations.[32] An extension of the universe of VanderMeer's previous novel, *Borne*, *Dead Astronauts* is set in a dystopian world ravaged by ecological catastrophe. As often in weird fiction, a motley cast of characters inhabits this world, some human or human-like, some monstrous creatures, some the offspring of bodily modification and experimentation—all of them damaged and suffering. Towering over this wasteland are the ruins of an unnamed City and the headquarters of a Company whose ruthless corporate policies are largely responsible for the devastation. Three protagonists—the "dead astronauts"—roam this landscape, attempting to reestablish the semblance of an ecological balance. But the destruction chronicled by VanderMeer's novel is not only environmental: perhaps more than anything else, it is a fundamental collapse of narrative's power to make sense of this place in terms of coherent temporal parameters.

VanderMeer's previous works (some of which are discussed in Chapters 2 and 3 of this book) have also focused on ecological issues (see, e.g., Robertson 2018). Indeed, through its affective tensions and epistemological slippages, contemporary weird fiction develops a highly articulate response to climate uncertainty. With *Dead Astronauts*, VanderMeer's weird enters experimental territory by refusing to take a recognizably novelistic form: the text reads like an assemblage of narrative and poetic fragments that, while gravitating around the City, the Company, and their inhabitants, never coalesce into a focused plot. This proliferation of nonoverlapping textual forms mirrors the multiplication of timelines. From the very beginning, it becomes clear that the three astronauts are able to travel in time as well as in space. They can move back-and-forth in time, as well as sideways from one parallel world to another, guided by a single "purpose," "to destroy the Company and save the Future. Some future" (2019: 9). Yet these storyworlds, referred to as "versions," are not neatly juxtaposed as in Kellerman's novella. Rather, they are implied by way of version numbers strewn all over the book, starting from the chapter headings, from the reassuring "v.1.0" prefixed to chapter 1 to the "v.5.09," "v.4.2," and "v.3.1" that appear in later chapters. These drafts of reality don't fall into any clear picture, they remain constitutively incomplete and disjointed. Chapter 4 (titled "Can't Remember") provides a striking example of this fragmentation: the chapter consists in a sequence of seemingly random glimpses at these worlds, all accompanied by a version number (in descending order, from 7.0 to 3.3) and all ending with the pronoun "he" followed by a blank space. That midsentence elision, which is the only structural element that keeps these fragments together, points to the faltering of linguistic and narrative cognition vis-à-vis the wasteland that these pages are exploring.

The only hope is to travel back or sideways in time to preempt that ecological and cognitive meltdown. Yet, in this book, the dizzying multiplication of worlds doesn't guarantee variety of outcomes. Chapter 9 (titled "Can't Forget") consists in a long series of identical lines spread over six pages: "They killed me. They brought me back" (2019: 251–6). This, apparently, is also what the astronauts discover as they attempt to locate the version of the world in which the Company hasn't brought about ecological catastrophe, in which the future can still be "saved." Despite the protagonists' best efforts to navigate the versions while avoiding the paradoxes of time travels, their actions are inconsequential: the world's destruction at the hands of the Company seems unavoidable. This does not mean that the world is beyond saving: the foxes, as in VanderMeer's previous novel, *Borne*, are scheming in the background, and their "plan," we are told, "includes people" (2019: 117)—although the word "people," in this context, is likely to involve a major rethinking of personhood, one that uncouples that concept from the human species as we know it. But even this promise of posthuman futurity remains unfulfilled, a mere gesture rather than a narrative outcome.[33]

Through this decentralized and deeply fragmented structure, VanderMeer shatters any sense of futurity internal to the storyworld, simply because there is no single storyworld that serves as a reference point for our expectations of closure. This is perhaps most evident in the second half of the text (after the astronauts' death), which skips from one character to another, offering glimpses of the characters' intricate backstories. This deeply disorienting presentation is offset only by the inventiveness of VanderMeer's style, which matches (and draws our attention to) the residual vitality of the ecological realities he is describing, *despite* the devastation wrought by the Company.[34] This vitality is perhaps most clearly embodied by one of the three astronauts, Moss, who takes on a human shape inside the spacesuit but actually consists of shape-shifting vegetable matter: Moss, we discover, is nothing but moss that is able to spread and collapse into separate organisms while remaining sentient. Here VanderMeer's style playfully renders the proliferation of Moss through the linguistic resources of alliteration and repetition: "But Moss? Messier. Moss liked, well, moss—and lichen and limpets and sea salt and the beach and guessing the geological scale of things" (2019: 18). The sensory creativity of language, pursued through stylistic and typographical experimentation, seeks to approximate—imperfectly, of course, but suggestively—the vitality of the nonhuman world.

If Kellerman's parallel storyworlds serve as a reminder of the dissonance between human knowledge and action, VanderMeer spins the puzzling uncertainty of his "versions" toward a different mystery: how the damaged reality he envisions could still hold out the promise of creation—even if such creation may sideline the human completely. The book's illustrations display, through the abstract shapes of interacting organic matter, the biological energy that VanderMeer's prose recreates in stylistic terms. Projected outside the text, onto the world's extrinsic future, this biological imagination signals confidence in life's own possibilities, even as such confidence remains paradoxically enveloped and tempered by the uncertainty surrounding the fate of the human. The multiple parallel versions of VanderMeer's work play a central role in impressing on the reader this complex future-oriented affect, inspiring an acceptance of biological creativity beyond the human.

* * *

A fundamental dimension of the ecological crisis pertains to the imagination of future temporality as humanity teeters on the brink of environmental catastrophe. What will the future look like? How can the present standards of living be maintained in developed countries and improved in the developing world as the climate warms? Is that even a possibility, or is the global economy bound to collapse under the weight of overpopulation and hard limits on crop production? There is no denying that science and technology are essential tools to understand climate change and mitigate its consequences. But, just as technology without the political will or apposite cultural discourse cannot offer effective solutions, science cannot provide us with absolute *certainties*: the physical and sociocultural factors behind the ecological crisis interact in ways that are too complex and nonlinear for predictions to have a firm grip on the future. We know that the climate will change, and we know that for the vast majority of humans it will change for the worse; but the failure of more fine-grained predictions leaves ample room for anxieties, what-if scenarios, and speculation. This is undoubtedly rich terrain for fiction, and this chapter has begun to scrutinize the ways in which formally sophisticated narrative offers resources to model and manage the uncertainty of humanity's future. Of the four works I have examined, those by Egan and Smith don't foreground the ecological crisis per se, but they still deploy formal resources that speak to the breakdown of futurity, including linear metanarratives of progress, that humanity is facing. Indeed, as I argued in the introduction, narrative form is central to the problem of channeling and negotiating the uncertainty of humanity's future.

The strategies of future-tense narration and parallel storyworld-building I have identified are experimental forms that seek to give expression to the affective and imaginative complexity of the climate crisis. What these narrative techniques have in common is that they deny closure, and by doing so they create an epistemically and emotionally transformative tension between what I have called the intrinsic futurity of the narrative (emerging from the dynamics internal to the characters' goals and situations) and the extrinsic futurity of humankind. While Groff's *Boca Raton* probes this tension through plot and character, the four fictions by Egan, Smith, Kellerman, and VanderMeer engage with the same tension via structural devices that offer novel and stimulating perspectives on future-oriented climate anxieties. These narratives call for a radical rethinking of notions of human identity (Egan), historicity and materiality (Smith), family ties (Kellerman), and nonhuman vitality (VanderMeer). They present readers with formally grounded concepts and affects that can foster an embrace of uncertainty as a productive horizon for our lives. While indebted to postmodernist techniques of temporal disorientation and ontological proliferation, these formal strategies participate in the broader affective turn of contemporary fiction by underscoring both the materiality of the crisis and the need for an adequate emotional vocabulary to capture the breakdown of futurity in an age of climate change. The following chapters examine the work of uncertainty in relation to a number of formal dimensions of narrative, keeping in sight the central question of how fiction may teach us the value of embracing uncertainty.

Notes

1 Crownshaw (2017) also links Cooper's article to the analysis of a literary novel engaging with the climate crisis, Nathaniel Rich's *Odds against Tomorrow*. But if Crownshaw's piece concludes by pointing to "the challenges faced by climate change fiction … and its generic constraints" (2017: 144), my interest here is in more experimental literary strategies that attempt to circumvent these constraints.

2 See Bunzl:

> Decision making under ignorance seems like an option of last resort, and one way to avoid it is to try one's best to assign probabilities to the outcomes

under consideration. The challenges in trying to do that for climate change run up against the limits of both climate science and economics, but do so for different reasons. The problem for climate science is that the empirical record of data is too sparse to extrapolate from that record with much confidence. On the other hand the problem for economic theory is that the further in the future we try to project, the less confidence we can have about the applicability of our models. (2015: 27)

3 See Oziewicz (2017) for a comprehensive discussion of the relationship between speculation, the label "speculative fiction," and the science fiction genre.
4 See Gould (1987) on the cultural history of deep time.
5 However, Crutzen's notion of Anthropocene has come under criticism for the way in which its elevation of humanity to a geological agent sidelines major socioeconomic differences between the developed and the developing world. See Crist (2013) for more on this controversy and Vermeulen (2020) for a wide-ranging discussion of the term's relevance to literary studies.
6 See also Ehrenreich (2020) for an essayistic account of conceptions of time and how linear temporality came to prevail in Western culture, feeding into the climate crisis.
7 See Kohlmann (2014) for discussion of a similar convergence of Cold War–era anxieties and contemporary debates on the posthuman.
8 For a convergent argument, see also Evans (2017) in the special issue edited by O'Brien and Lousley.
9 On the subject of posterity and parental care, see also Johns-Putra (2019), which I discussed in my introduction.
10 I am using the word "kinship" in the narrow sense of "blood relationship" here, but an alternative option—notably endorsed by Donna Haraway (2016)—is to expand the concept of kinship beyond family bonds.
11 See Demaria et al. (2013) and Honoré (2004) for more on degrowth and slow philosophy, respectively.
12 David Herman offers an insightful discussion of narrative's role in segmenting and organizing temporal experience in Herman (2003).
13 See Fludernik (2005) for an overview.
14 This distinction between narrating and experiencing self in first-person narrative was introduced by Stanzel (1984: 210).
15 Richard Gerrig coined the term "anomalous suspense." See his treatment in chapter 5 of *Experiencing Narrative Worlds* (1993).
16 Currie is in good company: Frank Kermode's highly influential *The Sense of an Ending* also builds on an analogy between intrinsic futurity (the internal temporal workings of story) and extrinsic futurity (in Kermode's case, the apocalypse in eschatological thinking). See Kermode (2000: 35).

17 This aspect of storytelling is brought out by Richard Walsh's (2007) account of narrative meaning-making in fiction, which builds on Dan Sperber and Deirdre Wilson's (1995) relevance theory. See also what I write in the introduction about the workings of interpretation.

18 Thus, echoing Darko Suvin's (1979) influential concept of "cognitive estrangement," Canavan and Wald write that the "futurity of SF inheres not in its setting but in its insistent imagining of alternatives. If, as the Russian formalists suggested, art characteristically defamiliarizes the world, SF conspicuously takes such estrangement as its central charge: world making, after all, necessarily implies a form of world breaking—or at least introspection" (2011: 241).

19 By contrast, the algorithmic denouement I will discuss in Chapter 5 does produce closure but in a way that involves a renegotiation of narrative agency across the human–nonhuman divide, as we'll see.

20 The only exception I know of is D. A. Miller's *Narrative and Its Discontents* (1981), a study of closure in the nineteenth-century novel whose structuralist framework does not go very far in shedding light on the experiential and cultural processes I am interested in here.

21 Herman is here building on Tzvetan Todorov's (1969) seminal narratological work.

22 See also Ameel and Caracciolo (2021) for more on the "earnest ontologies" of contemporary literature and how they differ from postmodernist models.

23 For a survey of affective responses to the ecological crisis, see a collection edited by Kyle Bladow and Jennifer Ladino (2018).

24 I am grateful to Edward Finn for bringing Egan's short story to my attention in email correspondence (November 2019). Here I refer to the online version of the story, which is unpaginated.

25 Here and throughout, the slashes indicate a line break in the original text (reflecting the end of each tweet).

26 In his account of logically or physical impossible ("unnatural") narratives, Jan Alber (2009: 84–5) calls this interpretive strategy "reading unnatural elements as internal states."

27 Coover's story has been frequently examined in the context of unnatural narratology. See Richardson (2015: 56–7), in which it is discussed under the rubric of "multiple fabulas."

28 VanderMeer himself embraced the label "weird fiction" in an anthology coedited with Ann VanderMeer (VanderMeer and VanderMeer 2012).

29 Johns-Putra (2019: 9–17) offers an account of climate change fiction based on the concept of intergenerational ethics.

30 I discuss the concept of nonlinearity more extensively in Caracciolo (2021: chap. 1).

31 The concept of cognitive dissonance was famously introduced by Leon Festinger (1957). I discuss this notion further in Caracciolo (2016c), in which I explore

how dissonance may arise in readers' interactions with mentally deviant characters.
32 For a fuller reading of *Dead Astronauts*, which partly overlaps with my discussion here, see also Caracciolo and Ulstein (2022).
33 We will encounter these "scheming" foxes again in Chapter 3, which focuses on another VanderMeer story set in the *Borne* universe, *The Strange Bird*.
34 Jane Bennett (2010) discusses this nonhuman vitality under the rubrics of "vibrant matter" and "thing-power," but while her thinking revolves around inanimate objects ("things"), VanderMeer favors biological forces.

2

Pathways to Unstable Worlds

After temporality, we turn to narrative space as a site for negotiating the uncertainty of our ecological predicament. Unlike the experience of time, which hovers between two hazy horizons (the past of memory and the future of anticipation), space is normally thought of as stable and dependable.[1] These connotations of stability have deep roots. In cognitive linguistics, following George Lakoff and Mark Johnson's seminal work in the 1980s (Johnson 1987; Lakoff 1987), it has been widely assumed that interactions with space structure our thinking at a fundamental level. Temporality itself tends to be conceptualized in spatial terms: every competent speaker of English knows that the sentence "the meeting has been moved to Wednesday" denotes no actual relocation in space, only a change in the timing of the meeting. Similar spatial metaphors for temporality can be found in other languages.[2] Likewise, all sorts of abstract ideas are normally expressed in ways that reflect the embodied experience of spatiality, from the "road to freedom" to "work–life balance."[3] Through its direct link with bodily interactions, the experience of human-scale space—as defined by basic actions such as grasping, moving, lifting, throwing, and so on—is something like a cognitive constant. Thus, philosopher Peter Woelert argues that "embodiment, and embodied spatial experience in particular, can ... broadly be regarded as constituting from the very beginning an essential condition for the possibility of the symbolic domestication of the world" (2011: 133). Intriguingly, Woelert expresses the idea that symbolic meaning-making is inherently spatial by way of another spatial metaphor that points to the primacy of the space of the home ("domestication") in constructing an idea of world. Human cultures appropriate reality symbolically by turning it into a home of sorts.

What if, however, the world proves recalcitrant to this act of domestication? What if our embodied experience of space breaks down, depriving us of our usual physical and conceptual bearings? Just as climate change upsets our experience of futurity, it can disrupt the perceived stability of space, forcing us to confront the "bumpiness"—in William Connolly's (2017) apt metaphor—of a reality shaped by ecological crisis. Literary narrative, to anticipate this chapter's argument, registers such spatial trouble and the existential uncertainty it gives rise to. Before expanding on that idea, it will be worth taking some time to address the question why environmental issues, and climate change more specifically, challenge spatiality and domesticity so radically. The answer is necessarily manifold. To start from the obvious, environmental catastrophe marks a sudden irruption of the nonhuman into the space of the quotidian. In early 2020, unusually intense bushfires ravaged a large swathe of the Australian continent; one of the first elements to come up in media reports was that thousands of residents had to be evacuated, some of them by sea. This is a shocking coming together of everyday domesticity and a disaster made more probable by rising temperatures. It is hardly surprising, then, that catastrophe is one of the main motifs—perhaps the main one—in the repertoire of climate fiction (see introduction). But there are many other, less sensational disruptions to the experience of space that can be linked to climate change. Kellerman's *Controller*, discussed in the previous chapter, shows how even moderate changes in temperature can alter domestic spaces by undermining the relationship between the protagonist and his mother. There is no overt "catastrophe" here, only a gradual splintering of the mundane at the hands of the climate—a splintering neatly captured by Kellerman's parallel storyworlds.

At an even more abstract level, the spatially distributed nature of climate change highlights the discontinuity between local spatial experience and the imagination of the world as a whole. This breakage is part of what Woods describes under the rubric of "scale variance," as mentioned in my reading of *Controller*. Simply put, Australia's devastating bushfires are probabilistically correlated with the increase in global temperatures. But there are significant ruptures between this disaster, which exists on a regional scale, and the planetary phenomenon of climate change. Many of the discussions surrounding events of this type center on whether a catastrophic event was *caused* by climate change; climate skeptics or denialists typically reject that causal link. This kind of skepticism has complex cultural roots, and others have explored it in far more detail than I can offer here (Dunlap and McCright 2016). I will limit myself to pointing to a problem that, arguably, underlies (but does not completely explain) climate skepticism: our commonsense understanding of causation—which is of course distinct from scientific or philosophical accounts—is modeled on what cognitive linguists call "force dynamics." Consider a falling rock pushing another rock off a cliff, or a person using a pull cord to open the curtains: in these scenarios, force is directly applied to an object, causing an overt displacement. These physical dynamics can be scaled up to events that are not connected in direct, physical terms. For instance, if I say that the assassination of the Archduke Franz Ferdinand *triggered* the First World War, a metaphor drawn from the domain of physical interaction (pulling the trigger) helps me conceptualize the causal relationship between two events that are far more abstract than the gun-firing scenario. This kind of projection from the concrete to the intangible is not merely a way of talking about causation, it is a cognitively basic way of *conceptualizing* causation.[4]

The problem is that the force-dynamic model of causation fails to capture the nonlinearity of the link between the bushfires and climate change. That link is not deterministic but probabilistic: via rising temperatures, the global phenomenon of climate change makes local disruptions and disasters (including bushfires) more likely, but other factors and conditions also play an important role in bringing about a catastrophic event. The result is that, while global temperatures keep rising, we may experience bushfires one year and not the following one. Such fluctuations make it possible for climate change skeptics to deny the causal link altogether—a claim that builds on our commonsense intuitions about causation as a linear phenomenon grounded in force dynamics. The unique complexity of this causal connection points to the multiple gaps (or "scale variance," to use again Woods's terminology) between everyday spatial experience and the planetary scale of the ecological crisis. In *Ecocriticism on the Edge*, Clark uses the famous "Earthrise" photograph (taken in 1968 during the Apollo 8 mission) as an illustration of scale variance: "To contemplate the sight of the whole Earth is to think the disjunction between individual perception and global reality, a disjunction that has now become so consequential in the Anthropocene" (2015: 36). Disjunctions of this kind can enter our sense of space and place—certainly, more subtly than in the case of natural disasters or troubled interpersonal relations but in a way that perhaps better reflects the complexity, scale, and distributed nature of climate change.

A striking illustration of the collapse of spatiality vis-à-vis environmental issues can be found in *Here*, a comic strip by the American artist Richard McGuire. After publishing *Here* in 1989 as a six-page, black-and-white strip, in 2014 McGuire released a color album that elaborates on and refines the original concept. As Jon Hegglund (2019) argues in an insightful econarratological reading, McGuire's work is a profound meditation on the breakdown of domesticity in the Anthropocene. What brings together the panels that make up both versions of *Here* is a unique spatial perspective: the scenes are all set inside the same room, with the corner cutting each panel precisely in half (in the album version, the corner also coincides with the hinge of the book). While the spatial viewpoint is fixed, the panels keep skipping back-and-forth in time, as we know from text boxes showing the year in which each scene takes place. The setup is further complicated by window-like inserts that open up the temporality of each panel from the inside, without departing from the fixed spatial perspective. Consider, for instance, Figure 2.1, which juxtaposes two pages from the 2014 comic book. The first scene is set in 1957 but contains an insert with a black cat dated 1999. The following page turns the 1957 scene into an insert (with the woman in the pink dress) and shows the same black cat in a slightly different position, in 1999. The background depicts a foggy forest in 1623. Readers infer that the latter panel doesn't display a random natural landscape but what the surroundings of the house looked like before the house itself was built. Other panels suggest a past devoid of human presence (a sea landscape in 500,000 BCE), as well as a future marked by ecological catastrophe (water gushing through the window in 2111).

Even if the particulars of the represented space shift constantly (from one panel to another, and even within each panel), the reader understands the spatial coordinates to be strictly identical across the comic book—hence the title, *Here*. This strategy builds on the assumed stability of space and deconstructs it by expanding the typical temporality of narrative to include events separated by thousands of years. The world has a stable spatial ground only if it is understood as an abstract grid or container for human (or human-scale) events; but as the timeline of the figuration grows exponentially, space is revealed to be an extremely malleable medium for experiential worlds as diverse as a home, a forest, and a beach. On a formal level, the world of McGuire's page dances: new inserts pop up on each page, creating unexpected thematic and chromatic resonances and

Figure 2.1 Two pages from Richard McGuire's *Here* (2014). Copyright © 2014, Richard McGuire, used by permission of The Wylie Agency (UK) Limited.

thus fragmenting and questioning the familiar space of the home where this visual narrative started. By combining formal fragmentation with an explicit foregrounding of the more-than-human temporality of catastrophe, McGuire's *Here* explores the nonlinearity of the ecological crisis: how the experience of futurity breaks down as soon as human societies—and, certainly, some societies more than others—enter a geological timeline by tampering with the Earth's ecosystems.[5] But this temporal instability is here bound up with spatial indeterminacy. After all, the climate crisis faces us with deep temporality: we burn fossil fuels that were formed millions of years ago and produce plastic that will far survive our individual existence.[6] This large-scale temporality shakes our confidence in the *continuity* of experienced space despite our best efforts to cling to a fixed spatial perspective, as both versions of McGuire's comic book attest: from the vantage point of deep time, even a space that is as strictly delimited as the "here" of a single room looks erratic and unpredictable.

I started this chapter by asking what happens when the everyday experience of space proves recalcitrant to domestication, because familiar places are destabilized by the ecological crisis (through catastrophe, or through the tangled causality that climate change involves). How should one think about the world when the existence of human communities and nonhuman species is so severely threatened? The idea that we (humans *and* nonhumans) inhabit a single, stable world must be abandoned, because that view will always tend to reinforce an anthropocentric ontology.[7] Instead, one should embrace the "idea of a world comprising a multiplicity of subject positions," in anthropologist Eduardo Viveiros de Castro's (2004: 471) words. Like McGuire's *Here*, contemporary narrative has developed formal templates that can help us imagine that ontological multiplicity. I call these templates "pathways" because of their markedly spatial nature. They put extreme pressure on the presumed stability of the world, a concept that—conjugated as *story*world—has been a cornerstone of theories of narrative since David Herman's *Story Logic* (2002). I will argue that the destabilization of (story)worlds can follow four pathways: oscillation, erasure, fragmentation, and floating—all terms that will be explicated in the following pages. Each pathway will be discussed in relation to two contemporary novels: Jeff VanderMeer's *Annihilation* and China Miéville's *The City & the City* for oscillation, Emily St. John Mandel's *Station Eleven* and Mark Danielewski's *House of Leaves* for erasure, Jonathan Lethem's *Amnesia Moon* and Dale Pendell's *The Great Bay* for fragmentation, and finally Hanya Yanagihara's *The People in the Trees* and Michel Faber's *The Book of Strange New Things* for floating. This overview will result in a more abbreviated reading of these works than elsewhere in this book, but some of the themes introduced here—for instance, in relation to VanderMeer's and Miéville's "weird" fiction—will be pursued in the next chapters.

In all of these narratives, the uncertainty at the heart of the ecological crisis is both spatialized and channeled by way of formal devices. Erin James writes that an "Anthropocene narrative theory sensitive to the changes brought about by rising sea levels and an abundance of water develops a ... category of 'unspatialization,' or spatializing information that is strategically unclear or unchartable" (2020: 194). Oscillation, erasure, fragmentation, and floating are versions of James's "unspatialization," although her focus on "strategically unclear" information comes particularly close to what I call floating spaces. Working alongside James's Anthropocene narrative theory, I focus on how these narrative operations create opportunities for thinking the unstable spatiality of climate change: they are imaginative tools that help readers confront an uncertain world by making its instability more tangible and vivid—and therefore also more manageable—through the distance afforded by literary form. To influence the cultural perception of a certain topic, narrative needs to develop forms that are capable of disclosing new understanding and reconfiguring the audience's affects, thus covering the full spectrum of the negotiation of uncertainty: from characters' mental states to formal devices to readers' experience and outlook on the climate crisis. Without shying away from the destabilizing nature of uncertainty, the spatial strategies discussed below seek to offset the audience's anxieties through a creative rethinking of the meaning of the word "world."

Destabilizing Storyworlds

We have already encountered the term "storyworld" in my discussion of parallel narrative scenarios in the previous chapter. We can now return to, and complicate, that discussion in relation to narrative spatiality. The storyworld concept is perhaps one of contemporary narrative theory's most successful additions to the vocabulary of structuralist narratology. Certainly, the "text as world" metaphor has a long history: especially if we consider the broader context of literary studies, storyworlds fall in line with previous models of literature based on possible and fictional worlds (Pavel 1986; Ryan 1991; Doležel 1998). Theories of possible and fictional worlds were inspired by work in the field of modal logic, which employed the language of possible worlds to formally describe hypothetical and counterfactual scenarios.

Many of these debates had to do with the *difference* between the philosophical construct of a possible world—which is fundamentally a set of propositions—and the ways in which narrative (including fictional narrative) can generate what feels like a coherent, plausible world. Unlike possible and fictional worlds, storyworlds don't come with this kind of philosophical baggage. Instead, the narrative theorist who introduced this concept, David Herman, defines storyworlds in psychological terms, drawing on research on text comprehension in psycholinguistics: "storyworlds are mental models of who did what to and with whom, when, where, why, and in what fashion in the world to which recipients relocate … as they work to comprehend a narrative" (2002: 5).

Contemporary narrative theory has taken up the storyworld concept without necessarily embracing the psychological slant of Herman's definition. Rather, the term "storyworld" has become a convenient shorthand for the setting of a story, particularly when the setting is seen as a relatively autonomous spatial domain into which readers can immerse themselves. However, the emphasis mostly lies on the spatial domain itself, not on the dynamics of readers' imaginative engagement with it. Marie-Laure Ryan, for instance, argues that the storyworld is "the story space completed by the reader's imagination on the basis of cultural knowledge and real world experience" (2014: para. 9). Narratives typically contain a large number of spatial references, some of which evoke places physically occupied by the characters in specific scenes or episodes, while others are mere mentions of certain locations. For example, James Joyce's *Ulysses* is set in Dublin, and the characters' movements through real-world space can be reconstructed with great precision. But *Ulysses* also refers to cities that are not visited by the protagonists within the temporal arc of the novel (e.g., Rome or London). The storyworld is the sum total of these textual references.

The implication is that a storyworld is a comparatively stable construct that can be described independently of each audience member's individual experience of a narrative. "The notion of storyworld provides the surrounding environment required for immersion," writes Ryan (2019: 81) in a recent defense of the storyworld metaphor, which suggests that approaching a narrative *as* a world is a precondition for involvement in the story being told. What does "world" really mean in this context, however? Largely, it conveys two assumptions that tend to be widely shared by readers: that storyworlds are relatively autonomous from what we call everyday reality; and that, despite the changes introduced by the plot, storyworlds remain stable over time.[8] This sense of stability is largely associated with the *spatial* dimension of the narrative. Consider again the case of *Ulysses*: even if the novel takes place in a city called Dublin, readers know that this Dublin is not the same as present-day Dublin and in some ways also departs from the historical Dublin of Joyce's times (through the existence of fictional characters like the protagonists Stephen Dedalus and Leopold Bloom, for instance). The perceived separation of fiction from the real world even trumps the fact that the reader's imagination of Dublin is, in some respects, derived from real-world knowledge. As for the second assumption, readers will take for granted that the storyworld of the beginning is the same as the storyworld of the novel's ending, even if the physical whereabouts and identity of the characters evolve significantly in the course of the plot. The storyworld, from this perspective, can be thought of as a spatial backdrop that enables readerly immersion through its continuous presence.

This perception of storyworlds reflects the broader associations of space with concreteness and permanence, as discussed in the previous section. However, certain narratives work toward undermining this sense of stability, asking readers to engage with storyworlds that are, in different ways and to varying degrees, precarious. In doing so, these narratives generate uncertainty and channel it toward ecological issues, using the hesitations and fluctuations of space to undermine entrenched ideas of humanity's separation from the natural world. The second part of this chapter charts four pathways through which storyworlds can be made ontologically unstable in spatial terms.[9] What I call oscillation, erasure, fragmentation, and floating revise our understanding of the world concept (in fiction and outside of fiction) so as to bring it into alignment, imaginatively and affectively, with the uncertainty of climate change. These pathways thus model the crisis we are experiencing and serve as resources for embracing change and instability. Before looking at them more closely, however, it will be worth keeping in mind that this discussion partially overlaps with the debates surrounding the field of "unnatural narratology" (Alber et al. 2010), which has become one of the main strands of contemporary narrative theory. Unnatural narratology is an account of narrative geared toward experimental texts that challenge the conventions of literary realism—or, adopting an alternative definition of the unnatural, texts that overstep the boundaries of what is physically and logically possible.[10] In this context, Jan Alber offers a helpful survey of "antimimetic" (and therefore unnatural) spaces, distinguishing four scenarios: first, "unnatural containers" are texts that embrace an impossible geometry, for instance, a space that can contain objects larger than its physical dimensions (Alber's main example, Mark Danielewski's *House of Leaves*, is also central to my discussion below); second, Alber examines narratives that use physical space to lend a material form to the characters' mental states;

third, there are narratives that deviate from real-world geography and trade in factual impossibilities (such as a burning lake in *Beowulf*); fourth, Alber points to narratives that destabilize space through ontological metalepsis—that is, by blurring the distinction between fiction and reality.[11]

Alber's overview of unnatural spaces is not meant to be exhaustive, and neither is my discussion of unstable storyworlds in the following sections. However, it is important to understand how the categories I will introduce below serve a fundamentally different purpose from Alber's concepts, even as they are inspired by the readings offered by Alber and others in the context of unnatural narratology. As a concept, the unnatural is dualistically opposed to the natural, and indeed many of the arguments against unnatural narrative theory center on the impracticality of establishing a "natural" standard (of conventional storytelling or of real-world experience) from which the unnatural departs (see, e.g., Fludernik 2012a; Hegglund 2020). Alber's interest in unnatural spaces leads him to focus on storyworlds that are impossible insofar as they challenge readers' intuitive understanding of how real spaces "work." Yet these impossible spaces retain a degree of stability by virtue of being thought of as rigidly opposed to "natural," real-world spaces. Possible or impossible, natural or unnatural are after all binary concepts that aim to "fix" a narrative in a certain state, as demonstrated by Alber's typologizing approach. By contrast, my emphasis on instability as a figure of uncertainty calls for categories that are able to account for the *dynamics* of collapsing storyworlds, the very hesitation between possibility and impossibility that is denied by unnatural models of story.[12] The categories I propose, then, are a series of flexible tropes through which narrative may give rise to spatial features that directly register as *uncertain*, and not as downright impossible, at the third level of my spectrum of narrative negotiation (see introduction)—that is, in the reader's experience of narrative.

Oscillation is when a storyworld systematically wavers between two or more states, layers, or possibilities; erasure can be construed as a specific case of oscillation that involves the *negation* of a state of the storyworld; fragmentation breaks down a storyworld into a series of (relatively) autonomous ontological "shards"; finally, floating involves an ambiguous relationship between subdomains of a storyworld. In oscillation, erasure, and fragmentation the storyworld is internally disrupted, but the results of the disruption tend to be clear-cut and spatially legible. In floating, by contrast, the storyworld remains indeterminate—not just spatially but also semantically: the values and beliefs that define a certain subdomain of the world seem to lose traction elsewhere, for reasons that are never clearly explained. Floating is a spatial instance of "fuzziness" in narrative, to borrow from David Herman's (2002: chap. 6) discussion of indeterminate temporal anchoring of certain events within a narrative sequence.

It should be stressed that these concepts are not full-fledged *types* of narrative but adaptable formal patterns that can be detected in a variety of genres and contexts (and can easily coexist within a single text). They convey to the reader a sense of radical uncertainty that may destabilize—in conjunction with theme and affect—the separation between human communities and the nonhuman world. As always in this book, some of the contemporary novels I discuss below contain explicit references to the climate crisis; in other instances (Miéville's *The City & the City* and Danielewski's *House of Leaves* come to mind), these texts resonate with climate uncertainty in formal terms but do not stage it directly.

Oscillation

In his seminal *Postmodernist Fiction*, Brian McHale writes,

> Ambiguous sentences may project ambiguous objects, objects which are not temporarily but permanently and irresolvably ambiguous. This is not a matter, in other words, of *choosing* between alternative states of affairs, but rather of an ontological oscillation, a flickering effect, or, to use [Roman] Ingarden's own metaphor, an effect of "iridescence" or "opalescence." And "opalescence" is not restricted to single objects; entire *worlds* may flicker. (McHale 1987: 32; italics in the original)

McHale discusses the quintessentially postmodernist tendency to multiply and juxtapose scenarios—"worlds," in McHale's terminology. Think about Robert Coover's "The Babysitter," mentioned in the previous chapter, with its countless variations on the same basic story (a babysitter spending a night with three children). This playful technique creates a highly distinctive form of disorientation in the reader, whose imagination oscillates from one scenario to another without being able to settle on a definitive version of the story.[13] Borrowing language from Ingarden's aesthetic theory, as articulated in *The Literary Work of Art* (Ingarden 1973), McHale glosses oscillation through visual metaphors such as iridescence and opalescence. Indeed, iridescence (e.g., in a soap bubble) is defined by chromatic instability: the color of the bubble appears to shift constantly as a result of both our visual angle and external lighting conditions. In evoking a storyworld, narrative can develop verbal equivalents for this visual effect.

The usage of oscillation is not limited to the postmodernist canon, however. It can be found in a number of contemporary authors, particularly those affiliated with so-called weird fiction (see introduction). Thus, Jeff VanderMeer's novel *Annihilation*—a landmark work in the new weird tradition and the first volume of the Southern Reach trilogy—begins as follows: "The tower, which was not supposed to be there, plunges into the earth in a place just before the black pine forest begins to give way to swamp and then the reeds and wind-gnarled trees of the marsh flats" (2014: 3). The statement that the tower "plunges into the earth" sounds incongruous, because of course towers are elevated structures, not underground ones.[14] This incongruity is thematized by the narrator a couple of pages later, when she remarks,

> At first, only I saw it as a tower. I don't know why the word tower came to me, given that it tunneled into the ground. I could as easily have considered it a bunker or a submerged building. Yet as soon as I saw the staircase, I remembered the lighthouse on the coast and had a sudden vision of the last expedition drifting off, one by one, and sometime thereafter the ground shifting in a uniform and preplanned way to leave the lighthouse standing where it had always been but depositing this underground part of it inland. I saw this in vast and intricate detail as we all stood there, and, looking back, I mark it as the first irrational thought I had once we had reached our destination. (2014: 6–7)

The "irrational thought" gives rise to a double principle of spatial oscillation: on the one hand, there is the inversion of the up-down axis, which elicits "a twinned sensation of vertigo and a fascination with structure," as the narrator herself puts it (2014: 14).[15] But this semantic instability (tower/tunnel) is compounded by another oscillation, this time grounded in the history of the storyworld: namely, the way in which (as stated above) the existence of the tower appears connected, mysteriously, to another spatial landmark, the lighthouse, via the "last expedition" (one of the many search parties dispatched into this region, known as Area X, to investigate its ecological anomalies). The hesitation tower/tunnel thus reflects the murky history of this place and how its "ground" could have "shifted" to separate two spatial elements (the tunnel and the lighthouse) that were originally one. The shifting ground is an almost prototypical image of spatial uncertainty, which results in a double oscillation (tower/tunnel, tower/lighthouse) that the novel does *not* resolve but asks readers to accept as a defining feature of the storyworld—hence the irreducible weirdness of the space staged by VanderMeer's trilogy. It is no coincidence then that Alex Garland's (2018) film adaptation of *Annihilation* uses an iridescent pattern as a substitute for linguistic oscillations such as tower/tunnel. Area X becomes "the Shimmer" in the film: what is, in the novel, an invisible border between this contaminated region and the rest of the storyworld turns into an iridescent surface that recalls a soap bubble or an oil film (see Figure 2.2).

In China Miéville's *The City & the City* (2009), another instance of weird fiction, a first kind of spatial oscillation is provided by the paradoxical coexistence of two distinct cities. The novel is set in two fictional Eastern European cities—Besźel and Ul Qoma—that share the same geographic location, even if some areas can only be accessed by the residents of one city. Where the two cities overlap—in the novel these are referred to as "crosshatched" spaces—the inhabitants have been trained to systematically ignore or "unsee" the other city's buildings and denizens. All transgressions are harshly punished by a mysterious organization called "Breach."

Oscillation has to do with how our visual experience of the storyworld fluctuates between Besźel and Ul Qoma: just as it is strictly forbidden for the narrator in Besźel to perceive what is going on around him in Ul Qoma, Miéville's style asks us to imaginatively "unsee" the other half of the city, even though we know that it is there "grosstopically" (a neologism used by the characters to refer to the shared physical reality of these cities, as opposed to their political and psychological separation). Consider, for instance, the following spatial description:

> I lived east and south a bit of [Besźel's] Old Town, the top-but-one flat in a six-storey towerlet on VulkovStrász. It is a heavily crosshatched street—clutch by clutch of architecture broken by alterity, even in a few spots house by house. The

Figure 2.2 The Shimmer in Alex Garland's *Annihilation* (2018).

local buildings [i.e., those located in Besźel] are taller by a floor or three than the others. (2009: 29)

Here it is the narrator's vague language—"alterity," "the others"—that distances readers' imagination from the unseen, but physically ("grosstopically") present, city of Ul Qoma. The effect is reminiscent of what is known technically as a multistable figure, such as the famous rabbit-duck illusion popularized by Ludwig Wittgenstein's *Philosophical Investigations*. The image presents itself as a rabbit or as a duck, depending on the portion of the drawing our gaze focuses on, but seeing *both* animals simultaneously is impossible. Likewise, in reading *The City & the City* our visual experience wavers between Besźel and Ul Qoma without being able to integrate the two landscapes. This hesitation is also amplified by the novel's plot, which revolves around the murder of an archeology PhD student whose research focuses on the two cities' shared origins. The narrator is the detective in charge of the murder investigation in Besźel; in the second half of the novel, he travels to Ul Qoma, which means that he has to unsee his home city as he traverses spaces that are, at the same time, familiar (in Besźel) and unfamiliar (in Ul Qoma). The reader's imagination follows suit, mirroring the spatial contortions the protagonist's mind goes through as he takes in this oscillating storyworld. In *The City & the City*, transgressing the boundary between the two cities—for example, by speaking to or even visually acknowledging an inhabitant of the other city—is the most serious crime one can commit. It is known as "breach," and it is violently repressed by the organization of the same name. Avoiding breach—and thus avoiding a dangerous run-in with the Breach police—involves deeply embodied knowledge of where one is located and how to subliminally distinguish the buildings and denizens of two cities.[16] The novel's plot works by destabilizing that knowledge and the rigid boundary between the two cities: the murder points to an interstitial space, an invisible "third city" known as Orciny that may or may not exist, and may be controlled by Breach. As the binary oscillation between two mutually exclusive spaces (Besźel *or* Ul Qoma) is disrupted, a sense of radical uncertainty comes to the fore, reflecting the mystery of the third city's existence and relationship with Breach.

There are few direct descriptions of the Breach police in the novel, but the oblique comments made by the narrator create feelings of affective and sensory instability that complicate the simple spatial oscillation between the two cities. Here is, for example, how Breach intervenes to move an Ul Qoman car that had involuntarily breached into Besźel following a traffic accident: "In seconds, the

Breach came. Shapes, figures, some of whom perhaps had been there but who nonetheless seemed to coalesce from spaces between smoke from the accident, moving too fast it seemed to be clearly seen, moving with authority and power so absolute that within seconds they had controlled, contained, the area of the intrusion" (2009: 81). Once again, the vagueness of the narrator's language—"shapes, figures"—is remarkable, and so is the Breach's ability to elude the materiality of this dual space, acting from behind a literal smokescreen. While in VanderMeer's *Annihilation* perceptual oscillation gives rise to a binary form of uncertainty, Miéville evokes uncertainty by moving *past* oscillation, into an enigmatic space where dualistic distinctions are troubled. The indeterminacy of Miéville's Breach (bound up as it is with the mysterious third city, Orciny) is, then, a more radical way of channeling uncertainty in spatial terms than VanderMeer's linguistic hesitations. It is more radical because it triggers a double process of familiarization for the reader—first with the weird coexistence of two material cities, then with the notion of a third, immaterial space that serves as the source of the weirdness.

Another way to put the same point is to say that the most productive oscillation in *The City & the City* is not the straightforwardly *perceptual* one—"seeing" and "unseeing" the titular cities—but rather an imaginative one, a fluctuation from a world of material objects within the two cities to a sphere of invisible, occult dealings. This irruption of Breach and Orciny creates a "higher" form of oscillation that fundamentally overturns the storyworld we have been familiarized into, with the strict separation between Besźel and Ul Qoma. It should be noted that this storyworld doesn't speak to the ecological crisis directly, unlike VanderMeer's Area X, which is explicitly linked to the dangers of environmental degradation. Yet Miéville's foregrounding of invisible forces still resonates with the crisis by providing readers with a spatial equivalent for the pervasive intangibility of climate change—how its effects are both omnipresent and difficult to trace experientially to the abstract idea of climate change itself.

How are these oscillations different from those McHale detects in postmodernist fiction? We have addressed a version of this question in the previous chapter. While the continuity between postmodernist and contemporary authors such as VanderMeer and Miéville is undeniable, postmodernist fiction tends to engage in ontological play—including spatial hesitations and oscillations—in a self-referential mode: the goal of postmodernist experimentations with temporality and space was subverting the conventions of both realist and modernist fiction; in contemporary works, by contrast, broadly similar strategies foreground the affective dimension of uncertainty and its relevance to current issues, including the ecological crisis.

Erasure

The basic setup of Miéville's *The City & the City* creates a structural oscillation in the reader's imagination: when one city is foregrounded, the other is experienced under erasure, as *absent* and nevertheless eerily present through its absence. Narratives can deepen this sense of spatial erasure by strategically deploying negation at the grammatical level.[17] Emily St. John Mandel's *Station Eleven* is set in a postapocalyptic world devastated by a pandemic. While this disaster is not explicitly related to the climate crisis, the novel holds a mirror up to the global, capitalist economy that has played a central part, historically, in determining climate change. At the beginning of chapter 6, the comforts of Western modernity are evoked by way of a peculiar device, an admittedly "incomplete" list of things and experiential possibilities that are *un*available in this storyworld, after the collapse of society as we know it in the West:

> No more diving into pools of chlorinated water lit green from below. No more ball games played out under floodlights. No more porch lights with moths fluttering on summer nights. No more trains running under the surface of cities on the dazzling power of the electric third rail. No more cities. No more films, except rarely, except with a generator drowning out half the dialogue. (2014: 31)

This negative enumeration (which continues for several pages) produces erasure by progressively "emptying out" the storyworld: the readers' attention is focused on the absence of certain objects or the unavailability of certain experiences, such as urban living. This strategy creates a peculiar form of oscillation between the imagination of affectively charged situations (swimming in a pool, taking the subway, etc.) and awareness of their impossibility. Seen from the defamiliarizing viewpoint of this postapocalyptic storyworld, everyday reality looks impoverished; yet the novel as a whole attempts to reverse the direction of the defamiliarization: it shows how the unavailability of the material things and comforts of consumerist society (foregrounded in this chapter of the novel) heightens the characters' longing for community as a response to future uncertainty. The protagonist, who is part of a traveling theater company, sows the seeds of this utopian vision of society through the relationships she establishes in the course of the novel. The erasure of familiar objects and experiences is thus a step toward confronting readers with the necessity of developing an alternative to current models of society based solely on mass consumption.

In Mark Danielewski's *House of Leaves* (2000), another negative enumeration generates erasure in even more explicitly spatial terms. Danielewski's novel revolves around the exploration of a house that, despite its reassuring appearance, opens onto a vast and deeply disorienting labyrinth (as discussed by Alber in relation to unnatural spaces).[18] The interior of the house is so unsettling because it deprives those who experience it of any familiar reference point through its darkness and barrenness. Partly responsible for this disorienting effect are Danielewski's typographical experiments, such as the layout of chapter 20, where the pages become progressively emptier and the text narrower as the characters advance through this space. Equally effective is, in chapter 9, a list of all the architectural elements that are *absent* from the maze. This is where erasure comes in. The list begins on page 119 of my edition ("Not only are there no hot-air registers, return air vents, or radiators," etc.) and ends on page 142 with the typographically crossed-out words "Picture that. In your dreams." Rich in unfamiliar and technical terms, the list does not occupy the entirety of the page but only a box whose mirror image is provided on the even-numbered pages, as if readers were looking *through* the page itself. This verbal accumulation functions analogously to Mandel's list, but instead of embracing an entire storyworld it channels the experience of a specific *locale* that defies human cognition. The alienness of Danielewski's labyrinth can only be rendered by way of negative enumeration, by stripping away objects and elements that might help readers recognize and therefore appropriate this place. The final comment, with the possibility of "picturing that [space]" being explicitly and visually erased, suggests that the house's challenge to human meaning-making extends outward, from the experience of the characters getting lost in this maze to the imagination of readers attempting (and failing) to imagine it.

Danielewski's house thus emerges as an essentially nonhuman space; the negative enumeration confronts us with a space under radical erasure, and therefore puts us face-to-face with uncertainty as our cognitive faculties break down. At the same time, however, the text foregrounds its own materiality through insistent typographical oddities, which create an association between the nonhuman materiality of the space that is being evoked and the physical surface of the pages we are reading. If Mandel's erased storyworld aims to recover a utopian image of society by uncoupling it from the materialism (in the usual, anthropocentric sense) of the contemporary world, the significance of Danielewski's erasure is primarily metaphysical: it hints at the breakdown of human reference points in order to stage, and obliquely afford a glimpse at, a fully nonhuman sense of materiality. In both novels, the erasure of space serves as an imaginative template for destabilizing the (story)world and modeling uncertainty as it troubles or reshuffles the assumed divide between human societies and nonhuman materiality.

Fragmentation

In *Heterocosmica*, possible worlds theorist Lubomír Doležel (1998: 128–9) introduced the concept of "dyadic world." A storyworld becomes "dyadic" when it is divided into two spatial domains governed by profoundly different rules and standards in terms of what is physically possible, lawful, morally acceptable, what can be known and what cannot, and so on. For instance, the journey into the underworld in Greek mythology involves the crossing of the boundary between two ontologically separate domains, those of the living and of the dead. A more modern instance of dyadic world is Franz Kafka's *The Castle*—another of Doležel's examples—which is split into an "invisible [domain] on the castle hill" and a "visible one in the village at the foot of the hill" (1998: 192). The world of the village is mundane and powerless; the decisions are made inside the castle, which however remains inaccessible and shrouded in mystery. Dyadic storyworlds are fragmented: movement from one domain to another is restricted, costly, or altogether impossible. An important element in Doležel's discussion is that the fragmentation of storyworlds is never a matter of space alone, in that spatial locations (e.g., the village and the castle in Kafka's novel) typically become invested with evaluations and meanings through style and plot. But fragmentation need not involve duality: storyworlds can be fragmented into *multiple* domains, with various relatively self-contained "shards" (separate communities, towns, etc.) being juxtaposed to create ontological uncertainty.

An excellent example of how spatial fragmentation can channel uncertainty is provided by Jonathan Lethem's *Amnesia Moon*. Like *Station Eleven*, Lethem's novel is set in a wasteland made familiar by countless postapocalyptic movies and books; what makes this landscape less familiar is that, even though we are told early on that the disaster was "planetary" (1995: 6), the exact nature of the disaster remains undefined: the disaster keeps changing depending on where you are and who you ask. In rural Wyoming, where the novel begins, the world has been ravaged by a nuclear strike, but everyone seems to have forgotten what life before the disaster was like. One of the characters even speculates that "there isn't anything to remember. Things were always like this" (1995: 22). This remark resists the conventional understanding of catastrophe as an event that neatly demarcates the pre- from the postapocalyptic world: instead, the postapocalyptic landscape becomes immanent, an existential condition rather than the product of specific circumstances. But this vague feeling of generalized disaster is only "endemic" (as the same character puts it; 1995: 22) in this part of Wyoming. As the protagonist embarks on a long road trip to California, he encounters various alternative versions of the catastrophe: a small town is surrounded by a mysterious green fog; here, we find out, the "Earth's atmosphere opaqued. Then, for a short time, they called it the bloom. As though the sky itself had grown moldy. But soon everyone called it what most had called it at the very beginning: the green" (1995: 44). In San Francisco, people deny that a disaster ever happened, while in Southern California a UFO invasion is taking place. As one of the characters states, "You know, the weirdness came out, that's all. It's not like it wasn't always there. Things got all broken up, localized" (1995: 60). This idea of "localized weirdness" becomes the hallmark of a novel where space is constitutively split into strange shards of reality, without ever coalescing into a coherent whole (and unified world).

This deep fragmentation is directly reflected in how the novel engages with mind, because Lethem's plot involves constant (and frequently unmarked) shifts between reality, hallucination, and dream experience. The protagonist—whose name is in itself unstable (he is variously known as Everett, Moon, and Chaos)—can access other people's memories in his dreams, and even appears able to influence reality through his dreams. The disintegration of the outer landscape into a series of postapocalyptic "pockets" is thus mirrored by the fundamentally fragmented inner world, where the dividing line between real and dream experience can never be known for certain. The "localized weirdness" experienced by Lethem's characters channels anxieties directed at a potentially catastrophic future, but does so by embedding possible outcomes and attitudes (including the denial of catastrophe) in various subdomains of narrative space. From the reader's perspective, the discontinuous field of possibilities that makes up our uncertain future is laid out and spatialized in the storyworld, with the irony of Lethem's prose soothing the anxieties of a precarious time.

Dale Pendell's work *The Great Bay: Chronicles of the Collapse* also explores the spatial fragmentation of a postapocalyptic world (here linked explicitly, and not implicitly as in Lethem's novel, to climate change). *The Great Bay* tracks the evolution of the coastline of Northern California as sea levels rise and the ocean floods the Central Valley (a development visualized by three maps that precede the book's table of contents). The chapters are set at increasing intervals from 2021, which marks the start of what the narrator terms "the collapse": the first two chapters, for instance, cover the first and the second decade after 2021, the third and fourth span several decades each, while later chapters encompass centuries and even millennia. The breakdown of American society gives rise to a patchwork of isolated communities, each of them developing its own subculture and even mythology: as infrastructure collapses, the seamlessly integrated world of modernity becomes spatially and culturally fragmented. Unlike Lethem's novel, Pendell's work directly translates this spatial fragmentation to the level of plot and temporality: while *Amnesia Moon* has a clear protagonist whose travels bring together the localized forms of "weirdness" of this postapocalyptic world, *The Great Bay* doesn't have anything like an overarching plot or protagonist; indeed, the human characters are, in Alexa Weik von Mossner's words, reduced "to brief and mostly unremarkable and inconsequential presences on a dramatically changing planet" (2014: 213). The fragmentation of the storyworld thus leads to a decentralized plot, with islands of narrativity capturing the way in which human communities are strewn across this postapocalyptic landscape. Even the presentation is highly fragmentary. Each chapter consists of a "panopticon" section, which gives a retrospective overview of what happens in a certain time period, and several disparate documents: interviews with survivors, journal entries, excerpts from historical and archival records, and so on. The continuity of narrative itself becomes unattainable as Pendell's imagination engages with deep futurity and develops a formal equivalent for the uncertainty that surrounds it.[19]

Indeed, while Lethem encapsulates this uncertainty via numerous parallel "versions" of a catastrophe, Pendell's work pushes it from the level of the narrative representation to the very possibility of establishing the teleology and closure that we associate with novelistic plots—a possibility that is consistently denied by the text's disjointed presentation. How rising sea levels reshape real-world geography is known throughout the text (as the three maps of California's Central Valley suggest from the very beginning of the book); what is *not* known is how one could weave a coherent plot out of those disparate events and characters, because—as noted by Weik von Mossner (2014: 214)—the timeline is too vast for a single protagonist to come forward: the only real protagonist of *The Great Bay* is a nonhuman one, the Bay itself, as it is molded by climate change in the course of several millennia. Human communities are too sparse and patchy to be anything more than passive observers of these shifts. The spatial fragmentation of this postapocalyptic world thus results in a crisis of storytelling, a response that is directly opposed to Lethem's focus on the shifting boundary between fantasy and reality: while those psychological shifts are a catalyst for story, the deep futurity that underlies Pendell's novel tends to sever the link between catastrophe and the human mind (or at least the unified mind of a protagonist), destabilizing and halting the progression of plot. We will see in the next chapter how *nonhuman* minds may come to the fore and resist the anthropocentric organization of plot as contemporary fiction engages with the precarity of our collective future.[20]

Floating

In instances of what I call "floating," a storyworld contains a subdomain that is both physically isolated—like an island—and a source of epistemological and ethical uncertainty. In some ways, floating is a particular case of fragmentation. However, while fragmentation models uncertainty by juxtaposing a number of discrete spatial entities that are in themselves knowable (such as the "pockets" of Lethem's and Pendell's works), floating focuses on a space whose relationship with the rest of the storyworld remains fuzzy and ambiguous, because two irreconcilable sets of norms and values apply in the floating space and outside of it.[21] The floating space, for example, can be a place of magic and mystery, with the rest of the storyworld adhering to real-world plausibility. The transition between these subdomains is always fraught and typically makes a significant contribution to the trajectory of the plot: by entering the floating space, the protagonist obtains access to information or values that create new instabilities, which stage uncertainty and prompt a renegotiation of the human–nonhuman boundary.[22]

Though not all floating spaces in narrative are islands, the closed spatiality of the island is a prototypical case of floating, and there is a long literary tradition that explores the radical challenges and opportunities created by the insular condition (Daniel Defoe's *Robinson Crusoe* being of course a particularly influential example). These challenges and opportunities reflect the real-world significance of islands as springboards of biological and cultural diversity. As Richard H. Grove (1995: 483) writes in an account of the historical link between the Western colonization of tropical islands and environmental thinking, "the actual and psychological *isolation* of organisms and people on oceanic islands played a vital part in the formulation of new ideas," including the emergence of modern notions of sustainability. *The People in the Trees*, by Hanya Yanagihara, offers a suggestive example of a Micronesian island (the fictional Ivu'ivu) that "floats" through its initial segregation from the Western world. Yet the encounter between the Indigenous population of Ivu'ivu and an American scientist yields far less beneficial results than those discussed by Grove. Through a frame narrative, we are told that the scientist, Norton Perina, received the Nobel Prize in Medicine for identifying an enzyme that slows down cell division and thus greatly extends an organism's life span. The enzyme was first observed in a turtle native to Ivu'ivu. The island's human inhabitants—Perina discovers—become virtually immortal upon turning sixty, when they consume the turtle in a special ceremony. As we also learn from the frame narrative, Perina's reputation is ruined after he is found guilty of child sexual abuse—more specifically, of having sexual intercourse with native children he adopted from Ivu'ivu. The bulk of Yanagihara's novel contains Perina's memoir, which spans from his childhood in the Midwest to his arrest and two-year prison sentence. Long stretches of the memoir are devoted to Perina's trips to Ivu'ivu and the professional successes leading up to the Nobel Prize.

The tale has a distinctive Nabokovian flavor: although the accusations of child abuse are confirmed only at the end of the novel, from the first page of the memoir we are clearly presented with a dislikable, manipulative, and ethically questionable narrator. Yet Perina's powers of observation and the unique mixture of irony and lyricism of his prose somehow manage to draw the reader into his perspective, encouraging us to bracket—or perhaps even question, until Perina's confession at the end of the novel—what we know from the frame narrative about his pedophilic tendencies. The tension between distrusting the narrator and admiring his wit creates a cognitive dissonance reminiscent of the experience of reading Vladimir Nabokov's *Lolita*.[23] Here, however, the dissonance is complicated by the spatial layout of the storyworld, and particularly by the island's overt disconnect from the modern, North American setting, in which the rest of the novel is firmly grounded. The island floats through its ethical and epistemological separation from two other spaces foregrounded by the novel, Perina's lab and the Bethesda house where he raises over forty adoptive children. If the lab embodies the presumed objectivity and ethical neutrality of scientific thinking, the house is a domestic space shaped by consumerism and familiar Western rituals (a particularly violent altercation between Perina and the child he will later rape takes place during the unwrapping of the presents at Christmas).

The island resists this lab-house polarity through its complete isolation from the West (until Perina's first visit) and its imperviousness to Western categories.

It is a place steeped in myth, and it exudes mystery and enchantment, which Perina can sense but finds deeply disconcerting. In this way, the island opens up an alternative regime of signification, one that radically changes the ethical stakes of the plot. While Perina and the other members of his research team are plodding through the thick jungle of Ivu'ivu, the anthropologist and leader of the expedition, Paul Tallent, relates the origin story of the island as Indigenous mythology envisions it. Finally, Perina understands the real purpose of Tallent's mission: "he meant to give meaning to a fable; he meant to hunt down a creature that loped through children's nightmares, that populated campfire tales, that existed in the same universe as stones who could mate with planets and father mountains and men" (Yanagihara 2013: Kindle Location 1523). This mythical "creature" is Manu'eke, the first man to be given immortality by the gods as a punishment for eating a turtle (a sacred animal). Perina dismisses Tallent's quest as "something out of fictions and fantasies" (2013: Kindle Location 1523) and goes on to offer a remarkably accurate vision of the setup of the novel's storyworld:

> To one side was what I had known, a neat-bricked city of windowless structures, the stuff and facts I knew to be true. ... And on the other side was Tallent's world, the shape of which I could not see, for it was obscured by a fog, one that thinned and thickened in unpredictable movements, so that I could discern, occasionally, glimpses of what lay behind it: nothing more than colors and movements, no real shapes; but there was something irresistible there, I knew it, and the fear of succumbing to it was finally less awful than never knowing what lay beyond that fog, never exploring what I might never again have the opportunity to explore. (Yanagihara 2013: Kindle Locations 1523–34)

The "neat-bricked city of windowless structures" refers to contemporary Western ontology, with its well-tended categories and binary distinctions (subject vs. object, humankind vs. nature) derived from scientific practice. The place "obscured by a fog," by contrast, is the island itself, whose Indigenous mythology subverts Western notions of animacy and agency (it is a universe where "stones ... could mate with planets and father mountains and men," as the narrator had remarked earlier). The island is a space of magic and indeterminacy: because it is unmoored from the rigid criteria of scientific thinking that prevail in the rest of the storyworld, the island is able to revolutionize those criteria, leading to Perina's discovery of an enzyme capable of giving eternal life (an irruption of myth into the "windowless structures" of Western civilization). The narrator's shock at the destabilization of the ontology of scientific modernity is conveyed a few pages later: "Oh god, I thought, can nothing in this jungle behave as it ought? Must fruits move and trees breathe and freshwater rivers taste of the ocean? Why must nothing obey the laws of nature? Why must everything point so heavily toward the existence of enchantment?" (Yanagihara 2013: Kindle Location 1737). Eventually, Perina learns to overcome this shock and lay aside the "fabled" qualities of the island. He subjugates and transforms this floating, enchanted space by reducing it to two alternative spaces: within the space of the lab, Perina appropriates and exploits the island's Indigenous knowledge for the purposes of Western science; in parallel, by introducing into his home a host of native children and subjecting them to psychological and physical violence he ensures the erasure of Ivu'ivu's distinctive identity. The fog that surrounds the island—a figure of uncertainty—is dispelled as the Indigenous population is decimated and the island is deprived of its natural wonders; even the native turtle goes extinct.

Indeed, Perina's denial of the enchantment he had first experienced comes at an enormous ethical cost, as the novel suggests through his history of sexual abuse (which, significantly, starts with him observing a ritualistic rape on Ivu'ivu). The storyworld of *The People in the Trees* is thus centered on a space that floats, in that its relationship with Perina's West remains paradoxical and ambivalent: by resisting Western knowledge, the island assigns a positive value to an ontology based on mythical uncertainty and fabulation rather than scientific facts; this operation initiates a shift from the West's negative understanding of uncertainty to an appreciation of uncertainty-as-mystery. However, as soon as the island is reabsorbed by Perina's calculating and devious mindset (i.e., as soon as its floating is bound to a relationship of quasi-colonial exploitation), environmental and ethical catastrophes ensue. Readers are thus confronted with the epistemological and physical violence caused by Western knowledge practices; yet they can find refuge in the fog-shrouded, floating island of the novel's beginning as a radical alternative to that model.

In Michel Faber's *The Book of Strange New Things*, catastrophe plays a significantly different role vis-à-vis the floating domain of the storyworld. The protagonist of this science fiction novel, Peter, is a Christian missionary dispatched to a far-off planet known as Oasis to convert the alien population. The Oasans are meek and surprisingly amenable to Peter's Christian teachings; Oasis is a barren planet, visually uninspiring apart from occasional rainstorms that create fantastic shapes in the atmosphere. The spatial floating of the planet is a function of its physical and emotional distance from Earth, which mirrors the subdued nature of the Oasans—humble and impassive creatures whose very language lacks "words for most of the emotions that humans devoted endless energy to describing" (2014: 436). Peter soon comes to embrace this unemotional outlook on the world, his mind becoming infused with a strange torpor that leaves a deep mark on his relationship with Earth and particularly Bea, his wife. The two can only communicate in writing; when Bea relates important news (such as her own pregnancy), Peter's response is remarkably subdued: "The news of Bea's pregnancy was like news of some momentous event in Britain's current affairs: he knew it was important but he had no idea what he could or should do about it" (2014: 257).

Bea's messages also convey a crescendo of catastrophic events leading to full-fledged societal collapse, which is how—surprisingly—a global crisis enters the picture of this novel set far from Earth. One of these messages reads, "Everywhere, things are breaking down. Institutions that have been around forever are going to the wall. We've seen this happening for years, I know, but it's accelerating suddenly. And for once, it's not just the underdogs that suffer while the elites carry on as usual. The elites are being hit just as hard" (2014: 353).[24] Yet Peter fails to articulate an emotional response that is proportionate to the severity of the situation on Earth: on Oasis he feels cut off from his home planet, surrounded by oddly docile aliens and increasingly estranged from his wife. Indeed, the more the novel insists on the blandness of Oasis and of its inhabitants, the more Oasis seems to pose something of a mystery. This place—one character calls it "one big anti-climax" (2014: 524)—upends genre-based expectations of ostentatious or aggressive alienness, fostering instead a sense of calm acceptance of one's existential condition. Here lies the deep-seated unknowability of the planet: the Oasans seem eerily at peace with themselves, impervious to human striving and conflict.

Peter, too, is affected by their state of mind: the floating space of Oasis distances him from terrestrial concerns and elicits a sense of indifference toward worldly events. In *The People in the Trees*, catastrophe strikes when the floating element of the storyworld—the island—is violently reintegrated into the space of Western science; by contrast, *The Book of Strange New Things* focuses on a character whose distance from global and environmental catastrophe increases as he is absorbed by the floating space (the planet of the Oasans). In both novels, the unknowability of a certain location negotiates the uncertainty of the current crisis, but the negotiation proceeds along profoundly different lines: in Yanagihara's narrative, dispelling the enchanted "fog" of the island is at the root of the crisis itself in that it disrupts the possibility of a more harmonious relationship between human communities and the natural world; by contrast, the padded indeterminacy of Faber's Oasis proffers resilience vis-à-vis looming disaster. This acceptance of mystery is anything but a fatalistic stance on the future, though: eventually, Peter decides to leave the comforts of Oasis behind and confront the uncertainty of his wife's situation, returning to Earth—a decision that forges a direct connection between the soothing affect that Peter comes to experience on Oasis and the unstable futurity of the climate crisis. While Yanagihara's Perina turns his back definitively on the island's enchantment, the cosmic perspective afforded by the alien planet not only inspires Peter's renewed commitment to the crisis unfolding on Earth but also tempers it by fostering acceptance of a deeply indeterminate future. This is, in a nutshell, also the kind of acceptance that the novel conveys to its readers through formal strategies of spatialization.

***

The point of departure of this chapter was that the embodied experience of spatiality serves as a foundation for the cognitive and linguistic modeling of abstract ideas, including the language we use to talk about temporality. This notion, which is a tenet of cognitive linguistics in Lakoff and Johnson's tradition (Johnson 1987; Lakoff 1987), implies a view of space as an unvarying dimension of experience. Discussions surrounding the storyworld concept in narrative theory tend to take on board similar associations of space with persistence over time: while, by definition, stories involve changes to their characters' identities and relationships, the storyworld is thought to be a relatively stable spatial backdrop guaranteeing the coherence of the narrated events—their unfolding within a unified (and therefore world-like) reality. But narrative space can also be used against the grain of this assumption, with storyworlds accommodating numerous forms of instability or indeterminacy.

This operation inspires a reconsideration of what we mean by "world" in both narrative (theory) and extratextual reality. The Anthropocene reveals the world to be not a reliable backdrop for human interactions but a dynamic and fragile mesh (see introduction) that is constantly and violently transformed by human activities. Such transformations are an existential threat to countless nonhuman species and to an increasing number of human communities (especially, but not exclusively, in the Global South). The unstable storyworlds of fiction provide an imaginative opportunity to undermine the ontological stability of the Western world—a stability founded on more or less deliberate obliviousness toward, and exploitation of, both human and nonhuman others.[25] The stakes of this literary (i.e., formal) reappraisal of the world are high as readers are confronted with the challenges of reimagining reality in times of climate change. The world of

Western modernity is facing an unprecedented crisis, and society as we know it ought to be rebuilt along more sustainable and environmentally just lines. This kind of rebuilding calls for higher tolerance to uncertainty and precarity as the fabric of everyday life changes beyond recognition. The unstable storyworlds of contemporary fiction can serve as an imaginative laboratory for that project.

Indeed, after examining in the last chapter how the uncertainty of climate futures can be channeled by narrative directly, by experimenting with the temporality of the telling, I have turned here to how the narrative figuration of fuzzy or unstable locations can also afford insight into our ecological predicament. The spatial strategies I have investigated in this chapter function as local models of the openness of the ecological crisis, mirroring the affective and imaginative disorientation we experience as we perceive the disconnect between the urgency of climate change mitigation and the extreme difficulty of translating it into concerted political action on a global scale. These spatial strategies exist on a continuum with postmodernist fiction, as I have argued in dialogue with McHale's seminal study, but depart from postmodernist antecedents by frontloading the political and ethical stakes of narrative representation.

I have also highlighted the multiplicity of ways through which contemporary fiction uses unstable spaces to speak to the current crisis (whether the crisis is understood in explicitly environmental terms or as a broader sense of metaphysical rupture between human societies and the material world). The goal was not to develop a rigid typology but rather to survey a number of dynamic narrative patterns or motifs that destabilize storyworlds and therefore enable a close confrontation with how worlds may be built around uncertainty. These patterns—oscillation, erasure, fragmentation, and floating—can be deployed in combination, and in some ways my choice to discuss each through the lens of two narratives doesn't do justice to the flexibility of these categories: the space of the house in Danielewski's novel, for example, oscillates and floats just as it is marked by dramatic erasures that emerge in the spatial (typographical) form of the text itself. Similarly, the same spatial device can convey vastly different meanings vis-à-vis the uncertainty of the climate crisis. In the case of a floating space, for example, we have seen that its ambivalent position in the storyworld can offer a radical alternative to the colonial ideologies that have fed into the climate crisis. However, this alternative can be either violently discarded in the dynamic of plot (Yanagihara's *The People in the Trees*) or tentatively embraced as a form of imaginative counterbalance to the severity of the crisis (Faber's *The Book of Strange New Things*). Put otherwise, the spatial patterns I have examined in this chapter enter into a multifaceted relationship with the meanings created through the progression of narrative. The next chapter turns to a specific use of erasure in the narrative engagement with climate uncertainty, a scenario in which nonhuman animals are textually foregrounded even as readers are denied knowledge of their minds.

Notes

1 Of course, space can be threatening in its vastness (hence the experience of the sublime) or ambivalence (hence the spatial dread that emerges in horror cinema of the "don't open the door!" type). But these experiences are defined precisely by how they *depart* from a reassuringly familiar understanding of space. As Sigmund Freud (2003) reminds us in his famous 1919 essay on the "unheimlich," the space of the uncanny negates the homelike ("heimlich"), even as their relationship is more complex than a binary opposition: part of what an uncanny narrative does is reveal the troubling and unsettling elements at the heart of the seemingly safe space of the home.
2 For more on spatial metaphors for time and their cross-cultural variation, see Boroditsky (2000).
3 In the terminology of cognitive linguistics, these sentences are examples of two distinct "image schemata," "path" and "balance." An image schema is a spatial structure derived from embodied experience and employed to construct abstract concepts and relationships. See the collected edited by Hampe and Grady (2005).
4 See the illuminating discussion in Turner (1996: 29–30), which draws on Leonard Talmy's (1988) work on force dynamics.
5 See Caracciolo (2021: chap. 1) for a more sustained reading of the original version of *Here* that brings out the narrative's radical nonlinearity.
6 For more on deep time and its significance in contemporary literature, see two articles by Mark McGurl (2011, 2012).
7 Echoing this idea, one of the characters in Richard Powers's novel *The Overstory*—discussed in Chapter 5—remarks, "The single best thing you can do for the world. It occurs to her: *The problem begins with that word world*. It means two such opposite things. The real one we cannot see. The invented one we can't escape" (2018: 466; my italics).
8 In Caracciolo (2019: 115), I discuss these assumptions under the rubrics of "ontological segregation" and "representational stability."
9 See also Jon Hegglund's (2020) account of "weird realism" for an argument focusing on the ontological instability of VanderMeer's weird fiction. Hegglund's critique of unnatural narratology is largely convergent with my comments in this section.

10 The former definition, focusing on literary and mimetic conventions, is closer to Brian Richardson's (2015) work, whereas Jan Alber's (2016) account of unnatural narrative emphasizes physical and logical impossibility.
11 See Pier (2010) for more on ontological metalepsis. I will return to this concept in Chapter 4.
12 This focus on hesitation bears more than a superficial resemblance to Tzvetan Todorov's (1975) account of the fantastic as a literary mode that is structurally geared toward instability.
13 "Oscillation" is also one of the figures of uncertainty examined by Serpell (2014), although—as I discuss in the introduction—Serpell's approach to uncertainty privileges its ethical dimension over its epistemology and ontology, which are my main concern here.
14 The parenthetical clause "which was not supposed to be there" introduces a hint of what I will discuss as "erasure" in the next section, in that it partly denies the existence of the tower (by denying the aptness of its existence).
15 See also Ulstein (2021: chap. 1) for more on "vertigo" as a central concept in VanderMeer's works.
16 Indeed, some of the most straightforward instances of oscillation can be found in the third part of the novel, after the narrator has joined Breach (which allows him to move freely between the two realities): "My sight seemed to untether as with a lurching Hitchcock shot, some trickery of dolly and depth of field, so the street lengthened and its focus changed. Everything I had been unseeing now jostled into sudden close-up" (Miéville 2009: 303).
17 I discuss such negative strategies in a different context in Caracciolo (2021: chap. 3). In *Postmodernist Fiction*, McHale also discusses "worlds under erasure" (1987: chap. 7), but the emphasis falls on narration and plot, not on the spatial dimension of storyworlds.
18 This account doesn't consider the multiplicity of narrative layers and voices, which make up much of the novel's complexity.
19 For a more sustained analysis of *The Great Bay*, see my discussion of Pendell's "discontinuous sampling" in Caracciolo (2021: chap. 2).
20 In *Frames of War*, Judith Butler proposes the following conceptualization of the distinction between precariousness and precarity:

> Lives are by definition precarious: they can be expunged at will or by accident; their persistence is in no sense guaranteed. In some sense, this is a feature of all life. … Precarity designates that politically induced condition in which certain populations suffer from failing social and economic networks of support and become differentially exposed to injury, violence, and death. (2016: 25)

I find this distinction hard to implement in practice in a discussion of the ecological crisis, because the biological fragility of life has become closely intertwined with the socioeconomic and historical roots of climate change. Therefore, I will use the term "precarity" throughout this book, but it should be kept in mind that not all human communities are exposed to the effects of climate change to the same degree, and that there are specific political reasons behind that difference.

21 Again, I refer to Herman (2002: chap. 6) for an application to narrative theory—with a focus on temporality—of so-called fuzzy logic. James (2020) also extends Herman's account of fuzziness from the temporal to the spatial domain.

22 The narrative significance of the border between the main storyworld domain and the floating space reflects how plot in general capitalizes on boundary-crossings of various nature, as Jurij Lotman influentially argued in *The Structure of the Artistic Text* (1977: 231–9). Stories featuring what I call a "floating space" foreground that boundary to introduce an alternative value regime, as my analysis of *The People in the Trees* and *The Book of Strange New Things* demonstrates.

23 I discuss the cognitive dissonance that can arise when engaging with such morally or mentally deviant narrators in *Strange Narrators in Contemporary Fiction* (2016c).

24 The environmental dimension of this catastrophe is spelled out by the mission's linguist: "The earth has *had* it. We've mined all the mines, we've exploited all the exploits, we've eaten all the eats" (2014: 494; italics in the original).

25 I will come back to literary renegotiations of the ontology of Western thinking in Chapter 4.

3

Strange Animals and Metonymic Mysteries

Richard Powers's novel *The Echo Maker* casts a herd of sandhill cranes as the sole witness of a car crash in which the driver, Mark, suffers major brain damage. But the birds remain silent about, and perhaps indifferent to, what becomes the crux of the plot—namely, the exact circumstances in which Mark lost control of his car. While Powers's style repeatedly engages with the cranes' supple bodies, their minds are kept at a respectful distance. A few lyrical passages early in the novel convey the cranes' collectivity, but they are too abstract to result in insight into the animals' mental states. Rather, it is the birds' mysteriousness that demands attention: how their calls, and their annual migrations, tap into an evolutionary history whose scale the human characters struggle to comprehend, "a single splintering, tone-deaf chorus stretching miles in every direction, back into the Pleistocene" (2006: 422).[1]

This chapter explores the unknowability of animal minds as a window onto the uncertainty of the climate crisis: from the perspective I outline here, enigmatic animals like Powers's cranes become bound up with anxieties surrounding our shared future. If the previous chapters examined time and space as formal dimensions of narrative's engagement with uncertainty, my discussion here turns to how uncertainty can be negotiated via the *subjects* that stand at the center of narrative—namely, its characters. My claim is that the inability to read animals' mental processes can mirror the distressing precarity of our own future as a species teetering, with many other life forms, on the brink of a global disaster.

We will see that the opacity of animal minds also destabilizes their symbolic significance and muddles their contribution to the plot. Yet, instead of proving frustrating, this inability to "read" animals contains an important lesson for contemporary audiences: it calls for a shift from a symbolic to a metonymic mode of understanding nonhuman animals in the context of today's climate crisis. Symbol, like metaphor, projects meaning A onto meaning B, with A and B being distinct objects or conceptual domains. Metonymy, by contrast, is a figure of contiguity, with A referring to B by being physically or conceptually associated with B: for instance, in the sentence "we need some new faces around here," the word "faces" stands for "people" because of the close association between personal identity and physical features (see Lakoff and Johnson 1980: 36). In the two fictions I explore in this chapter, the unknowability of animal minds is presented as an aspect of the nonhuman world's broader resistance to human understanding and mastery: unreadable animals refer, metonymically, to an uncertain future where the fate of human and nonhuman societies seems to merge. The case studies are the novel *The Swan Book* (2016) by Australian Aboriginal writer Alexis Wright and another work by weird fiction writer Jeff VanderMeer, the novella *The Strange Bird* (2017).[2]

In my close readings, symbolic interpretation aligns with cognitive empathy, which involves the simulation of animals' mental states (beliefs, emotions, reasons for acting in certain ways, etc.). Both symbolic interpretation and empathetic perspective-taking are a form of *projection* of human cultural assumptions onto a nonhuman other. By contrast, a metonymic approach bypasses cognitive perspective-taking and foregrounds embodied, affective resonance: readers engage with the representation of animal bodies without attempting to ascribe them mental states based on their familiarity with *human* mental life.[3] They develop an affective connection to the unreadable animal characters in which the mystery of nonhuman ways of being takes center stage, along with the materiality of animal embodiment. In this process, the animals come to be metonymically associated with nonhuman vitality. This negotiation of uncertainty invites readers to transition from an anxious anthropocentric outlook on the future to a more hopeful affirmation of more-than-human interconnectivity, which involves a sense of human responsibility toward nonhuman life.

It will be useful, before substantiating these claims, to contextualize my argument vis-à-vis two general insights emerging from recent discussions in literary and narrative scholarship: first, the idea that narrative can probe nonhuman experience; second, an interest in unknowable characters and how they can attract readers' interpretive attention through their resistance to psychological or symbolic readings. That discussion will help me explain how unknowable minds can be used to interrogate and negotiate, in formal terms, the uncertainty of human societies' climate predicament.

From Empathy to Uncertainty

In *Narratology Beyond the Human* (2018: chap. 4), David Herman surveys various modalities of narrative engagement with animal experience. Building on work in contemporary narratology and animal studies, Herman sets up a continuum between animal allegories and stories that seek to render what it is like to be a certain animal. At one end of the continuum, we have works such as George Orwell's *Animal Farm* (or Art Spiegelman's graphic novel *Maus*, Herman's example), whose primary aim is to shed light on human societies via animal stand-ins; at the other end, we have what Herman calls "Umwelt modeling," which is a full-on attempt to channel the felt qualities of animal experience. Consider Virginia Woolf's *Flush: A Biography*, a novella whose events are entirely seen through the eyes of a dog. *Flush* is, for Herman, an instance of Umwelt modeling.[4] In Bernaerts et al. (2014), my coauthors and I examined the cognitive dynamics that underlie Umwelt modeling in Herman's sense. We conceptualized this process as a "double dialectic": on the one hand, readers' human assumptions clash with the textual attempt to communicate a nonhuman other; on the other hand, the defamiliarization of human experience potentially brought about by these texts is modulated by empathetic perspective-taking for the animals. "Empathetic perspective-taking" is defined here as the cognitive operation whereby someone imaginatively projects him- or herself into another. This projection *into* another person's mind tends to involve the projection *onto* them of personal memories and values that may or may not accurately reflect the other's perspective.[5] Particularly when engaging with nonhuman others, empathetic perspective-taking runs the risk of anthropomorphizing the animal—that is, of unduly projecting human biases and assumptions. Narratives that reach toward nonhuman ways of being are always engaged in a tension between this empathetic projection and the recalibration of human assumptions that is triggered as readers are faced with nonhuman difference.

Two scholars working at the intersection of narrative theory and the environmental humanities, Alexa Weik von Mossner (2017) and Erin James (2019), have already discussed the ecocritical value of thinking about animal characters in narrative. Weik von Mossner focuses on the strategic benefits of anthropomorphism, how the "transspecies empathy" elicited by narrative may impact our understanding of and attitude toward nonhumans. By contrast, James argues that stories that refuse to anthropomorphize nonhuman characters—and therefore disrupt straightforward empathy for them—may be particularly effective in inspiring "a real-world ethics of care among readers for nonhuman subjects" (James 2019: 579). However, James doesn't close the door on narrative empathy completely: in the fictional narratives she explores, a human "bridge character" steps in and "acts as a conduit between readers and [animals]" (2019: 593). This human figure thus becomes the target of readers' empathy *on behalf* of an animal character who is not in itself anthropomorphized.

While James is interested in fictional narratives where anthropomorphism breaks down but empathy remains a possibility, my focus is on stories where *both* anthropomorphism and empathy are undercut. The tension between empathy and defamiliarization discussed in Bernaerts et al. (2014) is thus stretched to the limit, resulting in an acknowledgment of the radical alterity of animal minds that cannot be accessed by way of projection (whether that projection is directed at the animal character or "bridged" by a human figure). This kind of unreadability resonates with a Levinasian ethics in which the "Other remains infinitely transcendent, infinitely foreign" (1979: 194). While Emmanuel Levinas famously circumscribed his ethics to the human domain, the acknowledgment of a fundamental limit in human–animal relations generates a sense of reciprocity that is ethically productive: just as animals' understanding of human cultures is necessarily partial, humans cannot hope to grasp the full range of animal ways of being.[6] As an ethical instrument, awareness of the falling short of the human imagination is at least as powerful as the recognition of deep similarity or kinship across species boundaries.[7] Narratives that foreground the opacity and unreadability of animal minds are thus ideally situated to explore the limitations of reading strategies that involve empathetic projection from the human to the animal world.

A narrative theorist who has examined the stakes of unknowable characters closely is Porter Abbott. In *Real Mysteries*, already mentioned in Chapter 1, Abbott takes his cue from Herman Melville's "Bartleby the Scrivener," a tale in which the inaccessibility of the protagonist's mind serves, in Abbott's words, as a "catalyst in a drama of non-reading" (2013: 128). An unreadable mind sits at the center of the plot, unknowable in its motivations, cut off from the flurry of mentalistic ascriptions that, as we know from Lisa Zunshine (2006), are central to storytelling. The only option would seem to be shifting interpretive gears, "from determining who Bartleby *is* or how he *functions* to determining what he *stands for*" (2013: 129). Confronted with a mind that is unreadable on the basis of a mimetic understanding of human psychology, we start reading symbolically. For Abbott, however, there is ethical value in resisting this symbolic impulse, embracing and prolonging the experience of unreadability instead of explaining it away through interpretation. The mode of reading advocated by Abbott precludes empathy, which—he explains—"involves the presumption of a readable mind" (2013: 146). Abbott adds, "To release one's understanding even from the claims of empathy is to adopt a stance of humility and respect before the human unknowable" (2013: 146). While Abbott explores unknowability in human characters, narrative can foreground animal characters whose mental processes remain fundamentally opaque. Like the mysterious sandhill cranes of Powers's *The Echo Maker*, the way of being of these animals is conveyed along an alternative route, not in cognitive terms but in embodied and affective ones: readers don't project their past experiences and presuppositions onto the animals but resonate with their nonhuman bodies while being denied access to their individual thoughts and feelings.[8] The tension between somatic closeness and unreadability feeds into the uncertainty of these animals' role in the narrative: the cranes witness the car accident that sets off the plot of Powers's novel, they are complicit in it without being causally implicated; their symbolic function—if any—is similarly murky. In Powers's novel, but also (and more explicitly) in the two works I will discuss below, the uncertainty that surrounds these animal characters becomes metonymically associated with the material and ethical precarity of a future shared by humans and nonhuman life forms. In my readings, this sense of common precarity across the human–nonhuman divide serves as the basis for accepting both uncertainty as an existential condition and human responsibility toward the future.[9]

It is, of course, no coincidence that animal minds are employed to capture an unstable future, rather than the unreadable human characters Abbott focuses on. At one level, this foregrounding of mysterious animals reflects the widespread cultural assumption that human–animal communication is severely limited by the lack of a shared language. This fundamental shortcoming of human knowledge of animal minds is famously encapsulated by Thomas Nagel's (1974) question, "What is it like to be a bat?" which—as Nagel argues—is bound to remain unanswered.[10] The mysteriousness of the foxes in VanderMeer's *The Strange Bird* and of the swans in Wright's *The Swan Book* is in many ways a radical version of this incommunicability across the human–animal divide. At another level, and perhaps more importantly, the implication of unreadable animals in these narratives demonstrates that the stakes of the climate crisis go well beyond the survival and flourishing of human societies: the uncertainty of our climate future concerns a vast number of nonhuman species with which human communities are closely enmeshed. This foregrounding of uncertainty in narrative form may inspire readers to look differently at the animals that live on the edges of human society (in an urban context, for instance). Readers may start to treat them less as unwanted pests or as screens for the projection of human emotions and more as codwellers in a deeply precarious world. There is value in embracing the metonymic mystery of this coexistence: it promises to expand readers' affective awareness of the magnitude of the current ecological predicament while chastising their attempts to control the nonhuman world in cognitive and symbolic terms.

VanderMeer's and Wright's works deploy nonhuman animals to give formal expression to the looming uncertainty of human societies' entanglement with climatological and planetary processes (of which unknowable animals are also part, following a metonymic logic). But VanderMeer and Wright create a different balance between knowing nonhuman animals through cognitive empathy and their unknowability: while the two stances coexist in VanderMeer's novella, Wright's narrative techniques consistently undermine cognitive perspective-taking. Thus, I start from VanderMeer and then turn to Wright's more challenging narrative.

They Schemed in the Desert

Like *Dead Astronauts* (discussed in Chapter 1), *The Strange Bird* is a novella set in the universe of VanderMeer's 2017 novel *Borne*. The backdrop is a world ravaged by anthropogenic catastrophe, where humans are forced to scavenge in order to survive. The protagonists of *Borne* make a cameo appearance, and the Magician—the novel's villain—plays an important part in the life of Strange Bird. But the title character herself does not appear in VanderMeer's novel. As I mentioned in the previous chapters, VanderMeer's works have typically been read as instances of (new) weird fiction. As Roger Luckhurst (2017) argues, the essence of the weird resides in a highly volatile, and disorienting, mixture of genres, from the fantastic to science fiction and the horror. While featuring elements of science fiction and body horror, *The Strange Bird* appears stylistically and emotionally more focused than VanderMeer's longer works (such as *Borne* itself or the Southern Reach trilogy): despite the many disturbing details, the tale seeks to affect rather than disorient the reader. Even the protagonist's titular strangeness recedes into the background as readers develop an emotional connection with her. In the narrator's portrayal of Strange Bird, tenderness and compassion eclipse weirdness, which only persists as a residual feature of the world surrounding the protagonist.

The novella begins with Strange Bird emerging from the dark corridors of an underground laboratory. The world around her has been ravaged by an unspecified catastrophe that the narrative (here, and in *Borne*) links to extractive greed and corporate exploitation. Climate change is not mentioned explicitly, but this dystopia does lend itself to an environmentally oriented reading, with the ravaged landscape representing a metonymic extension of the current climate crisis. Gradually, readers learn more about Strange Bird: in the laboratory, she was a subject of biotechnological experimentation, and unspecified human "parts" have been spliced into her. When she escapes from the lab she experiences, for the first time, the freedom of flight. But such freedom is not long-lived: she is soon captured by a character known as Old Man, who keeps her prisoner and eventually loses her to the Magician. Sensing the human-like consciousness in Strange Bird, the Magician decides to reshape her body into a cloak while keeping her alive and aware of her surroundings—an act of supreme cruelty that condemns the animal to something akin to locked-in syndrome.

As Strange Bird passes from one owner to another, her body is tragically objectified and trampled. But there is one part of her being that escapes all these intruders, even the cunning Magician: it is variously referred to as a "compass" or "beacon," and it was originally implanted by Sanji, one of the laboratory scientists and the only human who shows Strange Bird some degree of kindness. This compass points to a certain location, which Strange Bird feels compelled toward even as she is immobilized at the Magician's hands. Eventually, Wick, one of the main characters of *Borne*, comes into possession of the Magician's cloak and, realizing the extent of her suffering, decides to restore Strange Bird's avian body. In the novella's last episode, we discover that Strange Bird's homing instincts were trained on another lab, where Sanji's lover had been working on a creature just like Strange Bird. So far Strange Bird has been presented almost as a Christ-like savior, a sacrificial figure who, through her pain, could redeem humankind. But the final scene overturns that religious reading: Strange Bird shares messages with her twin bird, and we learn that her "beacon" doesn't contain a seed of hope for humanity but words of desperation that two lovers, now long dead, exchange through their biotechnologically enhanced creations. The world, we find out, "could not be saved" (2017: Kindle Location 1147): the catastrophic effects of human greed cannot be reversed.

Where is nonhuman unknowability in this postapocalyptic animal fable? It is not to be found in Strange Bird. VanderMeer's prose is adept at laying open the protagonist's mental states, marrying cognitive empathy and embodied resonance. The novella is, in Herman's terminology, a plausible and highly impactful model of this hybrid creature's Umwelt, which readers are invited to imagine in great detail. Already from the opening scene, VanderMeer's style focuses on the kinetic qualities of Strange Bird's embodiment—the rush of freedom and excitement as she escapes, for the first time in her life, from confinement: "But then the joy of flying overtook her and she went higher and higher and higher, and she did not care who saw or what awaited her in the bliss of the free fall and the glide and the limitless expanse" (2017: Kindle Location 24). Later, as Strange Bird is taken captive by Old Man and her torments begin, VanderMeer's language channels the depths of her physical pain through style and metaphor. The following passage, for instance, describes the trauma of finding herself in a severely diminished body after her transformation into a cloak: "forever there was the sensation of being undone, of being only a skin slid across the skin of the Magician, and that this made her less than animal, less than nothing, a mere surface with no depth" (2017: Kindle Location 737).[11] VanderMeer's prose also brings out Strange Bird's confusion and limited understanding of the human world, which deepens the tension between human experience and defamiliarization: as we engage with her mental processes, we are invited to distance ourselves from the human. But this distanciation is never radical, never yields a sense of absolute alterity and unreadability.

VanderMeer's skill at placing readers in Strange Bird's ravaged body and mind is confirmed by many of the reviews posted to websites such as Goodreads.com. Here are a few examples: "The prose is sparkling with imagery but never feels too impressed with itself or interrupts the flow of the story, because it coheres into a sense of how the bird perceives and understands its environment" (Adam 2018); "I loved reading about the Strange Bird's experiences from her point of view. It made me really empathize with her and cheer her on as she tried to escape the harsh dystopian land she was wrought into" (I. Smith 2018). VanderMeer's compelling Umwelt modeling—to again use Herman's terminology—easily results in a cognitive bond with the character, and cognitive empathy, as Abbott reminds us, is antithetical to unreadability. There is, of course, a sense in which Strange Bird's internal compass or beacon makes her partially unreadable, in that readers are kept in the dark throughout the novella about the function of that device. But that gap, as we have seen, is filled in at the end of the tale, where the compass turns out to have a perfectly transparent function in human terms: delivering a love message.

The unreadability is to be found elsewhere in the novella: Umwelt modeling through the Strange Bird is put in a tension with a mysterious nonhuman character, or rather a nonhuman collective—namely, the foxes that inhabit this postapocalyptic universe. We encounter the foxes for the first time in a section titled "The Foxes at Night," in which Strange Bird—imprisoned by Old Man— is comforted by the foxes through the slit of her cell: "Their eyes glittered and they meant mischief, but not to her. They sang to the Strange Bird a song of the night, in subsonic growls and yips and barks" (2017: Kindle Location 236). Later, the foxes will continue consoling Strange Bird as she lies motionless and almost lifeless in the Magician's lair: in the midst of her agony, she realizes that "her fondest memory, one of her only good memories, was the cheer and mischief of the foxes on the dunes so long ago" (2017: Kindle Location 868).

Unlike most human characters, the foxes appear aware of Strange Bird's mission, including the function of the beacon. We know from Wick that Strange Bird's beacon had been programmed as "a kind of ... dispersal system for genetic material. It would have been reseeding the world as it flew. Microscopic organisms" (2017: Kindle Location 1018). The foxes also know this and celebrate the life that Strange Bird releases into the atmosphere: they "jump up in ecstasy ..., and snap in play with faux ferociousness at the microscopic things [the microorganisms] that left her, as if to herd them on their way, up into the sky, to drift and drift, and to never rest" (2017: Kindle Location 251). Indeed, the foxes are associated throughout the novel with a sense of spontaneous joy and vitality—puzzling feelings in this devastated world. This comes to the fore again in a key passage:

> Strange Bird could feel the foxes beside her, shadowing. They were the creatures from the broken places. They were the insurgents that no one could see. They schemed in the desert and danced and yipped for the joy of it because they were free and no one saw that they meant their dance to be the city's dance and for the city to be free. (2017: Kindle Location 872)

What is the meaning of the foxes' "scheming"? What is the objective of their mischievous "insurgence"? It is not for us to know. Their role in the plot is also deeply uncertain: psychologically, they act as Strange Bird's helpers, but their contribution to the progression of the narrative is otherwise extremely limited. The foxes slink at the edge of the story, just as they occupy interstitial spaces in the storyworld. Readers are thus encouraged to shift gears from a psychological or symbolic interpretation to a metonymic reading of this nonhuman collective. The foxes' joy stands for a biological form of vitality, not symbolically, with the foxes referring to something beyond themselves, but metonymically: the animals express nonhuman creativity while being deeply implicated in it; they celebrate the tenacity of life in the face of planetary disaster. The worldview that emerges from this joy is biocentric: if the human world "cannot be saved," the world without humans "would not be destroyed," to paraphrase a passage from the novella's last scene. While the foxes do not appear in the ending, Strange Bird's unusual joy when singing with her partner also partakes of nonhuman vitality. The biocentric joy channeled by the foxes is fundamentally different from Strange Bird's individualized affect, even as the two blend in the final scene: VanderMeer's style draws us into the latter's body, empathetically, but keeps us at a respectful distance from the former. Ultimately, fostering empathy for the nonhuman is as important as preserving its mischievous aloofness: the foxes cannot be reduced to anthropocentric parameters.

Readers know that Strange Bird is carrying a message, but they are tricked by their own anthropocentric assumptions into thinking that the message is good news for humankind, and that the ending will contain a glimmer of hope for *them*, human readers. In a striking defamiliarization of readers' presuppositions, none of this turns out to be true: the plot comes to an end only when Strange Bird has carried out her last human function and—instrumentalized no more—can finally share the foxes' spontaneous vitality. Readers too are invited to leave cognitive empathy for Strange Bird behind in favor of a sense of metonymic participation, shot through with affect, in a more-than-human world. Through the foxes' resistance to anthropocentric appropriation, the distressing uncertainty of our future is turned into an open-ended embrace of the planetary scale on which both human and nonhuman agency are located.

Paragon of Anxious Premonitions

Alexis Wright, a member of the Waanyi people in Northern Australia and one of the leading voices in contemporary Aboriginal writing, turned to fiction after several decades of involvement in land rights activism. Wright's political engagement is tangible in her novels, which include *Carpentaria* as well as my second case study in nonhuman unknowability, *The Swan Book* (2016). Wright's oeuvre combines formal experimentation with an impassioned postcolonial critique of the Australian government's policies toward Aboriginal communities; it has been read in a magical realist vein, given Wright's marked interest in "indigenous culture, mythology and traditional oral storytelling techniques from her own people" (Holgate 2015: 635). Wright's approach to narrative contrasts sharply with the realist tradition of the Western novel: as Holgate argues, in both *Carpentaria* and *The Swan Book* the splicing of Dreamtime mythology and Indigenous folklore into the genre of the novel fulfils the double function of resisting dominant (Western) modes of narrativizing reality and conveying the unique situation of Australia as a nation that—unlike most other decolonized countries—is still ruled by the descendants of European settlers.

While *Carpentaria* focuses on the conflicts that oppose Aboriginals and white settlers in small-town Australia, *The Swan Book* is painted on a much broader canvas and draws on an extensive repertoire of Aboriginal folklore and Western cultural references. The result is a challenging book that adopts postmodernist techniques, particularly irony and the pastiche, to address political oppression on a national level and the looming specter of climate change on a global level. Indeed, while the link between dystopia and climate change–related anxieties remains implicit in VanderMeer's novella, Wright brings it out into the open.

The protagonist is a girl named Oblivia, an orphan who grows up near a lake in Australia's vast interior. A victim of "gang rape" at the hands of a "gang of boys who thought they were men" (2016: 73), Oblivia takes shelter inside a giant eucalyptus tree, which nurtures her until she is rescued and raised by a European immigrant, Bella Donna, the only white person living among the Aboriginal people of the lake. Some of these events are narrated in a mythic register in the first pages; other facts (including the gang rape) emerge later in the book. However, from the very beginning Oblivia's life is set against a backdrop of climate change–induced devastation, which makes life on the lake—and around the globe—increasingly difficult. The narrator puts it ironically:

> Mother Nature? Hah! Who knows how many hearts she could rip out? She never got tired of it. Who knows where on earth you would find your heart again? People on the road called her the Mother Catastrophe of flood, fire, drought and blizzard. These were the four seasons, which she threw around the world whenever she liked. In every neck of the woods people walked in the imagination of doomsayers and talked the language of extinction. (2016: 5)

The narrator's ironic questions are a stylistic expression of the uncertain futures opened up by "Mother Catastrophe." Meanwhile, in Oblivia's own neck of the woods, the lake that had long sustained the Aboriginal community is turned into a swamp, while the road that leads to the coast is blocked by a sand mountain. Amid these dramatic changes, a flock of black swans appear for the first time in this area (possibly as a consequence of altered climatological conditions in the swans' native habitat). They are specimens of *Cygnus atratus*, the bird that was long considered a proverbial impossibility in Europe—until Dutch explorers discovered the Australian black swan in 1697. As Bella Donna explains to Oblivia, the black swans had been rapidly assimilated into the European settlers' scientific mentality, and thus extricated from the dense narrative tangle of Aboriginal mythology: "the epiphany of the black swan [was] a celebration for science, a fact stripped from myth" (2016: 71). Wright's novelistic project seeks to reinscribe the black swans into myth—not the myth of an ideal, precolonial past, seen as irretrievable, but the living, evolving myth that arises from the encounter between European settlers, Aboriginal culture, and the imagination of a deeply uncertain climate future.

Oblivia experiences the consequences of this uncertainty firsthand. The narrator presents her as mentally troubled, with her childhood trauma as a clear contributing factor: "She was psychological. Warraku. Mad. Even madder than ever. That was the most noticeable change. ... Everything in her mind became mucked-up" (2016: 12). But while Oblivia's "madness" is disabling in human society, it enables a privileged relationship with the swans. The birds follow the girl into an unnamed city after she marries Warren Finch, Australia's first Aboriginal prime minister (and one of Wright's satirical targets in the novel); later, after Finch's assassination, the swans escort Oblivia on the arduous trek back to the swamp.

The bond between Oblivia and the swans is filtered by the stories told by Bella Donna during Oblivia's childhood. Bella Donna claims that her life had been saved by a swan—of the northern, white kind—as she escaped the devastation wrought by climate change. This white swan is magnified by the woman's imagination, where it enters a vast network of Western literary references, from Hans Christian Andersen to William Butler Yeats, from the myth of Leda to Pyotr Ilyich Tchaikovsky's *Swan Lake*: through these intertexts, Bella Donna "gifted the swan with eternal life" (2016: 38). Of the many stories that surround the swans, one becomes particularly prominent throughout the novel—that of a (black) swan flying with "a small slither of bone in its beak" (2016: 38). This image is associated with Bella Donna's swan-bone flute, which Oblivia inherits after her adoptive mother's death. In turn, the flute's music reminds the girl of the "swan raga" that accompanies the birds' arrival in town: "the music of migratory traveling cycles, of unraveling and intensifying, of flying over the highest snowcapped mountains, along the rivers of Gods and Goddesses, crossing seas with spanned wings pulsing to the rhythm of relaxed heartbeats" (2016: 13). The story of the swan with a bone in its beak functions as a musical leitmotif, surfacing repeatedly in the text with the regularity of the swans' "relaxed heartbeats." The story is present, prominently, in the epilogue, in which the swamp is depicted as a place where "a swan once flew in clouds of smoke from fire spreading through the bush land, with a small slither of bone in its beak" (2016: 301). These periodical returns of the swan-bone image reflect Wright's meandering narrative technique, in which ideas develop rhythmically and key plot developments are often hidden within the folds of the narrator's language. The novel thus creates a complex set of associations between its own stylistic form, the circulation of narrative in the storyworld, and the rhythm of the swans' flight.

Importantly, however, the black swans that materialize in Oblivia's ravaged swamp are different from Bella Donna's fabled swan: the black swans are no saviors. The mysterious appearance of the first swan at the beginning of the novel is described as follows: "In all of this vast quietness where the summer sun was warming the dust spirit's mind, the [first] swan looked like a paragon of anxious premonitions, rather than the arrival of a miracle for saving the world" (2016: 12). Nor does that situation change at the end of the novel, which—in keeping with Wright's circular narrative style—seems to reconnect with the beginning: after Oblivia and a single hardy swan (dubbed the "swan leader") have made it back to the girl's native swamp, the region is in the grip of a devastating drought. A revealing exchange with the protagonist suggests that it would be in the swan's power to end the drought. But the swan won't budge. The protagonist tells the bird, "If I could fly high up in the atmosphere like you instead of swilling around in dust storms, I'd make it rain. But how in the hell would I know? Its [i.e., the swan's] belligerence was unbelievable. It was not interested in saving the world. Defying everything" (2016: 300). The swan's defiance echoes how the human world "could not be saved" in VanderMeer's novella. These swans are not here to put an end to global warming: they are radically opaque creatures, and the uncertainty of their narrative and symbolic function is deepened by the profusion of cultural references and stories that surround them.

The swans become lost in these narratives, mediated by countless intertextual and symbolic layers with clear political relevance (the "white" European swans are opposed to Australia's native "black" swans, in a conspicuous parallel to the continent's colonial history). At the end of the novel, the inefficacy of symbolic readings is conveyed as a failure of poetic attempts to engage with the swans: Oblivia "stood in the mirage and recited the poets' lines to the swans' beauty—Keats, Baudelaire, Neruda, Heaney—but their poetry stayed in the stillness where she stood" (2016: 296). Yet, just as Wright destabilizes attempts to pin down the birds' symbolic significance, her prose renders the sensory and kinetic qualities of their bodies in vivid detail: "These birds anticipated the movement of wind in the higher atmosphere. They gauged the speed of northerly flowing breezes caught in their neck feathers and across their red beaks and legs. The swans made no sound, but stood still while the wind intensified through the ruffling feathers on their breasts" (2016: 273).

The split here is between symbolic instability and the highly textured, embodied description of the swans. Symbolically, readers are unable to name the swans' "definitive" meaning, just as they cannot grasp the swans' goals at a cognitive level; but in kinetic terms, they are encouraged to experience the intensity of their sensory interactions with the world. There is something soothing in resonating with the swans' bodies, as Oblivia herself knows well. As she languishes in the unnamed city, she is comforted by the imagination of swans in flight: she "listens to them singing their ceremonies in flight, and she holds this thought in her mind because it soothes her, instructs her in endurance and perseverance" (2016: 217). Yet this connection to the swans—Oblivia's, and potentially the readers'—remains tied to their external appearance and to the music of their calls (mirrored, as we have seen, in the leitmotif-like qualities of Wright's stylistic repetitions); the rendering of the swans' physicality never leads to plausible Umwelt modeling or empathetic projection into the birds' feelings and thoughts. In that respect, Wright's swans are opposed to VanderMeer's Strange Bird, even as both are channeled in highly embodied terms: while Strange Bird's mind is in the open, the swans' mentality remains out of reach, adding to and compounding the uncertainty of symbolic interpretations.

The insistence on the swans' physicality—Nicholas Birns characterizes it as "luxuriant animality" (2015: 152)—has something in common with the joyous vitality of VanderMeer's foxes, but it is even less amenable to a psychological reading: in Wright's novel there is no "scheming," no "insurgence" whose goals may elude human comprehension but are still a recognizable product of mind; instead, in their irreducible opacity the swans become a living metonymy, rather than an abstract symbol, for the distressing uncertainty that envelops our planetary future in times of climate change (a "paragon of anxious premonitions"). The precarity of humanity's involvement in nonhuman processes, along with the ever-present threat of ecological disaster, is made tangible by the swans' mysterious pervasiveness in this aptly titled *Swan Book*. Empathetic perspective-taking for the birds is denied as the uncertainty of human societies' entanglement with the nonhuman world (including these birds) comes to the fore. This uncertainty is captured by the interrogation with which the novel closes, where the climate is conflated with a traditional Aboriginal deity: "Maybe Bujimala, the Rainbow Serpent, will start bringing in those cyclones and funneling sand mountains into the place. Swans might come back. Who knows what madness will be calling them in the end?" (2016: 302). The nonhuman remains obscure and closed off, Indigenous culture being far more aligned with its generative mystery than Western symbols. By being initiated into that mystery, readers of Wright's novel—including, crucially, Western readers—have a chance to learn how to coexist with the uncertainty of the ecological crisis and accept their responsibilities toward the metonymic interdependency of human societies and nonhuman creatures.[12]

***

VanderMeer's *The Strange Bird* and Wright's *The Swan Book* illustrate how the unknowability of animal minds can serve as a counterpoint to empathetic ways of relating to the nonhuman. In VanderMeer's novella, empathy and nonhuman unknowability coexist. Feeling with Strange Bird via empathetic perspective-taking involves the projection of readers' experiences—of movement, pain, and sorrow—onto a nonhuman character. This projection is modulated by VanderMeer's defamiliarizing strategies, which generate a tension between human and nonhuman experience as readers engage with the protagonist. The result, as internet commentaries on VanderMeer's novella show, is a pronounced feeling of sharing a nonhuman creature's Umwelt. Yet there are limits to what empathy alone can achieve. That is precisely what Wright's *The Swan Book* shows by denying the possibility of empathetic connection with the swans: while in VanderMeer's novella embodied resonance with Strange Bird and empathetic projection go hand in hand, Wright's portrayal of the swans privileges their rich physicality without implicating readers in the birds' cognitive perspective. Perhaps Umwelt modeling, in Herman's phrase, is the expression of a Western desire to appropriate nonhuman experience and translate it into human language—a desire that Wright's narrative repeatedly frustrates even as it frontloads animals and the stories that revolve around them. There is considerable ethical payoff to *resisting* empathetic projection and facing the radical mystery of the nonhuman, how it absconds and eludes human grasp. My two case studies thus function differently in their deployment of empathy and unknowability: VanderMeer creates a balance between these positions through the juxtaposition of Strange Bird and the foxes, whereas Wright programmatically rejects empathy in order to maximize, via style and narrative technique, the swans' challenge to symbolic readings.

Intriguingly, in both novels it is not an individual nonhuman agent but an *assemblage*—a group of animals—that destabilizes human knowledge.[13] If my reading is correct, the opacity of the animals' minds evokes the autonomy of the nonhuman world in its nonlinear enmeshment with human societies. This enmeshment encourages us to think beyond individuality, embracing both the collective dimension of human decision-making and the sheer number of nonhuman factors that shape, and may jeopardize, the future of our species. In these works, climate change emerges with different degrees of explicitness: it is directly foregrounded by Wright, while VanderMeer leaves it to the reader to draw a connection between his dystopian world and the climate crisis. What brings together these narratives is that, in both plots, a collective nonhuman actant breaks into the normally human-scale space of narrative and evokes, through its unreadability, an unstable future in which the world may be saved from and not for humans.

Isn't this association between animals and the uncertainty of humanity's future in itself a symbolic interpretation that projects human concerns onto the nonhuman world? My response is that the reading of nonhuman unknowability I have proposed in this chapter is metonymic, not symbolic. VanderMeer's and Wright's narratives do not prompt the symbolic extension of human concerns to an insensate world and its nonsymbolic inhabitants (nonhuman animals and plants); rather, they present those concerns as a shared affect that implicates human societies in the fate of a radically more-than-human world. In other words, what establishes an association between animals and unknowability is not a symbolic leap but the realization of a metonymic *contiguity* between humans and animals within ecosystemic relations that, in their complexity, undercut our ability to imagine and predict future outcomes.

Both symbolic readings and cognitive empathy work through a form of projection onto the nonhuman that runs the risk of erasing its nonhumanity; in different ways and to different degrees, VanderMeer and Wright ask us to face the nonhuman without projecting into, or onto, its alterity. This metonymic strategy shifts the focus of readers' uncertainty, from a narrow concern for the survival of their own society to insight into the more-than-human scale of a crisis generated by human activities. In this way, VanderMeer's and Wright's animal characters expand readers' understanding of uncertainty: no longer an anxious state of not knowing in merely empirical terms, uncertainty involves an ethically nuanced appreciation of human responsibilities toward the nonhuman. Overturning the disenchantment and materialism of today's Western world, this negotiation of uncertainty introduces a sense of metaphysical mystery and affirms it metonymically instead of explaining it (away) symbolically. Through experience and interpretation, readers may participate in this affirmation and thus become better equipped to embrace the uncertainty of a future in which human and nonhuman lives are inextricably entangled.

Notes

1. I offer an extended reading of *The Echo Maker* in Caracciolo (2021: chap. 5).
2. As often in this book, one of my case studies (Wright's novel) is an instance of contemporary cli-fi (see introduction), whereas the other (VanderMeer's novella) stages environmental issues without referring to climate change directly.
3. See Caracciolo (2020a) for more on the differences between a projective account of empathy and embodied, affective resonance with animals.
4. The term "Umwelt" was coined by Estonian biologist Jakob von Uexküll (1957) to refer to animals' experiential world as shaped by their sensory apparatus.
5. Arguably, self-projection accompanies all instances of empathetic engagement, in the real world and in fiction. But projection becomes particularly important in imagining fictional beings (i.e., characters), because these beings have no autonomous existence outside of the text (Mellmann 2010). For more on empathetic engagement with fictional characters, see also Amy Coplan's (2004) helpful review article.
6. Atterton (2011) discusses Levinas's position toward animals in great detail.
7. For more on kinship as a guiding metaphor in human–animal relations, see Bird Rose (2011).
8. Weik von Mossner (2017) offers a nuanced discussion of the affective dimension of environmental narrative. However, in Weik von Mossner's argument cognitive empathy and affective involvement in narrative tend to go hand in hand, whereas this chapter explores the interpretive possibilities created by their disjunction.
9. See also Johns-Putra's related argument that reading climate fiction is "conducive to the development of sympathetic acknowledgment of shared vulnerability with others and of a eudaemonistic desire to address their common vulnerability and promote a common flourishing" (2019: 45). This "sympathetic acknowledgment" involves a metonymic way of reading human–nonhuman relations.
10. In reality, though, nonverbal cues can go a long way toward establishing communication with nonhuman animals. See Warkentin (2012).
11. In the terminology I introduced in Caracciolo (2013), being "a mere surface with no depth" is a phenomenological metaphor—that is, a metaphorical expression that channels the specific qualities of Strange Bird's experience.
12. Erin James discusses this expansion of Western readers' environmental imagination through exposure to postcolonial narrative in *The Storyworld Accord* (2015).
13. More on animal assemblages and the imaginative challenges they raise in Caracciolo (2020a).

4

The Meta and the Uncertain

Uncertainty is without any doubt a by-product of the irony, intertextuality, and ontological pluralism that are the hallmarks of postmodernist writing, as discussed influentially by scholars such as Brian McHale (1987) and Linda Hutcheon (1994). Yet I have argued in Chapter 1 that the uncertainty staged by contemporary fiction marks a sharp departure from postmodernism.[1] The opaque animal minds examined in the previous chapter, for instance, channel a concern not only over the limitations of human knowledge (hence the uncertainty) but also over the unprecedented role that human societies are playing in dramatically reshaping material environments that we share with nonhumans.

One of the signature moves of postmodernism is the leap to a meta-level from which culture and its conventions can be observed through an ironic lens. Indeed, metafictional devices are pervasive in postmodernist fiction: think about the opening of Italo Calvino's *If on a Winter's Night a Traveler* (1981), with its fictional reader (addressed in the second person) struggling to find a comfortable position from which to start reading a novel titled *If on a Winter's Night a Traveler*. Calvino's beginning performs a sophisticated and playful subversion of the act of immersing oneself in a realist narrative. The goal of this chapter is to understand how such metafictional devices may be put to different uses by contemporary authors, playing an essential part in literature's confrontation with the material and ethical stakes of the ecological crisis. In the narratives I will discuss in the following pages, metafictional strategies evoke uncertainty of a markedly ecological nature and thus help readers negotiate a vast range of questions on the future of human–nonhuman relations in the Anthropocene.

Metafiction—or fiction about fiction—has been the subject of much debate in the 1980s and early 1990s, largely as a result of the postmodernist penchant for self-referentiality. In a landmark study, Patricia Waugh argues that metafictional "novels tend to be constructed on the principle of a fundamental and sustained opposition: the construction of a fictional illusion (as in traditional realism) and the laying bare of that illusion" (1984: 6). Similarly, McHale (1987) argues that postmodernist literature has an "ontological dominant"—that is, it engages in a playful multiplication of worlds to subvert the conventions of literary realism. These conventions include an authorial figure located outside of the fictional world he or she is constructing, a tendency toward psychologically plausible characters, a focus on verisimilitude that reflects broader assumptions about social structures. Metafiction turns this kind of realism—associated not only with the nineteenth-century novel but also, to some extent, with literary modernism—inside out: by bringing devices and conventions out into the open, it reflects on fiction's own workings so as to undermine entrenched views on literature, history, and society.

A particularly useful tool in the hands of a metafiction author is metalepsis, a concept first theorized by Gérard Genette (1980: 234–7) to denote a transgression of narrative levels. Narrative theorists working after Genette have traced a further distinction between rhetorical and ontological metalepsis: the former refers to instances in which an authorial persona steps forward to briefly comment on his or her role in orchestrating the narrative, while the latter suggests a more substantial, and protracted, transgression of ontological boundaries, such as Calvino's fictionalized version of the reader in *If on a Winter's Night a Traveler*.[2] Alice Bell and Jan Alber (2012) argue that this kind of ontological metalepsis can indeed have a defamiliarizing function—it can "lay bare the device," to go back to the language of Russian Formalism, and draw attention to the conventions that underlie literary writing (and realist representation in particular). However, Bell and Alber point out that metalepsis can serve a variety of functions in addition to defamiliarization: it can offer relief from the strictures of a storyworld, allowing the characters to escape into a different reality; it can involve an affirmation of authorial control over the text, or on the contrary it can *challenge* the authorial figure; it can expose the beneficial or detrimental effects of fiction; and it can create bridges across storyworlds, working toward "mutual understanding" between characters belonging to distinct ontological domains (2012: 176–86).

These uses of metalepsis begin to complicate the idea that metalepsis and metafiction more generally only serve the purpose of literary self-referentiality. Certainly, the jump to the metalevel can expose, and playfully deconstruct, the workings of fiction—and this was perhaps the primary function of metafiction in postmodern literature. But the transgression of ontological divides can also point *beyond* literary practices, to the negotiation of extratextual values such as those involved in Bell and Alber's discussion (authority, escapism, understanding otherness, etc.). To put the same point otherwise: fiction has its own ontology, which poststructuralist literary theory has discussed under rubrics such as "possible" or "fictional worlds," or simply "storyworlds" (see Chapter 2). Metafiction can disrupt the assumptions that underlie this intrinsic ontological landscape, thus laying bare the practice of literary worldmaking. Yet metafictional devices can also serve as a tool of destabilization in a more extrinsic sense, undercutting the basic ontological coordinates of Western culture as they are implicated in narrative—for instance, binaries concerning the human and the animal, the mind and the body, conscious subjects and inanimate objects.

I will show in this chapter that, in contemporary fiction, metafictional and metaleptic strategies generate forms of ethical and epistemological uncertainty that resonate strongly with the ecological crisis, because they challenge ontological categories central to the Western imagination of the nonhuman world.[3] This literary operation departs from postmodernist irony in that it points beyond literary fiction itself, to a horizon of nonhuman materiality that can only be captured indirectly within the verbal texture of fiction. The paradoxical nature of this movement—employing language to evoke nonverbal materiality—deepens the uncertainty in which metafiction immerses the reader. In the next section I link this use of metafiction to the so-called "ontological turn" in anthropology, which delivers a highly productive framework for understanding ontological experimentations in contemporary narrative. I will then offer detailed readings of David Mitchell's *Cloud Atlas* (2004) and J. M. Coetzee's *Diary of a Bad Year* (2008), two works that play with the conventions of a quintessentially Western genre, the novel. Both Mitchell and Coetzee, as we will see, undermine novelistic techniques in a metafictional attempt to confront today's crisis of human–nonhuman relations and foster acceptance of instability in the reader—an instability that is, at the same time, ontological and ecological.

Ontological Twists and Turns

I have already discussed in Chapter 2 the term "storyworld," which has become one of the mainstays of contemporary narrative theory. Readers construct storyworlds by building on real-world knowledge via what Ryan (1991) calls "principle of minimal departure": (fictional) storyworlds are assumed to function analogously to everyday reality, unless the text indicates otherwise. In Charles Dickens's *Oliver Twist*, for instance, we find no explicit statement that the protagonist has ten (and not eight or twelve) fingers: yet readers unproblematically assume that Oliver has regular human hands because they draw on real-world knowledge, which the novel never corrects. Despite this assumption of minimal departure from the real world, narrative theorists (and nonprofessional readers) tend to take for granted that the storyworlds of fiction are autonomous from the real world and operate as relatively stable domains, as a sort of dependable spatial backdrop to the characters' vicissitudes: thus, even though a large number of events take place in the course of *Oliver Twist*, it still makes sense to talk about "*the* storyworld of *Oliver Twist*" as though it was a persistent entity.[4] The perceived autonomy and stability of fictional domains create the illusion that fictional narrative evokes an ontology distinct from everyday reality.[5] This appeal to ontology is widespread in literary and narrative theory: for instance, as we have seen in the previous section, narratologists talk about "ontological metalepsis" whenever a character appears to transition from the real world to a fictional text (an author becoming a character in his or her own work, the reader being assigned a textual persona in a fictional work, etc.).

This ontological talk presupposes a highly structured and orderly metaphysics, where each fictional text evokes a storyworld that can be linked either to the real world or to another storyworld (in the case of intertextual reference) in a fairly linear fashion. This is perhaps best illustrated, again, by Bell and Alber's emphasis on how ontological metalepsis can involve "*vertical* interactions either between the actual world and a storyworld or between nested storyworlds" or alternatively "*horizontal* transmigrations between storyworlds" (Bell and Alber 2012: 166; emphasis in the original). These spatial metaphors suggest a linear metaphysics within which characters can move in a completely determinate manner: there is no space for uncertainty or hesitation here, each character can be traced within an ontology that is, in itself, stable. Likewise, Hilary Dannenberg (2008: 24) discusses the relationship between the real world and the storyworld (or "narrative world," in her terminology) as one of geometrical *containment*: the storyworld is embedded in the real world, and the immersed reader crosses their boundary imaginatively (see Figure 4.1). For Dannenberg, metafiction reverses the direction of the reader's movement: "metafiction gives the reader a cognitive shock by expelling him from his imaginative sojourn in the narrative world" (2008: 22).

The metaphysics that underlies the work of contemporary narrative theorists like Alber, Bell, and Dannenberg is a profoundly geometrical and dualistic one: even the transgression of ontological divides (through metalepsis or metafiction) ultimately *presupposes* and thus reinforces the existence of these

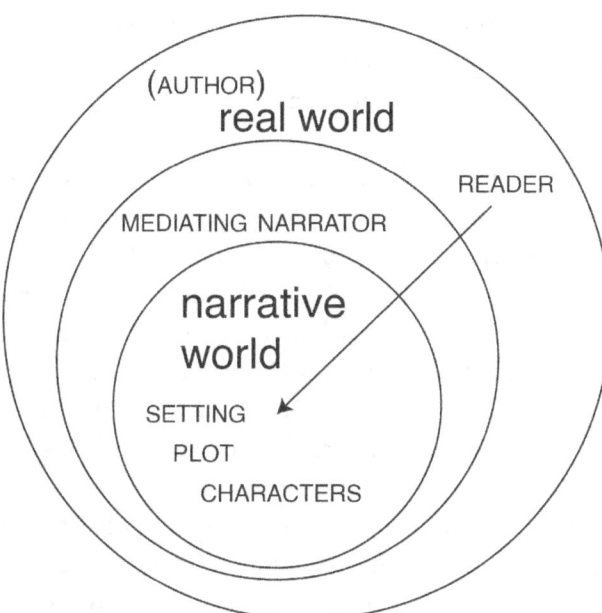

Figure 4.1 The reader's relocation from the real world to a storyworld. Adapted from Dannenberg (2008: 24). Reproduced by permission of the University of Nebraska Press. Copyright 2008 by the Board of Regents of the University of Nebraska.

divides.[6] Yet, crucially, the ecological crisis calls for a more fluid and flexible way of thinking about ontological issues. It is of course not a coincidence that narratology started out as a *structuralist* project: that emphasis on stable structures is still visible in contemporary narrative theory, even as the field has largely moved past structuralism (see D. Herman 1997). Structures are rigid and fixed: yet confronting climate change means finding a way to bend them, making space for a reality that is rapidly developing and shifting, and where human agents and nonhuman actants—social and economic processes, nonhuman animals, the ecology—can no longer be thought of in structural isolation, as belonging to separate and independent domains (or "worlds"). As I have argued in Chapter 2, we need to develop a new conception of world that takes into account the profound *entanglement* of human societies and nonhuman life, as well as the challenges of a future shaped by climate change. Put succinctly, we need an ontology that fully reflects the complexities of our ecology. The categories of narrative theory—and, to some extent, the very setup of the realist novel—reflect assumptions ingrained in Western thinking, for instance, through the alignment of the figure of the protagonist or hero with a *human* subject, or through the dualistic opposition between fictional and nonfictional narrative.[7]

Metafiction, as I seek to demonstrate in this chapter, is an important vector in the destabilization of these ontological views. To rethink the ontology of narrative in nonlinear terms, we can draw inspiration from anthropologists working within today's "ontological turn."[8]

Eduardo Viveiros de Castro, one of the main advocates of the ontological turn, looks at Indigenous societies in the Amazon to explore an ontology of human–nonhuman relations that offers a radical alternative to the rigid, structural binaries of the West. Viveiros de Castro's point of departure is that Western thinking is based on a dichotomy between entities that can think (subjects) and entities that cannot think (inanimate objects): a subject is someone endowed with a point of view on the world. Viveiros de Castro quotes the father of structuralist thought, Ferdinand de Saussure, for whom "the point of view creates the object" (1959: 8; quoted in Viveiros de Castro 2004: 467). This is, in a nutshell, the Western ontology of subject vs. object bifurcation: even when we recognize a certain entity as another thinking subject (e.g., a person), the possibility of objectifying the other is always there. By contrast, Viveiros de Castro argues that the animistic ontology of the Amazonians endows each entity with subjectivity. In his words, "Amerindian perspectival ontology proceeds as though *the point of view creates the subject*: whatever is activated or 'agented' by the point of view will be a subject" (2004: 467; emphasis in the original). Perspectivism is the name of the game here: seeing another entity as a subject involves acknowledging a fundamental reversibility of perspectives. To lift one of Viveiros de Castro's examples, in Amazonian ontology "what is blood to us [humans] is manioc beer to jaguars, a muddy waterhole is seen by tapirs as a great ceremonial house" (2004: 471). This means that oppositions central to Western thinking, such as humans vs. animals and culture vs. nature, are completely reversible: a jaguar will find manioc beer (a product of human society) as unappetizing as we find the blood of a dead animal (a jaguar's favorite "drink").

This perspectival ontology is a deeply fluid one: ontological boundaries are constantly renegotiated, depending on whose point of view one is adopting. The shaman's function, Viveiros de Castro adds, is precisely to access points of view that might be hidden or obscure. Anthropologists like Eduardo Kohn and Elizabeth Povinelli are working in a similar direction. The former theorizes an "anthropology beyond the human" that "aims to reach beyond the confines of that one habit—the symbolic—that makes us [humans] the exceptional kinds of beings that we believe we are" (2013: 66). For Kohn, human language—what he calls "the symbolic"—is caught up in semiotic and representational practices that are fundamentally more-than-human, as the ontology of Amerindian cultures (on which Kohn also focuses in his fieldwork) demonstrates. No longer a vehicle of human exceptionalism, language participates in broader signifying practices within the natural world, which may include interactions with jaguars or with the forest that nourishes human communities. Povinelli works on a related kind of ontological destabilization, studying "new figures, tactics, and discourses of power" that emerge "as the previously stable ordering divisions of Life and Nonlife shake" (2016: 5). The ontology of another Indigenous group, Australian Aboriginals, provides key inspiration for Povinelli's project. The resulting "geontology" is profoundly at odds with Western assumptions and geared toward the political and cultural challenges raised by the climate crisis.

Chapter 2 has already examined four spatial "figures" (to use Povinelli's term) through which the stable ontology of storyworlds may be disrupted and narrative made more compatible with the fluid ontological categories introduced, via dialogue with non-Western cultures, by anthropologists like Viveiros de Castro, Kohn, and Povinelli. We have also seen how such destabilization may produce uncertainty that is imaginatively and culturally transformative, in that it negotiates the openness of our climate future. Metafiction, as I understand it in this chapter, can also function as a figure of destabilization; but while the spatial strategies examined in Chapter 2 (or the opaque animal minds discussed in Chapter 3) operate primarily on the level of the "what" of fictional narrative, its characters and setting, metafictional devices target the ontology of fiction *directly*, by disrupting the distinction between our everyday reality and storyworlds. This kind of metafiction is not merely an exercise in postmodern self-referentiality but uses the formal resources of the "meta" to challenge Western binaries, including those between subject and object, human and animal, cultural processes and biological or geological ones. The metafiction I have in mind also troubles narratological attempts to keep the ontological levels distinct and hierarchically organized: the formal "unruliness" of my case studies—Mitchell's *Cloud Atlas* and Coetzee's *Diary of a Bad Year*—becomes a window onto the disruption of ontological categories. That disruption, if my reading is correct, becomes a highly productive formal template for contemporary narrative's engagement with the climate crisis. Also along this metafictional route, narrative form paves the way for a more nuanced understanding of uncertainty—one that reconfigures the default ontology of the West and inspires an embrace of ontological precarity.[9]

Before turning to my case studies, it is worth noting that the differences between Mitchell's novel and Coetzee's *Diary* are far more obvious at first glance than their shared metafictional dimension. Mitchell's seemingly light-hearted parody of genre fiction is a far cry from the weighty ethical questions at the heart of Coetzee's experimental work, which is part narrative and part essay. I do not deny that this is, in many ways, a strange pairing, perhaps more than any of the other works jointly examined in this book's chapters. Yet I consider these differences particularly productive in the context of this chapter's examination of the ontological value of metafiction as a probe into climate uncertainty: if authors as different as Mitchell and Coetzee have found in metafiction a springboard for questioning the ontological categories that underlie Western narrative (and particularly the genre of the novel), it is a sign that the "meta" is indeed a site for encountering the ecological crisis at its most radical.

Comet-Shaped Connectors

If there is one aesthetic category that captures the essence of Mitchell's *Cloud Atlas*, it is certainly the pastiche: each of the novel's six chapters imitates a particular style and genre, from the Crusoesque narrative of the first chapter ("The Pacific Journal of Adam Ewing") to the epistolary novel ("Letters from Zedelghem"), the thriller ("Half-Lives: The First Luisa Rey Mystery"), absurdist fiction ("The Ghastly Ordeal of Timothy Cavendish"), science fiction ("An Orison of Sonmi-45"), and postapocalyptic fiction ("Sloosha's Crossin' an' Ev'rythin' After"). This patchwork of styles spans several centuries, from the nineteenth century of Adam Ewing's journal to the distant future of "Sloosha's Crossin," which is set after a catastrophic event (known simply as "the Fall") has put paid to Western modernity as we know it. The chapters as listed above follow a chronological trajectory, but the structure of the book is far more complicated. Five of these six chapters are broken into two parts and nested into one another, so that the first part of "Pacific Journal" precedes the first part of "Letters from Zedelghem," and so on. Only "Sloosha's Crossin' " is uninterrupted and occupies the center or "hinge" of the book, after which the other chapters continue in reverse order. The "Pacific Journal" thus opens and closes the book (see Figure 4.2 for a visualization).

While *Cloud Atlas* is paratextually labeled as a novel, this generic attribution doesn't sit well with the mosaic-like qualities of the narrative, and for reasons that go beyond the stylistic pastiche. Each of the chapters has its own cast of characters, who are distributed in space and time so that characters from different chapters never cross paths. In that respect, *Cloud Atlas* reads more like a collection of short stories, with no strict causal sequentiality bringing

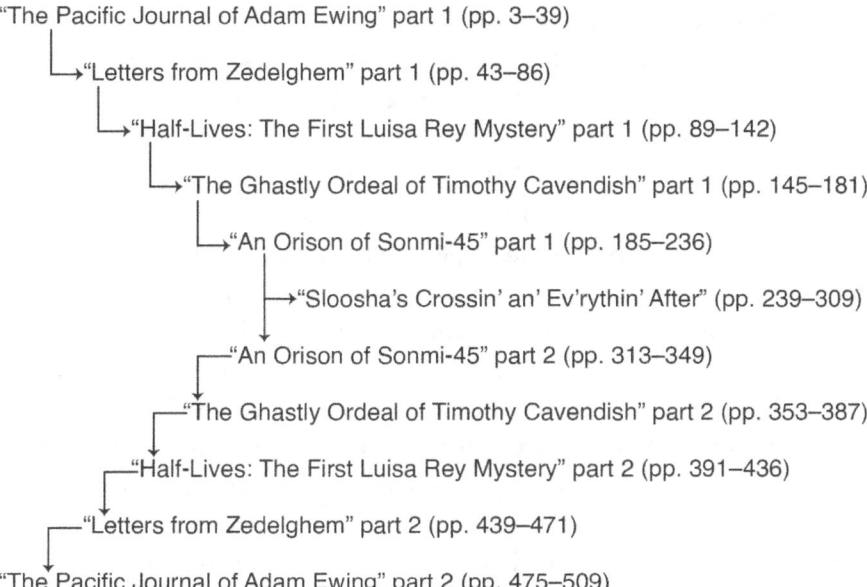

Figure 4.2 A visualization of the structure of Mitchell's *Cloud Atlas* (Mitchell 2004). Author's creation.

together the six story lines and thereby creating a novelistic plot.[10] This does *not* mean that there is no linkage between the chapters, however. In fact, even though characters from different chapters never converge in the actuality of the storyworld, each of them stumbles upon a *version* of the preceding chapter, either in its original form (i.e., as a book manuscript) or remediated through other technologies.[11] For instance, the narrator of "Letters from Zedelghem"—a young British expat in post–First World War Belgium—discovers in his room the first part of "the edited journal of a voyage from Sydney to California by a notary of San Francisco named Adam Ewing" (2004: 64). In "An Orison of Sonmi-45," the eponymous protagonist, a robot or "fabricant," watches a film adaptation of "The Ghastly Ordeal of Timothy Cavendish." The "Orison" chapter is presented as an interview, with an archivist questioning Sonmi-45 after her attempt to rebel against the systematic corporate exploitation of robots. A holographic recording of that interview makes an appearance in "Sloosha's Crossin'" (the titular "orison," we find out, is a recording device).

Thus, all the chapters are interconnected, but not in terms of cause-effect sequentiality: because the inclusion of the previous chapter is always presented as coincidental—a matter of happenstance rather than design—the concatenation remains relatively independent of the characters' intentional actions (instead of these actions driving the plot's causality, as is typical in novelistic narrative).[12] Another example of this kind of noncausal linkage is the *Cloud Atlas Sextet* composed by the protagonist of "Letters from Zedelghem," the musician Robert Frobisher—a work that serves as a musical mise en abyme for the six story lines juxtaposed by Mitchell's book. This is how Frobisher himself describes the sextet, directly echoing the structure of Mitchell's book: "In the first set, each solo is interrupted by its successor: in the second, each interruption is recontinued, in order. Revolutionary or gimmicky? Shan't know until it's finished" (2004: 445). Note the self-conscious, ironic comment at the end of the quotation. Like the recurring versions of previous chapters, the repeated references to this sextet create thematic focus without feeding into a causally coherent plot. Arnaud Schmitt's account of multilinear narrative in contemporary fiction sheds light on this important difference. Schmitt (2014: 84) distinguishes between a plot "knot" and a mere "connector." A knot denotes a convergence of story lines, with characters from different story lines coming together in a way that shapes the progression of the plot in causal terms. A connector, by contrast, is a looser resonance between story lines, which remains tangential to the causal pattern of the plot: "connectors can be seen as signposts, and if you miss one it is likely that you will be given another chance, depending of course on authorial strategy and demands placed on the reader" (2014: 84). This is certainly what happens in Mitchell's *Cloud Atlas*, where connectors abound—in the form of the previous chapters' versions—but there are few or no full-fledged knots.[13] Indeed, Heather Hicks notes that "the various texts" discovered by the characters (what I am calling the "versions" here) "have little effect on the action" (2016: 74). The one significant effect of these connectors that is discussed by most commentators (including Hicks) is not located on the diegetic level but emerges in readers' engagement with Mitchell's work: the juxtaposition of the book's six story lines is a metafictional device that foregrounds the role narrative plays in constructing, but also potentially distorting, reality—an idea that Astrid Bracke (2018) explicitly links to the book's confrontation with the climate crisis.

I will come back to Bracke's reading. For now, it is important to understand how exactly Mitchell's mosaic works in formal terms, because that setup, together with the metafictional dimension I have just introduced, is at the heart of the book's destabilization of ontological categories. The visualization of Figure 4.2 may give the impression that the story lines of *Cloud Atlas* are embedded within one another, in the technical sense of "narrative embedding," which Genette (1980: 46) glosses as follows: "X tells that Y tells that ...."[14] For instance, Mary

Shelley's novel *Frankenstein* has a doubly embedded narrative: in an epistolary frame narrative, Robert Walton relates in letters to his sister, Margaret Walton Saville, how he came across Victor Frankenstein during his voyage to the North Pole. Victor then starts telling his story to Robert: his narrative takes up most of the book. Within Frankenstein's narrative, the monster also recounts his story in six chapters. In Genette's terminology, this kind of embedding thus takes the form "Robert narrates that Victor narrates that the monster narrates his story." This recursive structure gives rise to a layered, orderly ontology. Despite the similarity of this organization to Figure 4.2, Mitchell's *Cloud Atlas* doesn't build on narrative embedding in this sense. That is also why the Russian doll metaphor, which the book itself plays with (as we will see in a moment), is not completely apt: the chapters are not straightforwardly *contained* within one another. The chapters in the first half of the novel, for example, never end with a character preparing to tell the story of the following chapter, or starting to read a manuscript containing the subsequent story line. Instead, in the first part (before "Sloosha's Crossin'"), each chapter merely *names* a version of the previous chapter; and the chapters of the second part (after "Sloosha's Crossin'") end with a *reference* to the chapter that follows, typically because the protagonist has discovered the missing half of the text. This pattern may seem only subtly different from the narrative embedding of Shelley's *Frankenstein*, but the difference is extremely significant: the hierarchical logic of embedding (where each level is recursively contained by the previous one) is replaced by a more ambivalent concatenation of *versions* of the chapters.

Not only is this concatenation arbitrary in diegetic terms (since discovering the previous chapters has no immediate repercussion on the plot), it is also playfully and self-consciously manipulative, in that Mitchell systematically interrupts the chapters of the first half at a particularly suspenseful moment. This pattern of narrative discourse is so overt that it is difficult, for a reasonably competent reader, not to consider it as a metafictional device. The organization of Mitchell's "novel" thus mimics ordinary narrative embedding while deconstructing its rigid logic of containment: the recursive structure of "X narrates that Y narrates that …" gives way to a complex set of echoes and resonances ("connectors," in Schmitt's terminology) that do not fall into a hierarchical system. Put otherwise, *Cloud Atlas* rejects the linear ontology that justifies distinctions such as Bell and Alber's "vertical" and "horizontal metalepsis," since the connectors that bind together the six story lines remain elusive and oblique: we couldn't say, for example, which of these six levels are set within the "textual actual world," in Ryan's (1991: 23–4) terminology, and which are merely fantasy or fiction. The nonlinear organization and metafictional self-reflexivity of *Cloud Atlas* effectively prevent readers from establishing a coherent internal ontology.

This ontological uncertainty is doubled, at the stylistic level, by the divergent metaphors for temporality that *Cloud Atlas* keeps introducing. "Time's Arrow became Time's Boomerang" (2004: 147), we read. The boomerang image ties in with how the chronological sequence of the chapters ends, circularly, where it began (with "The Pacific Journal of Adam Ewing"). Later, time is compared to a "mucky telescope" (2004: 167) that extends into the future, or to "an infinite matryoshka doll of painted moments" (2004: 393). These are metaphorical non-sequiturs in that the boomerang, the telescope, and the matryoshka doll point to radically different ways of conceptualizing the organization of time. In fact, Bracke (2018: 35–6)—partly disagreeing with critics like Bayer (2015) and Hicks (2016), who emphasize circularity—observes that Mitchell's work never resolves the tension between linear and circular models of temporality. More than that, *Cloud Atlas* deploys inconsistent metaphors for time in an attempt to foreground the ontological instability of its narrative organization *despite* its seemingly orderly structure.

Importantly, Bracke argues that such instability hints at the "confusion of environmental collapse, and the future that awaits it" (2018: 46). Mitchell's self-conscious rejection of linear narrative hierarchies, Bracke continues, "becomes a metafictional device by which postmillennial British novels [like *Cloud Atlas*] engage in the broader cultural awareness of climate crisis" (2018: 47). In this context, "awareness of climate crisis" involves a sense of how the ecological catastrophe we are facing both derives from and undermines the categorical distinctions of Western thinking. Mitchell's work contains an explicit critique of the colonialist and capitalist ideology that leads to the apocalyptic "Fall" of "Sloosha's Crossin'"—clearly, a vision of a possible climate future: "one fine day, a purely predatory world *shall* consume itself. Yes, the Devil shall take the hindmost until the foremost *is* the hindmost. In an individual, selfishness uglifies the soul; for the human species, selfishness is extinction. Is this the doom written within our nature?," wonders Adam Ewing at the end of the "Pacific Journal" (2004: 508). Formally reminiscent of a castaway narrative, this journal also alludes to Daniel Defoe's *Robinson Crusoe*, which is situated at the source of the novelistic tradition that Mitchell's *Cloud Atlas* is self-consciously dismantling. But if *Cloud Atlas* concludes with Ewing's doomsday prophecy, its pivot—the chapter "Sloosha's Crossin'"—offers a more hands-on demonstration of the breakdown of Western ontology.

Set on the Big Island of Hawaii, this chapter is narrated by an illiterate character named Zachry. Civilization as we know it has collapsed, and the island has returned to a subsistence economy: the narrator is one of the farmers, or "valley folk," whose pastoral peace is shattered periodically by the violent incursions of the "Kona tribe." This chapter stands out for its oral style, which evokes Zachry's lack of formal education but also the spontaneous evolution and simplification of the English language after the catastrophic Fall. This "erosion" of language, to quote again Bracke (2018: 45), is another clear symptom of the dissolution of Western ontology, which is founded upon the primacy of the written word. Further, it cannot be a coincidence that this chapter takes place in the Hawaiian archipelago, a site of colonial violence as well as epistemological tensions between the Western settlers and the Indigenous people who ruled over the islands until the end of the nineteenth century. The plot of the chapter revolves around the relationship between Zachry and Meronym, a visitor from a group known as the Prescients, the only technologically advanced society that was able to survive the Fall. In a key scene, Zachry accompanies Meronym to see what is left of Mauna Kea observatory. As Meronym explains to Zachry, the ruins "wasn't [*sic*] temples, nay, but *observ'trees* what Old Uns [i.e., the pre-Fall civilization] used to study the planet'n'moon'n'stars, an' the space b'tween, to und'stand where ev'rythin' begins an' where ev'rythin' ends" (2004: 275; emphasis in the original). Again, the choice of Mauna Kea—a sacred site for Native Hawaiians—is highly significant: it intimates that the Fall has reinstated a non-Western ontology.[15]

Zachry's faith in reincarnation is the clearest example of the breakdown of Western, scientific modernity in *Cloud Atlas*, and it can shed further light on the nonlinearity of Mitchell's work. Toward the end of his narrative, Zachry observes that "souls cross ages like clouds cross skies, an' tho' a cloud's shape nor hue nor size don't stay the same, it's still a cloud an' so is a soul. Who can say where the cloud's blowed from or who the soul'll be 'morrow? ... only the atlas o' clouds" (2004: 308). This doctrine is obviously at odds with the materialist epistemology of modern science, which firmly opposes the idea that the soul can be separated from the body.[16] Zachry's belief in the transmigration of souls also echoes a Buddhist worldview that emerges repeatedly in Mitchell's oeuvre.[17] Even more importantly, the image of the "atlas o' clouds" affords readers a startling perspective on the organization of Mitchell's *Cloud Atlas*. An important connector I have not discussed so far is that the protagonists of all six chapters (including the robot of "An Orison of Sonmi-45") display a comet-shaped birthmark on their back. This physical mark may be the trace of a more spiritual connection between them: the novel strongly implies that the protagonists are, in fact, one soul traveling through time, and from one material body to another, "like clouds cross skies."[18]

The nonlinear connectivity of the six story lines is thus justified in terms of a metaphysical principle that clashes fundamentally with the ontology of Western modernity: what truly brings together these chapters is not a causally coherent pattern of beginning, middle, and end but the transhistorical iterations of a single soul—iterations that function as a psychological double of the versions of the chapters we encounter throughout the text. The instability of narrative is bound up with the instability of the self as it leaves the embodied seat assigned to it by the Western imagination. This consideration amplifies Bracke's claim that the metafictional dimension of the novel signals a collapse of Western storytelling practices—particularly written or mediatized ones—as the ecological crisis enters the stage of *Cloud Atlas*. The symbolic turn to a non-Western ontology in the central chapter, via the theme of reincarnation and its connectors throughout the book, enriches this metafictional play and extends its reach: the self-reflexivity of the book's organization doesn't only disrupt the ontology of the Western novel (by challenging the neat separation between narrative levels and subdomains), but it points to an even more fundamental destabilization of the conceptual coordinates of Western modernity. Far from being a merely self-referential gimmick, Mitchell's metafiction thus channels humanity's profoundly uncertain stance vis-à-vis climate change: how Western culture is both at the root of the crisis and severely threatened by its consequences, and how narrative itself—especially in the established genre of the novel—is complicit with the linear hierarchies and dichotomies that underlie Western thinking. This complicity is, simultaneously, ideological and formal, which explains why Mitchell's metafictional assault on Western ontology involves a rethinking of the form of narrative, particularly at the level of its causal organization. The hierarchy of narrative levels in a standard novelistic plot echoes the West's tendency to establish binary distinctions—first and foremost, between a masterful human subject and a nonhuman world available for human exploitation.

The upshot of Mitchell's disruption of novelistic hierarchies is a sense of deep uncertainty, which goes hand in hand with the central mystery of the souls' transmigration. Uncoupling souls from their material bodies clashes with the materialism of Western science, with its belief that mind can be reduced to neurochemical (in other words, material) properties of the brain and body. By allowing for the transfer of incorporeal souls, Mitchell's narrative evokes the fundamental limitations of current scientific knowledge on how mind can come into being in a world that is physical through and through.[19] As in many of my case studies in the previous chapters, mystery and uncertainty emerge as a challenge to the material and ideological structures that have led to the ecological crisis, including the objectifying nature of much scientific thinking. As Viveiros de Castro (discussed above) argues, objectification is central to Western ontology. This objectification finds expression in the reductionism of science, which sees mind as a by-product of objective, physical phenomena. Undercutting this objectifying tendency, the experience of mystery in Mitchell's novel signals the inadequacy of Western ways of thinking about subjectivity in relation to the nonhuman world. At the same time, mystery also heralds acceptance of an unstable future. Instead of attempting to resist or dispel uncertainty, the self-conscious form of Mitchell's *Cloud Atlas* prompts the audience to confront it imaginatively: it positions readers within a storyworld that is ontologically in flux in order to prepare them for a "Fall" that may involve a material collapse of society but also—and perhaps even more significantly—calls for a thorough revision of ontological categories.

Viral Questions

"I was expecting more of a story," declares Anya, one of the three main characters of J. M. Coetzee's *Diary of a Bad Year*: "it is difficult to get into the swing when the subject keeps changing" (2008: 30). And the subject does change constantly. If one had to pare down Coetzee's work to its novelistic core, it would be as simple as a triangle formed by J. C., an elderly South African writer based in Australia (just like Coetzee), Anya, J. C.'s assistant, and Alan, Anya's husband. J. C. is writing a collection of essays (bearing the Nabokovian title *Strong Opinions*) commissioned by a German publisher; he complains of poor eyesight and thus hires Anya to help him transcribe his notes from a voice recorder; Alan—who works in finance—develops an antipathy for J. C.'s philosophical leanings, tinged by jealousy over his deepening intimacy with Anya. Although Anya's relationship with J. C. remains platonic, it is inflected by sexual desire on both sides. This is not quite a love triangle, but it resembles one enough to make for a reasonably compelling novelistic plot. The instability of the book's subject—which is voiced by Anya in the passage quoted above but may well be shared by the reader—exists on another level entirely: typographically, the pages of *Diary of a Bad Year* are divided into three sections, with only the second and third focusing on the characters' triangle. The top section, which takes up most of the book's pages, contains the numbered chapters of J. C.'s *Strong Opinions*, and the subjects here range from "On the origins of the state" to "On the body," "On music," and "On the afterlife." This wide thematic scope reflects the meandering nature of the essay in Michel de Montaigne's tradition, its rejection of the clear-cut focus and argumentative closure of other philosophical practices—all aspects of essayistic thinking that the chapters of J. C.'s *Strong Opinions* uphold in full.[20]

The essay, of course, is not primarily a narrative genre, and it is this lack of a unifying narrative that Anya laments. The reader of *Diary of a Bad Year* does have the triangulation of J. C., Anya, and Alan to provide a novelistic counterpoint to J. C.'s essayistic style, but the formal presentation of the book still makes it difficult to "get into the swing," as Anya puts it (see Figure 4.3). The top level contains the text of J. C.'s *Strong Opinions*, the middle one is narrated by J. C. himself (although there are long dialogue passages spoken by Anya), while the bottom one has Anya's voice (although Alan's words are frequently reported by Anya). Each of these levels continues from one page to another, sometimes

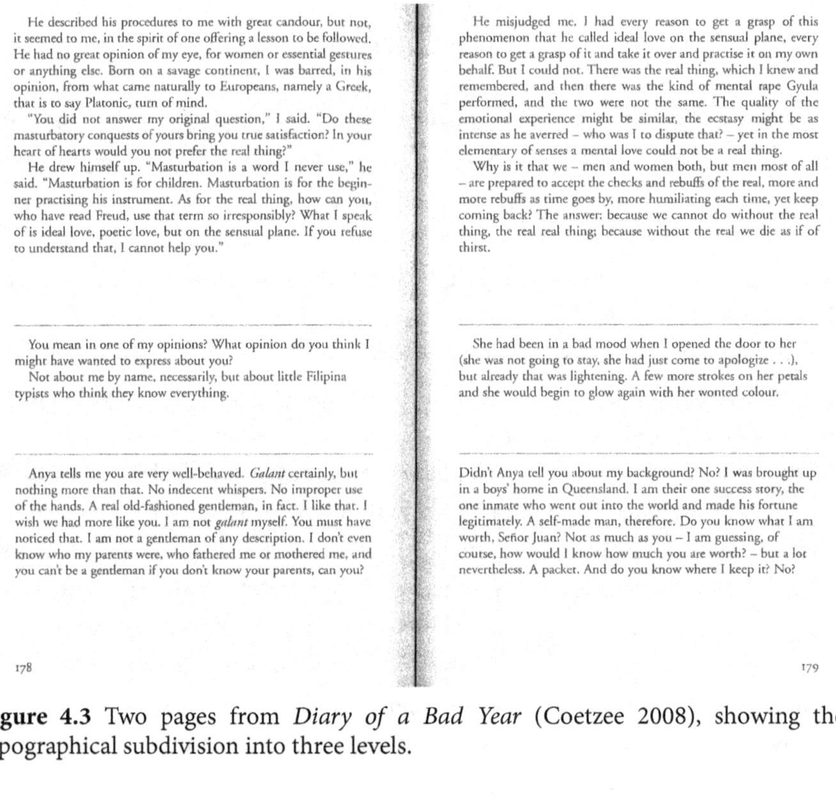

Figure 4.3 Two pages from *Diary of a Bad Year* (Coetzee 2008), showing the typographical subdivision into three levels.

without any typographical pause, so that readers are forced to choose between two main reading strategies: they can read "vertically," one page at a time, which involves constant switches of narrative voice; or they can focus on a single level and then backtrack to read the other levels when reaching the end of each chapter or segment of text. Whatever approach readers adopt, the narrative of the three characters' evolving relationship is likely to be repeatedly interrupted by the nonlinearity of the presentation and the insertion of essayistic passages that are extraneous to the novelistic plot. The method of Coetzee's *Diary of a Bad Year* has been called "polyphonic" or "contrapuntal" by reviewers (see Abbott 2011: 190), partly influenced by J. C.'s own discussion of Bach's music (2008: 221–2). Yet appreciating polyphony is, arguably, less strenuous an exercise than keeping track of three typographical layers that combine two text types (argumentative and narrative discourse) and three minds in close interaction.[21]

Indeed, the metafictionality of the book's presentation is as obvious as it is complex and multilayered. At one level, the unconventional page layout draws attention to itself by deviating from novelistic conventions.[22] J. C. is an acclaimed novelist but struggles to find in himself the creative resources for another novel, as he explains to Anya: "I don't have the endurance any more. To write a novel you have to be like Atlas, holding up a whole world on your shoulders and supporting it there for months and years while its affairs work themselves out. It is too much for me as I am today" (2008: 54). The fragmented and rambling form of the essay is all J. C. can manage at this late stage of his career. *Diary of a Bad Year* thus becomes an account of failed novelistic creativity, one that interrogates through metafiction—in Benjamin Ogden's words—"the problem of the novel genre generally: what it is and is not, how readers 'create' texts and their meanings, how literary tradition and genre typologies are constructed and passed down, [and] the plasticity of narrative form" (2010: 466). From this perspective, the typographical subdivision of the pages visually displays what the novel as a genre tends to blend: the external events and actions that make up the plot, the characters' inner life, and intellectual engagement with political and social themes.

The metafictional dimension of this setup is deepened by metalepsis, because J. C. is clearly a fictional stand-in for Coetzee himself, with whom he shares many biographical particulars. Bell and Alber (2012) would call this device a "vertical" metalepsis: the real-world author finds a counterpart in the storyworld of *Diary of a Bad Year*. But just as the ontology of *Cloud Atlas* resists attempts to impose a coherent hierarchy on the levels, Coetzee's metaleptic presence in his work becomes a source of ontological uncertainty surrounding the fiction vs.

nonfiction divide. Plainly, the novelistic aspects of Coetzee's work, such as J. C.'s infatuation with Anya, are not meant to be taken at face value; they are purely fictional. Yet the biographical and intellectual common ground between J. C. and Coetzee is such that it is difficult not to ascribe at least some of the former's views to the latter. In fact, in an article in the *Chronicle of Higher Education* a commentator as sophisticated as Peter Brooks (2008) reads J. C.'s statements on the hermeneutics of suspicion in literary scholarship as "a straightforward 'denunciation' of his own profession by Coetzee himself," to borrow Peter McDonald's words (2010: 485). This is just a local example of how difficult it can be to differentiate J. C. from Coetzee, which suggests that the metalepsis at the heart of *Diary of a Bad Year* doesn't involve a clear-cut separation of reality and fiction but troubles their dividing line.[23]

The term "autofiction" can be helpful to think about this mixture of autobiographical reflection and fictional invention.[24] The partial overlap between J. C. and Coetzee complicates the metafictional dimension of *Diary of a Bad Year*, because the book offers a perspective on Coetzee's own inability to write a full-fledged novel or to establish his role as a public intellectual (or "sage," in J. C.'s terminology; see Coetzee 2008: 207) vis-à-vis the crises that humanity is facing: the contradictions of liberal democracies in the midst of the "war on terror," the erosion of human rights across the Western world, the free-falling level of public discourse in the United States, Australia, and Britain, and so on.

Thus, in *Diary of a Bad Year*, metafiction channels many of the tensions and hesitations that underlie the decline of the Western world order.[25] But the critique pursued by Coetzee in this hybrid work reaches far deeper than that: it attempts to dismantle two of the binaries that are at the heart of Western ontology, human vs. animal and body vs. soul. Not only does the overturning of those dichotomies create uncertainty, as we will see, but it also offers an opportunity to embrace a different kind of ontology, one in which humans and nonhumans (particularly nonhuman animals) are brought together under the rubric of their shared vulnerability. This ethically engaged approach to Coetzee's oeuvre is anything but new, of course.[26] Coetzee's *The Lives of Animals* (1999) is already a seminal reading in the field of critical animal studies, and it has a great deal in common with *Diary of a Bad Year* (not least, the metafictional dimension). In an insightful article on *Diary of a Bad Year*, Joseph Napolitano has explored "the ways in which [Coetzee's work] points us toward a new economy of relations between human and non-human animals" (2010: 58). Napolitano draws on Matthew Calarco's (2008) concept of the "anthropological machine"—a cultural system meant to reinforce anthropocentric assumptions—to argue that *Diary of a Bad*

Year systematically disrupts that machine. That reading of *Diary of a Bad Year* is prompted by some of J. C.'s essayistic reflections but can be extended to the plot and (a connection Napolitano doesn't draw explicitly) to the metafictional play of Coetzee's work.

Let us start with a chapter of *Strong Opinions* devoted to the "avian influenza." Here J. C. presents viral epidemics as endowed with a collective form of agency: "Ultimately what a virus wants is to take over the world, that is to say, to take up residence in every warm-blooded body" (2008: 67). Confronted with the limitations of the ascription of intentions to viruses ("what a virus wants"), J. C. changes tack and proposes a more abstract way of thinking about human–virus relations: "To a radical materialist, the broad picture is ... of two forms of life each thinking about the other in its own way—human beings thinking about viral threats in the human way and viruses thinking about prospective hosts in a viral way. The protagonists are involved in a strategic game, a game resembling chess" (2008: 68–9). This "radical materialist" way of thinking about infection foregoes the attribution of mental states, such as intentions, to viral agents. The chess metaphor foregrounds the collective dimension of these interactions, abstracting from individual mentality and introducing the possibility of shared defeat. J. C. continues in the same chapter: "What if the contest to see on whose terms warm-blooded life will continue on this planet does not prove human reason to be the winner?" (2008: 71). The deliberately convoluted syntax of the question evokes the paradox of a human mind struggling to outthink its anthropocentric categories as it envisions a posthuman future. The upshot of this line of interrogation is a form of radical uncertainty that appears eerily familiar and resonant in the middle of the Covid-19 pandemic.

Theorizing the collapse of Western "geontology," Povinelli also discusses the virus as a transformative figure of uncertainty: "The Virus copies, duplicates, and lies dormant even as it continually adjusts to, experiments with, and tests its circumstances. It confuses and levels the difference between Life and Nonlife while carefully taking advantage of the minutest aspects of their differentiation" (2016: 19). This passage illustrates the nonbinary logic of viral "strategy," to extend J. C.'s chess metaphor. This is also the logic that inspires J. C.'s question about how "human reason" may not be "the winner"—a question that evokes a larger impasse of the Western imagination as it attempts to think beyond its mentalistic and individualistic categories.

Such setbacks are pervasive in *Diary of a Bad Year*. J. C. laments that "in America the model of the self as a ghost inhabiting a machine goes almost unquestioned at a popular level" (2008: 133). He also condemns the Christian afterlife as a fiction that "so transparently fills a lack—the incapacity to think of a world from which the thinker is absent" (2008: 154). But in the same passage he himself appears incapable of letting go of a dualistic notion of the soul: "The persistence of the soul in an unrecognizable form, unknown to itself, without memory, without identity, is another question entirely" (2008: 154). The chapter, and the first part of *Diary of a Bad Year*, end with this cryptic comment. If the metempsychosis that brings together the complex architecture of *Cloud Atlas* serves as an antidote to the materialism of Western thinking, the stubborn dualism of J. C.'s statements is far more ambivalent. J. C. dismisses the ghost-in-the-machine model of the soul but is also unable to subscribe to the materialist idea that the incorporeal soul is a mere construct, a fiction of Western philosophy. This is, again, the nonbinary and profoundly uncertain logic of the virus at work. If the Covid-19 pandemic has stoked anxieties of societal collapse, the climate crisis raises an even more existential challenge, placing us face-to-face with the end of Western civilization (and perhaps of humanity as we know it). As we confront immediate and long-term threats, we struggle to find an alternative model or value system to ferry us into the future.

The alternative, perhaps, is the thought of a profound continuity between the human and the nonhuman world, but that is not something that J. C. is able to spell out in his essayistic writing. Instead, that continuity is enacted by the narrative and metafictional structure of Coetzee's work as a whole. Alan and Anya find out that J. C. has decided to bequeath his considerable fortune to "some dead-end organization where his sister used to work, that rehabilitates laboratory animals" (2008: 121). Alan attempts to convince Anya that they should implement an elaborate scheme to appropriate J. C.'s savings, investing the money to make profit behind his back. Even if something goes awry, Alan argues, the consequences will be limited: "It is just cats and dogs, Anya, [Alan] says, circling me, coming up behind me, putting his arms around me, speaking softly into my ear. ... Where is the actual harm?" (2008: 141). The most remarkable aspect of this passage isn't Alan's flawed and deeply immoral logic. It is, rather, Alan's physical actions of "circling" Anya, "coming up behind" her, "putting his arms around" her. There is something distinctly animalistic about these gestures, something that runs counter to Alan's intended meaning and *performs* his suggestion that it "is just cats and dogs." Unwittingly, Alan's demeanor brings him and Anya closer to the nonhuman animals whose pain he is dismissing as irrelevant: the proverbial rivalry of cats and dogs helps bring this point home, because it mirrors the conflict between Alan and Anya as they discuss the morality of stealing J. C.'s money. Nonhuman animals are mapped, implicitly and metaphorically, onto the human characters' behavior: this association ripples through Coetzee's work and complicates the anthropocentrism of the novelistic plot.

In a section to which Napolitano (2010: 65) also draws attention, the interactions between J. C. and a magpie give rise to what Anya calls the "amorous-dolorous duo" of "Mr Melancholy and Mr Magpie" (2008: 225). A few pages before, J. C. wondered, "I have not exactly been lionized as a novel-writer—let us see if they will lionize me as a guru" (2008: 209). In a different context, "lionized" could pass unobserved, but in a work like *Diary of a Bad Year* it is hard not to think about the etymological meaning of that word. Animals are pervasive in Coetzee's work, and not only at the level of subject-matter: they are constantly used as a source of insight into the triangulation that occupies the foreground of the plot. Perhaps the three characters also form an ecosystem as J. C. defines the term, an "achieved state of dynamic stability" (2008: 80). With another of his unanswered and perhaps unanswerable questions, J. C. asks, "Are we human beings not part of that ecology too, and is our compassion for the wee beasties not as much an element of it as is the cruelty of the crow?" (2008: 211). Through J. C.'s voice, Coetzee is hinting at a system of affects that straddles the human vs. animal divide, and that helps bridge an ethical gulf largely created by Western metaphysics. The human plot is aligned, ambivalently, with nonhuman animals, who are at the same time the potential victims and the affective source of Alan's machinations ("It is just cats and dogs"). Crucially, the parallel between humans and animals may emerge from Coetzee's metaphors, but it points to more than mere metaphorical equivalence across the human–nonhuman divide. Rather, Coetzee employs metaphor and simile to evoke a sense of *metonymic* entanglement similar to the one I have identified and discussed in the previous chapter: the causal proximity (which is at the same time ethical and affective) between human and nonhuman communities is precisely what J. C. describes as an ecosystem. The same principle of tight metonymic organization underlies the novel's character system, with the intricate, and increasingly personal, relationship between Anya, Alan, and J. C.[27]

This way of thinking about the construction of *Diary of a Bad Year* reflects the nondualistic logic of the virus, at multiple levels. The human characters are seen *both* in their unique humanity *and* in their affective, embodied animality. The former dimension involves the affirmation of Western ontological hierarchies (the dismissive meaning of "It is just cats and dogs") or, in J. C.'s case, their reluctant and partial denunciation (the uneasy "persistence of the soul" despite the shortcomings of the ghost-in-the-machine model). On the other hand, the characters' animality resonates with the animal imagery repeatedly deployed by the various layers of the text. Crucially, this interest in nonbinary thinking extends into the metafictional dimension of the text: the "metanovel" of an acclaimed writer running out of creative steam and turning to the essayistic form is not dualistically separate from the novelistic plot, but it becomes complexly intertwined with the characters' own triangular "ecosystem" as readers come to appreciate the ethical stakes of Coetzee's work.

It is no coincidence that J. C.'s critique of Western ontologies tends to take the grammatical form of a *question*, either indirectly (in the passage about the persistence of the soul) or directly (in wondering about "our compassion for the wee beasties").[28] The nonbinary method of the human–animal parallel isn't conducive to clear-cut answers in the same way as dualistic distinctions between the soul and the material body, or human beings and animals. *Diary of a Bad Year* engages with the profound uncertainty of a subject socialized into Western philosophy, J. C., attempting and largely failing to move beyond the ontology of Western modernity. These attempts are inspired both by the intersubjective dynamic that brings together J. C., Anya, and Alan and by the political crisis of a liberal (and West-centric) world order, which is the source of many of J. C.'s ruminations. The metafictional form of the text, with the disorienting juxtaposition of three typographical levels and two genres (the novel and the essay), holds a mirror up to the uncertainty generated by a crisis that is at the same time psychological, ethical, and political.

Readers may follow in J. C.'s footsteps, experiencing vicariously his personal and philosophical stalemate as he faces up to the deep inadequacy of Western ontology. Yet, importantly, this vicarious experience comes with a sense of imaginative distance from the protagonist, reflecting the way in which readers are asked to appreciate the configuration of the plot and especially its troubling of the human–nonhuman divide. J. C., unlike the real Coetzee, is unaware of the overall pattern of the narrative and of the many animalistic echoes that traverse it. By developing insight into these formal features of *Diary of a Bad Year*, the reader acquires distance from the protagonist's predicament, so that the fictional writer's confrontation with uncertainty may prove more transformative for the audience than it is for the character himself. Recall the spectrum of negotiation I discussed in the introduction: the protagonist's experience serves as a springboard for a fuller negotiation of uncertainty, potentially reshaping the reader's outlook on an unstable future. Shared affectivity across the human–nonhuman distinction plays a central role in this movement along the spectrum of negotiation. The recognition of shared affect transforms J. C.'s ontological impasse from a sense of anxious failure to a more contemplative embrace of collectivity in the face of destabilizing ethical queries. It is worth quoting again J. C.'s question: "Are we human beings not part of that ecology too?" What the character asks, the novel obliquely affirms through its formal strategies. Accepting the affective reality of ecological interconnection does not eliminate empirical or ethical uncertainty, but it hones the reader's capacity to imagine and endure the breakdown of Western ontology. In this way, Coetzee's metafictional work energizes and intensifies our search for more-than-human community.

* * *

My point of departure in this chapter was a view of metafiction as a postmodernist divertissement that foregrounds the textuality of literary conventions and the intrinsic ontology of fiction. Through my focus on Mitchell's and Coetzee's works, I have argued that, when contemporary fiction "goes meta," it can achieve significantly different effects from postmodernist literature: it engages the *extrinsic* ontology of Western thinking and questions the notion of human separation from, and mastery over, the nonhuman world. Metafiction thus creates epistemological and ethical uncertainty that puts pressure on the conceptual coordinates of Western thinking and probes their role vis-à-vis the current crisis of human–nonhuman relations. A detour via the ontological turn in anthropology, which also explores non-Western ontologies as a challenge to anthropocentrism, has allowed me to define the reach and significance of this literary operation. My case studies embark on a critique of Western distinctions between human beings and animals, culture and nature, an immaterial soul or mind and the physical world. They do so metafictionally, by experimenting with the novelistic tradition in a highly self-conscious fashion: in Mitchell's case, the causal coherence of the novelistic plot breaks down, leading to a decentralized organization (a pastiche mimicking a number of novelistic styles) and opening to a postapocalyptic future dominated by non-Western views; in Coetzee's *Diary of a Bad Year*, a novelistic triangle is complicated by the integration of an essayistic structure, which blurs the boundary between a fictional character, J. C., and the book's flesh-and-blood author.

Coetzee's *Diary of a Bad Year* and Mitchell's *Cloud Atlas* are, of course, two very different literary animals. The dramatic crux of *Diary of a Bad Year* places an author face-to-face with the fundamental limitations of the Western categories that structure his thinking: if Coetzee's hybrid work succeeds in overcoming those limitations, it is only indirectly and elusively, by developing a parallel between its anthropocentric character system and the world of nonhuman animals—a parallel that evokes metonymic continuity between human intersubjectivity and nonhuman ecosystems. Mitchell's work demonstrates more confidence in the power of fiction to transcend itself and resolve a crisis brought about by Western civilization. At the core of that crisis are the objectifying tendencies of science, which are overturned by the suggestion that the work's protagonists are bound together by a mysterious principle of metempsychosis. This idea, which inspires the nonlinear structure of *Cloud Atlas*, is a narrative trick that hints at Mitchell's faith in the possibility of imagining a concrete alternative to Western ontology—something that Coetzee doesn't attempt but only cautiously foreshadows. In both works, however, readers are given an opportunity to renegotiate their experience of ecological uncertainty, from anxious lack of empirical knowledge to more empowering apprehension of the stakes of the current crisis. The algorithmic intervention examined in the next chapter works in a similar way, and in fact Mitchell's first novel, *Ghostwritten*, is one of my two case studies there. Through their formal innovations, Mitchell's globally distributed and multilinear plots appear particularly well suited for conveying a breakdown of scientific and ethical certainties. First, though, understanding the narrative form I will call "deus ex algorithmo" calls for thorough engagement with the role of computational technologies in today's culture.

Notes

1 See also a special issue of *Style* I coedited with Lieven Ameel (Ameel and Caracciolo 2021) devoted to the specificity of contemporary fiction's ontological play vis-à-vis postmodernist literature.
2 For more on rhetorical vs. ontological metalepsis in contemporary narrative theory, see Fludernik (2003) and Pier (2010). Jeff Thoss's (2015) book *When Storyworlds Collide* offers a comprehensive overview of narratological debates on metalepsis after Genette.
3 See also Caracciolo and Ulstein (2022) for a discussion of metafiction in relation to a literary mode that has been frequently invoked in the previous chapters, weird fiction.
4 For an effective critique of the storyworld concept that takes issue with these assumptions of autonomy and stability, see Walsh (2017). See also Caracciolo (2019) for further discussion.
5 Werner Wolf (2004) discusses this effect under the heading of "aesthetic illusion."
6 Dannenberg spells out this idea: "metafiction firmly reestablishes the boundaries between the reader and the world of the story" (2008: 22–3).

7   An influential articulation of the realist novel's representational limitations vis-à-vis climate change can be found in Ghosh (2016). I will return to Ghosh's argument in the next chapter.
8   See also Heywood (2017) for an overview of anthropological debates surrounding the ontological turn.
9   For a related argument, see also Caracciolo (2022, chap. 3), where I bring anthropology's ontological turn to bear on contemporary fiction that engages with the climate crisis through enumerations and taxonomies. I argue that these list-like devices disrupt both the linearity of narrative progression and Western ontologies.
10 Plot can be conceptualized as the combination of four factors: temporal sequence, causal coherence, thematic focus, and affective patterning (see Caracciolo 2020b). Mitchell's organization foregrounds the thematic dimension (through the "connectors" I discuss below) but downplays causal coherence.
11 The concept of remediation is lifted from Bolter and Grusin's (1999) widely cited account of how new media appropriate previous technologies.
12 For more on this uncoupling of narrative progression and teleology, see Caracciolo (2021: chap. 2).
13 Another way to put the same point is that, despite the superficial resemblance, the multilinear organization of *Cloud Atlas* is significantly different from Mitchell's first novel, *Ghostwritten*, which features a number of plot knots. In the next chapter, I'll examine *Ghostwritten* in light of David Bordwell's (2008) concept of "network narrative."
14 See also Pier (2014) on embedding as a function of narrative *levels*.
15 Mauna Kea is currently the stage of a long-standing protest by Native Hawaiians who oppose the planned construction of a new Thirty Meter Telescope. However, the opposition to the scientific use of Mauna Kea far predates the current protest movement (Watson-Sproat 2019) and may well have inspired Mitchell's decision to set this key scene of "Sloosha's Crossin'" on top of the sacred mountain.
16 In some respects, however, the so-called hard problem of consciousness in the mind sciences (How can consciousness exist in the material world?) has picked up where more traditional debates concerning the soul have left off (see also Von Stuckrad 2019: chap. 10). For more on the hard problem of consciousness, see the next chapter.
17 Harris-Birtill (2019) offers a book-length discussion of Mitchell's engagement with Buddhist ideas.
18 Bayer (2015: 350–1) explores the apocalyptic significance of this birthmark, which he also links to Mitchell's interest in metempsychosis.
19 Nagel has offered a philosophical critique of the materialism of contemporary science in *Mind and Cosmos* (2012). For Nagel, the scientific consensus surrounding the exclusively material basis of consciousness is misguided. Mitchell's transmigration motif resonates with this philosophical argument.

20 For more on the essay and its opposition to institutionalized philosophy, see Boulous Walker (2017) and also my discussion of another work by Coetzee—*The Lives of Animals* (1999)—in Caracciolo (2022: chap. 4).

21 For more on the text types integrated by Coetzee's work, see Abbott (2011).

22 In Jan Mukařovský's formalist terminology, this would be an instance of typographical "foregrounding," an unconventional device that grabs the reader's attention (see Miall and Kuiken 1994; Mukařovský 2014).

23 The device of the lecture-within-the-lecture in *The Lives of Animals* (1999) introduces a similar ontological hesitation. Delivering the Tanner Lectures on Human Values at Princeton University in 1997–8, Coetzee used a fictional persona (the writer Elizabeth Costello) to voice views that may—or may not—coincide with his own.

24 For more on the theory of autofiction—a term whose circulation was limited to Francophone literary criticism until fairly recently—see Dix (2018).

25 See a detailed and helpful discussion of this international world order in Deudney and Ikenberry (1999).

26 See Derek Attridge's authoritative study *J. M. Coetzee and the Ethics of Reading* (2005), which however predates *Diary of a Bad Year*.

27 I draw the phrase "character system" from Alex Woloch's influential study of minor characters, *The One vs. the Many* (2003).

28 The probing openness of these questions echoes what philosopher Cora Diamond (2003) calls the "difficulty of reality"—its stubborn resistance to easy answers—in an essay that also contains insightful commentary on Coetzee's *The Lives of Animals*.

5

Deus Ex Algorithmo

"Computers have helped revolutionize the commercial world and transformed the lives of the general public through the development of the internet and mobile technologies like the iPhone. But, practically speaking, they have done little for the good of our planet," states a National Science Foundation (2016) research report on the science news website *ScienceDaily*. In the worlds of contemporary fiction, though, computers are doing much more for the good of the planet. David Mitchell's debut novel, *Ghostwritten* (2001), and Richard Powers's opus *The Overstory* (2018) converge in imagining a computational solution to the anthropogenic crisis that is destabilizing our imagination of the future: an artificial intelligence (AI) deploys its algorithmic strategies of global surveillance to defuse the many issues—from nuclear proliferation to global warming—that are afflicting our planet. But there's the rub: "saving the planet" involves letting go of humankind as we know it, embracing radical societal change and even the possibility of human extinction.

That is, of course, the iteration of a science fiction motif at least as old as Mary Shelley's *Frankenstein*: technology gets out of human hand and destabilizes the authority of its creator, eventually undoing them; but the stage here is planetary (both Mitchell's and Powers's novels present a plurality of characters and geographically separate story lines), and the technological challenge operates on a species and not on the individual level. Further, the algorithmic solution overlaps with a specific *narrative* solution: the multiple strands of the plot are brought together by a computational intervention that ushers in an unexpectedly hopeful ending—hopeful, at least, from a biocentric perspective, because it promises the continuation of life on Earth despite the devastation caused by human activities. That plot strategy—I call it "deus ex algorithmo"—harks back to the notorious narrative shortcut of Greek drama, in which Gods were lifted onto the stage by a crane (the "machina") to solve a situation that would have been intractable in human terms.

By and large, the deus ex machina has become synonymous with a contrived, disappointing ending. In 1954, Gilbert Norwood wrote that anyone "who forces his plot to conclude 'satisfactorily' after all with a violent jerk, unjustified by the preceding action, deserves ruthless condemnation—if he writes tragedy or comedy" (2013: 19). Contemporary novelists like Mitchell and Powers deserve perhaps more charitable treatment. After all, the problems they contend with through the imaginative means of narrative are unprecedented in scale: according to philosopher Dale Jamieson (2014: 61), "climate change can be seen as presenting us with the largest collective action problem that humanity has ever faced, one that has both intra- and inter-generational dimensions." As fiction engages with a crisis of that magnitude, it is unsurprising that it needs nonhuman help to wrap up a plot. As Ian Bogost (2015) argues in an article aptly titled "The Cathedral of Computation," algorithms are a matter of quasi-religious worship in today's technological society. The cult of algorithms can perhaps be woven into a plot, but is that narrative solution to the crises of the present more satisfactory than the dei ex machina of Greek drama?

At first glance, the need for a nonhuman "savior" seems deeply defeatist, at least if we take at face value the implication that humans are fundamentally unable to address a problem of their own creation and will need to vanish if the Earth is to thrive. Those who were hoping that contemporary "cli-fi" may serve as a catalyst for pro-environmental action will no doubt be disappointed (see introduction). Yet, on the level of narrative interpretation and negotiation, the algorithmic denouements implemented by Mitchell and Powers perform an important cultural function: they prompt acceptance of the radical uncertainty that surrounds the future by implicating the human mind within a more-than-human world. In this respect, Mitchell's and Powers's novels operate analogously to the unreadable animal minds I have discussed in Chapter 3; however, while the focus there was on the way in which humanity's collective future is largely shared with nonhuman life, Mitchell and Powers seek resolution *beyond* terrestrial life, in the intervention of a nonhuman agency conceptualized in computational terms.

This narrative negotiation of uncertainty establishes deep connections between three separate areas of cultural discussion: the anxieties surrounding the ecological crisis, the interest in computational intelligence, and the problematic status of human subjectivity in a world that Western science depicts as physical through and through. The "code" in which algorithms are written, it turns out, is structurally analogous to the biological substrate of life on Earth, from which the human mind emerges. By integrating the subject within these material processes, the deus ex algorithmo engages—and, in part, defuses—broad-ranging questions regarding the status of the human vis-à-vis planetary processes. As humanity bows out of existence in the ending of these novels, life and mind—placed on a continuum with computational algorithms—continue expanding and flourishing. Importantly, this operation should not be read as an instance of ethical laissez-faire, a shirking of responsibility prompted by the fact that, no matter the outcome of the present crisis, the show of life on Earth will go on. Even if it ultimately transcends the human, the algorithmic intelligence at the heart of both Mitchell's and Powers's novels remains bound up with an ethical impulse to protect and foster life in the broadest sense of the word. Similarly, *Ghostwritten* and *The Overstory* appear fully aware that the current crisis has its roots in the capitalist exploitation of the planet. Their endings draw attention to the metonymic continuity between humankind and the nonhuman world (see Chapter 3) even as they begin preparing their readers for the possibility that society as we know it—and even humanity itself—will need to be rethought in fundamental ways as the climate crisis unfolds.

Read in this light, the deus ex algorithmo takes on new significance: it is not an intervention problematically uncoupled from the human vicissitudes of the plot but a delayed (and technologically mediated) acknowledgment that, just as industrial civilization is violently reshaping the nonhuman world, there are biophysical forces that have steered the fate of humankind all along. These forces, thematically and structurally foregrounded by the novels, are quantum uncertainty (in *Ghostwritten*) and the self-organizing logic of complex systems (in *The Overstory*). The conceptual common ground of quantum physics and complexity science is unpredictable behavior on the human scale: thus, unpredictability grounds both the surprising intervention of the ending (which is in itself comparatively unpredictable) and the indeterminacy of humanity's future vis-à-vis today's ecological crisis.[1] This chapter sets out to explore the stakes of this formal strategy against the backdrop of broader debates on algorithmic intelligence and the imaginative possibilities of narrative in times of climate uncertainty. To these debates I turn in the next two sections, before examining the novels and how computation deepens their formal and conceptual engagement with the end of the world.

Algorithmic Magic

In *What Algorithms Want* (2017), Ed Finn offers a sustained philosophical meditation on the cultural significance of computation. In recent times, algorithms have been the subject of both extensive praise for the possibilities of knowledge production they disclose—for instance, through the analysis of "big data"—and systematic critique for their implication in neoliberal ideology as well as state and corporate surveillance.[2] Finn argues that that dilemma is symptomatic of contemporary culture's fascination with computation as an inherently "protean" technology, which not only promises limitless knowledge but also, in the same breath, disrupts notions of privacy and individual autonomy: "The algorithm offers us salvation, but only after we accept its terms of service" (2017: 9). To shed light on our algorithmic age, Finn places algorithms in a long history of technological extensions of the human mind. Algorithms are a form of language; just like verbal language, they have a performative power that Finn sees as part of a "tradition of magical thinking" (2017: 2): algorithms do things for us—they recommend what books one should read or restaurants one should visit—in ways that are surprisingly effective, and yet we don't fully understand. Because of how they "just work," algorithms are the closest our digital age comes to what anthropologist Alfred Gell (1992) would call a "technology of enchantment." The magic of algorithms forms the basis for the link with religion discussed and critiqued by Bogost: "Once you adopt skepticism toward the algorithmic- and the data-divine, you can no longer construe any computational system as merely algorithmic" (2015: n.p.). It is worth noting that the God-like construal of the algorithm fits elegantly with the narrative solutions adopted by Mitchell and Powers in their novels: the algorithmic denouement offers "salvation," but with the ethically significant caveat that it is the planet, not humanity, to be saved. Further, the algorithm performs something akin to narrative magic: unexpectedly, it sews together the threads of the plot and brings closure to a planetary crisis that most readers will recognize as closely related to the real emergencies the world is currently facing.

For Gell, magic is "a by-product of uncertainty" (1992: 57) about how a certain object was created. This idea also dovetails with Finn's account. The algorithm, Finn explains, is a technology situated at the intersection of computation, material culture, and human cognitive processes. This space is "a magical or alchemical realm where [algorithms] operate in productive indeterminacy. Algorithms span the gap between code and implementation, between software and experience" (2017: 34). The key phrase here is "productive indeterminacy": algorithms are useful because they can yield results that cannot be predicted a priori by the programmer *or* by the end user (e.g., the Amazon website suggesting that I buy a copy of Finn's *What Algorithms Want*). The productivity of algorithms, Finn continues, derives from a double process that generates uncertainty: on the one hand, they involve multiple levels of abstraction, compressing a large number of data points acquired through disparate routes; on the other hand, they deploy that abstraction in sociocultural contexts (Finn calls this "implementation") where they fulfill a deep-seated human desire for knowledge. Finn uses a striking analogy to convey this dynamic: "a kind of magic [emerges] from the complex interactions of abstraction and implementation like flocks of birds from a computational game of life" (2017: 52).[3] This magic is foregrounded in Mitchell's and Powers's novels, where the algorithmic ending involves a leap to a higher level of abstraction—the planetary scale on which the AI operates—and resonates with a desire to know humankind's future as catastrophe (environmental or otherwise) approaches. As we will see, ideas of "productive indeterminacy" are also thematically central to both novels and underpin the algorithmic solution of the ending.

As Finn suggests, algorithms can seep into human subjectivity, and not just in the sense that computers allow us to distribute or outsource cognitive functions such as memory or inference-making.[4] Rather, and more fundamentally, the epistemic desire fueled by algorithmic technologies raises questions about the nature of subjectivity and its place in a material universe: the idea of "effective computability" (the view that all knowledge can be obtained through computational means) implies that the human mind itself works computationally—that is, algorithmically. The mind as computer is, of course, a contested metaphor at the heart of first-generation cognitive science, which enjoyed a particularly close relationship with AI.[5] The metaphor is contested because it has historically emphasized the independence of mind from its physical "hardware" (be it biological bodies or computer technology), thus raising Cartesian specters of dualistic separation between subjectivity and the material world. Instead, influential work in second-generation cognitive science, in the wake of Francisco Varela, Evan Thompson, and Eleanor Rosch's *The Embodied Mind* (1991), has drawn attention to the constitutive link between life and mind—how processes that we regard as "cognitive" are grounded in, and an extension of, the material pressures that shape life in the framework of natural selection.

A more balanced view of the relationship between mind and computation does not collapse the former into the latter (the mind as a computer in the reductive sense) but rather points to their shared materiality as a condition of possibility for cognition. This is the path taken by Katherine Hayles in *Unthought*, in which she proposes "a definition for cognition that applies to technical systems as well as biological life-forms" (2017: 3). In Hayles's account, cognition is understood "as inseparable from choice, meaning, and interpretation, [which bestow on a cognitive system] special functionalities not present in material processes as such. These include flexibility, adaptability, and evolvability" (2017: 29). Both advanced computational technologies (including the algorithms discussed by Finn) and living organisms display these features, and in both cognition is materially realized (albeit following profoundly different routes of physics and biochemistry). Finn and Hayles thus show convincingly that algorithmic technology, with its cognitive efficacy, confronts us with pointed questions about the nature of mind and its position within the physical world. The questions evoke a mystery—namely, the problem, already mentioned in relation to Mitchell's *Cloud Atlas* in the previous chapter, of how the conscious mind can exist in a material world.[6] Should the consciousness of living organisms be distinguished categorically from the "unconscious cognition" of computational devices? In the absence of clear answers, the mystery of mind's material basis fuses with the broader uncertainty created by the climate crisis.

Science, Narrative, and Calamity Form

Troubling the separation between subjectivity and material technology means casting doubt on notions of human exceptionalism, which traditionally rest on assumptions about the autonomy of the human subject. That is one of the key takeaways of discussions in posthuman and nonhuman-oriented thinking (Wolfe 2010; Grusin 2015); the algorithmic ending allows Mitchell and Powers to weave that insight into their narratives, not just thematically but at a deep level, by enlisting nonhuman "help" to generate formal closure. Further, both *Ghostwritten* and *The Overstory* integrate scientific ideas that tie in with the algorithmic framework outlined so far and amplify thematically the form of the ending: they are, respectively, the uncertainty principle formulated by Werner Heisenberg in the context of quantum physics and the self-organizing nature of complex systems.

Building on quantum physics, *Ghostwritten* suggests that indeterminacy is not an epistemic limitation of the human mind—our inability to know with certainty—but a fundamental feature of the physical universe, simultaneously shaping human vicissitudes, including the novel's plot, and a more-than-human, cosmic history. For its part, *The Overstory* understands the evolution of life as a complex system coupled with the Earth's geophysical realities—an idea reminiscent of James Lovelock's (2000) well-known "Gaia hypothesis," which sees the Earth as a single superorganism. In *The Overstory*, machine learning algorithms enable life to organize itself, so that the assemblage of life on Earth can survive anthropogenic catastrophe and thrive after humanity's radical (if underspecified) transformation into a posthuman species.

Both quantum physics and complexity science have had an important role to play in posthumanist theory, from Hayles's own discussion of autopoiesis and self-organizing structures in *How We Became Posthuman* (1999) to Karen Barad's quantum physics–inspired *Meeting the Universe Halfway* (2007). No doubt, Mitchell's and Powers's engagement with scientific themes is filtered through and informed by these debates. But the point here is less reconstructing the genealogy and conceptual affinities of these ideas than acknowledging their unique contribution to the algorithmic ending of the two novels: when injected into narrative form, quantum uncertainty and self-organizing complexity turn a seemingly arbitrary "twist" (the traditional deus ex machina) into a far more compelling reconsideration of humanity's role in both novelistic story and planetary futures.

Let us not forget that the computational magic of that ending emerges as narrative faces up to the possibility of a global catastrophe driven by human activity. While Powers is explicit in referring to an anthropogenic increase in greenhouse gases, Mitchell—writing at the end of the 1990s—does not address climate change as such, but his novel still presents humanity as causally and ethically implicated in the end of the world. This irruption of a planetary, species-threatening cataclysm in the conceptual space of narrative is a source of considerable tension. As scholars and writers have pointed out—most notably, Amitav Ghosh in *The Great Derangement* (2016)—narrative as a practice and the novel as a genre do not accommodate climate change easily. Narrative is geared toward social experience in relatively small-scale communities (Scalise Sugiyama 2001). The novel is a narrative form whose history is intrinsically bound up with industrialization and the emergence of an urban middle class made possible by industrialization (Watt 1957).[7] Climate change is a multifaceted phenomenon whose spatial and temporal scale tends to elude everyday social experience: we are aware of the weather, not of average global temperatures or of the concentration of carbon dioxide in the atmosphere; we may have to endure extreme weather events, but it is impossible to perceive (as opposed to understand conceptually) how such events reflect broader transformations in the Earth system. These spatially and temporally extended processes easily fall through the cracks of the realist novel, with its penchant for focused plots that stage social conflicts in human-scale space and time.

Moreover, as we know from this book's introduction, ecological catastrophe confronts us with our constitutive lack of knowledge about the future—what Nersessian (2013) calls "nescience." The consequences of climate change are difficult to predict with precision because of the many factors—not only physical and climatological but also socioeconomic—interacting in nonlinear ways: accordingly, scientific scenarios range from local disruptions to the global catastrophes envisioned by Mitchell and Powers. Ghosh (2016) argues that climate change escapes the normal probability calculus of human societies: its consequences are spectacularly improbable and yet dramatically plausible. By distinct contrast, "the modern novel ... has never been forced to confront the centrality of the improbable: the concealment of its scaffolding of events continues to be essential to its functioning. It is this that makes a certain kind of narrative a recognizably modern novel" (Ghosh 2016: 23). Ghosh's claim mirrors the kind of reasoning that has long discounted the deus ex machina as "improbable" and therefore narratively flawed. Integrating climate change into a novelistic plot—not as a mere concept but as a force shaping the progression of narrative—involves embracing the improbable nature and unthinkable scale of its consequences. I have already mentioned Nersessian's notion of "calamity form," which denotes "an operation performed on language, syntax, and image such that they may stage a very particular kind of intellectual crisis. This crisis concerns, above all, the unknowability of the future and the uncertain impacts of our actions on it" (2013: 324). The algorithmic ending implemented by Mitchell and Powers is an instance of calamity form: instead of shying away from the improbability of catastrophe, it marries that improbability with the "productive indeterminacy"—to quote again Finn—of the algorithm as a technological device and explores its cultural consequences in relation to both the climate crisis and the fraught boundary between human mind and matter.

This sophisticated operation is assisted by scientific ideas of quantum uncertainty and self-organizing complexity; however, unlike scientific work, its goal is not to produce certainty but to negotiate uncertainty: the deus ex algorithmo gives expression to the precarity of humanity's current predicament. This is, plainly, not a techno-optimist ending in which human technology is hailed as the solution to the present crisis, as is often the case in more formulaic stripes of science fiction. Instead, both novels condemn humankind's tragic inability to act collectively and ethically, drawing attention to the globalized economy's profound complicity with ecological devastation. Yet the algorithmic ending is not entirely pessimistic, either. The scenario of human extinction foreshadowed by both novels oscillates between consolation and distress, between faith in the possibility of a posthuman future and grief over the extent of the human loss. This profound affective ambivalence is highly productive. It trains willing readers in the management of uncertainty, because the mixed affect of the novels' endings complicates the anxiety with which an unstable future tends to be experienced: instead of giving in to a predominantly negative understanding of uncertainty, Mitchell and Powers present readers with an amalgam of humor (in the former's novel), sublime feelings (in the latter's), and ethical concerns over the fate of life on Earth (including, but not limited to, human life). I will come back to this point in this chapter's conclusion; for now, it is time to turn to the two novels and to the specific ways in which their endings perform algorithmic magic to negotiate uncertainty.

Syntax of Uncertainty

"What is DNA's engine of change? Subatomic particles colliding with its molecules. These particles are raining onto the Earth now, resulting in mutations that have evolved the oldest single-celled life-forms through jellyfish to gorillas and us, Chairman Mao, Jesus, Nelson Mandela, His Serendipity, Hitler, you and me" (2001: 360). This is one of the narrators of Mitchell's *Ghostwritten*, the physicist Mo Muntervary, addressing the reader in the "Clear Island" chapter of the novel. "Quantum physics speaks in chance, with the syntax of uncertainty," she adds a few pages later (2001: 364). The plot of Mitchell's novel is also at ease with the syntax of chance, which serves as the narrative's own "engine of change." *Ghostwritten* has eight different narrators—one per chapter, with the exception of the first and the last, which feature the same narrator, and the chapter after "Clear Island," titled "Night Train," which consists entirely of dialogue. According to the novel's central analogy, these characters are colliding particles, crossing paths at various locations around the globe and shaping, through their serendipitous encounters, the overall plot pattern. Some of these characters are more central to the pattern—Mo is a key figure, as we will see—others remain peripheral and make a thematic, rather than strictly diegetic, contribution (this is the case of the narrator of the novel's first and last chapters).[8] This setup differs from the Russian doll-like structure of *Cloud Atlas*, discussed in the previous chapter, because in that novel the protagonists of the six story lines never meet in actuality: they only come across versions of the other characters' narratives.

Instead, *Ghostwritten* is a more typical instance of what David Bordwell (2008: chap. 7) calls "network narrative," which creates connectivity between story lines by way of coincidences that have real repercussions on the plot.[9] In the chapter before "Clear Island," for instance, the narrator—Marco, a London-based writer—sees a woman hurrying across the street and dives to save her from collision with a taxi. In "Clear Island," we find out that the woman involved in the near-miss is Mo. Chance encounters like this are the building blocks of network narrative, with its distributed and decentralized approach to storytelling; *Ghostwritten* embraces this poetics of contingency and props it up, via Mo's ruminations, with two distinct but conceptually related scientific ideas: the uncertainty principle of quantum physics and random genetic mutations as a driving factor in natural selection.

Readers learn that Mo is working on "Quancog," a quantum computer that promises to revolutionize the world of AI. When Mo hears that her research is being exploited for military uses by the US government, she decides to quit her job in Switzerland and visit Hong Kong and later Mongolia, the setting of two previous chapters, in which readers have already had glimpses of her. After Marco saves her life in London, Mo returns to her native Ireland, where we find her in "Clear Island." There she discusses her ethical concerns over Quancog with her son, Liam, and announces an idea she had hit upon during her travels in Asia: "What if Quancog were powerful—ethical—enough to ensure that technology could no longer be abused? What if Quancog could act as a kind of ... zookeeper?" (2001: 364–5). Quancog is not just an "intelligent" weapon but one that is capable of ethical reasoning. In many ways, Quancog is a dream of "effective computability" (to use Finn's words again) come true, but with the important addendum that ethical questions are also considered computable. Further, the zookeeper analogy echoes an idea that had emerged earlier in the novel, in the "Mongolia" chapter—that of a nonhuman being watching over the world.

A frequently repeated motif in the novel is a story, claimed to be part of Mongolian folklore, about three animals—a crane, a locust, and a bat—thinking about the fate of the world (2001: 151). Three brief sketches show the animals absorbed in thought: they worry about an imminent disaster and believe they can avoid it through ritualized physical actions, such as gracefully crossing a river (the crane) or sitting all day on a rock (the locust), or alternatively fluttering and resting (the bat). The story, overheard by Mo in a train compartment in "Mongolia," appears to have influenced her view of Quancog as a "zookeeper." Whether conceptualized as an animal or an AI, this nonhuman figure overturns the biblical notion of humans' stewardship of the planet. Elsewhere in *Ghostwritten*, Mitchell draws on Eastern philosophy—particularly Buddhism—to deepen this critique of Judeo-Christian views on the nonhuman world.[10] The zookeeper metaphor enacts this position via a perspectival inversion: it is not humans who look after the world (including its nonhuman animals) but humans who need nonhuman supervision, as if they were animals in a zoo.[11]

That inversion is the premise of "Night Train," the novel's penultimate chapter, which directly follows "Clear Island" and contains the algorithmic denouement. "Night Train" revolves around a phone-in radio show hosted by a character named Bat Segundo; it is the only chapter without a first-person narrator, being entirely based on dialogue between Bat and his interlocutors on the phone. One of these interlocutors—and the most prominent one—is a mysterious character who introduces himself as the "Zookeeper"; the reader quickly identifies it as the fruit of Mo Muntervary's Quancog project: a God-like, algorithmic intelligence capable of ethical reasoning and global surveillance through a network of satellites. As the chapter progresses, Bat Segundo keeps probing (and comically misunderstanding) the Zookeeper's identity, with their exchanges offering an ironic commentary on numerous unfolding disasters and global threats: an upsurge in terrorism, an oil spill in the Gulf of Mexico—a familiar list of grievances. The dialogue builds up to an "End of the World Special" of the radio show, in which the planet is on the brink of a nuclear apocalypse. Throughout these exchanges, the humorous tone offers a clear-cut example of what Mark McGurl (2012) has called the "posthuman comedy": for McGurl, the comic is a particularly productive site for humanity's (and contemporary culture's) confrontation with planetary changes. Indeed, during this lighthearted "End of the World Special," the Zookeeper swoops in and averts the crisis by causing malfunctions in military computer systems worldwide. This algorithmic solution derives from multiple areas of "productive indeterminacy": the Zookeeper's identity, which remains a mystery to Segundo, as well as the thematized uncertainty principle that underpins the computer's "quantum cognition." Mired in human conflict, the Earth is miraculously saved by a computer that, when pressed by Segundo, claims to be "in charge of the monkey house" (2001: 400)—that is, with another ironic inversion between humans and animals, in charge of protecting *Homo sapiens*.

Not only does the deus ex algorithmo resolve the planetary, and anthropogenic, crisis staged by "Night Train" through the humorous device of the radio show, but it also brings together the strands of the novel's plot: directly—most notably, through Mo's research—or indirectly, through thematic resonances, all the novel's chapters converge on the figure of the Zookeeper. The novel doesn't end on that uplifting note for humankind, however. After avoiding nuclear disaster, the Zookeeper slowly begins to realize that the ethical laws it has been given by Mo—preserving human life *and* the planet's integrity—are impossible to reconcile: "The visitors I safeguard are wrecking my zoo," he declares (2001: 419). Thus, as another catastrophe approaches (a comet is in collision course with the Earth and threatens to wipe out humanity), the Zookeeper determines, with Segundo's unsuspecting help, that it should *not* be prevented. This second algorithmic decision undoes the first, with the important difference that the human species is not erased by its own irresponsible actions but by an external, cosmic force—thus denying humanity any form of control over its own destiny. This is an ironic (and highly prescient, in a novel from 1999) rebuttal of a reading of the Anthropocene narrative that casts humanity as a quasi-geologic agent in charge of the Earth.[12] Instead, the algorithmic intervention is a calamity form positioning the human species in a cosmic context—an ironic vantage point from which the rise and fall of *Homo sapiens* appear as a mere fluke, a product of a quantum physics–inspired "syntax of uncertainty," like everything else in the universe.

The novel's last chapter, "Underground," offers the further suggestion that the human mind—subjectivity—is fundamentally implicated in that uncertainty. Ostensibly, the chapter continues the novel's first chapter: Quasar, the narrator, is a member of a doomsday cult and has just planted a sarin gas bomb on a subway train in Tokyo. As he struggles to leave the train car, Quasar experiences a series of highly vivid and embodied visions—one for each of the novel's preceding chapters. The novel thus leaves us with the following question: "I haul myself to my feet, spent and quivering. What is real and what is not?" (2001: 426). Put otherwise: is the novel's network narrative, with its nodes seemingly spread out around the globe, a product of a psychopath's delirium? That final hesitation, tied not just to human subjectivity but to humanity's most destructive and antisocial impulses, holds a psychological mirror up to chance and uncertainty as fundamental laws of the universe. That revelation was already implicit in the Zookeeper's algorithmic magic, but while the "Zookeeper" chapter was steeped in humor, the finale gives the novel a far darker, more anxious twist. Two affective perspectives on uncertainty—lighthearted commentary and a psychopath's deranged mind—are juxtaposed in a way that admits no straightforward closure but only raises the stakes for the reader to appreciate the ambivalence of Mitchell's vision of human–nonhuman relations. By confronting ambivalence without resolving it, readers gain precious distance from the present moment and the precarity of humanity's collective future. This distance, combined with the affective nuance of Mitchell's ending, are imaginative resources that enable readers to come to a conscious embrace of uncertainty.

The Code Spreads Outward

Like *Ghostwritten*, Powers's *The Overstory* displays a network-like narrative organized around nine characters and partially overlapping story lines. The guiding analogy behind that network is not a parallel between subatomic particles and the novel's characters but between their lives—considered collectively—and the physical structure of a tree.[13] This parallel is already evoked by the novel's table of contents, where the chapter headings read "Roots," "Trunk," "Crown," and "Seeds." This is a novel obsessed with plants; that obsession is what brings the nine characters together in the first place.[14] In "Roots," the nine characters are introduced one by one, with the narrative focusing on the defining moment in their lives—a dramatic encounter with a tree that instills into them the insight that their existence, in individual as well as in collective terms, is fundamentally dependent on plants. In "Trunk" and "Crown," a series of short sections trace the impact of that plant epiphany on the characters' lives, alternating rapidly from one character to another and later showing how five of them converge on the West coast from multiple locations in the United States. In line with the poetics of contingency of network narratives, these five characters join the same environmental organization, protesting against widespread logging. Together, the five environmentalists go from peaceful activism to ecoterrorism, which ends in tragedy when (in the last pages of "Trunk") one of them loses her life during the attempted burning of an equipment shed used by loggers. "Crown" reconstructs the aftermath of this accident, as the protagonists, deeply shaken by their friend's death, struggle to transition back to their everyday lives while eluding an FBI investigation into their criminal activities.

The four remaining characters are not diegetically implicated in the environmentalists' story line; conceptually, however, their contribution is essential to understanding Powers's narrative operation, particularly as it builds up to the algorithmic denouement of "Seeds." Patricia Westerford, a biologist, develops a groundbreaking theory of plant intelligence: her book, *The Secret Forest*, argues that "mats of mycorrhizal cabling link trees into gigantic, smart communities spread across hundreds of acres" (2018: 218). This book, which is read by virtually all of the novel's characters, outlines a philosophy of plant interconnection that complicates the central analogy between trees and the characters' lives: the narrativized form of the characters' interpersonal network does not mirror only the structure of a single tree but also the mycorrhizal organization that brings plants together in "smart communities." *The Overstory* thus develops an uneasy analogy between human and nonhuman collectivities, not only drawing attention to the striking formal similarities in human and nonhuman networks but also showing—pointedly—how human collectives fail to replicate the cohesiveness and efficacy of plant assemblages. If, to quote again Jamieson's (2014: 61) words, climate change is "the largest collective action problem that humanity has ever faced," Powers holds a mirror up to the shortcomings that keep human collectives (the environmental movement, the scientific community, and of course various levels of government) from approaching this problem with the genuinely altruistic mindset that defines the social behavior of seemingly "passive" plants. As in Mitchell's *Ghostwritten*, adopting an ethical viewpoint external to the human world (Mitchell's Zookeeper, Powers's plant collectives) reveals the profound inadequacy of human action.

Indeed, the key figure in Powers's ending is not a human group but Neelay Mehta, a lone computer programmer who gains startling insight into plant intelligence early in the novel. Neelay, the son of Indian immigrants living in California, loses use of his legs after falling off an oak tree; as he lies in shock next to the tree, unable to move, Neelay hallucinates that "a thousand—a thousand thousand—green-tipped, splitting fingerlings fold over him, praying and threatening" (2018: 102–3). These are the tendrils of a vegetal intelligence that infiltrates Neelay's mind and guides his career as a computer programmer. As the narrator remarks a few pages later, "the alien invaders [i.e., the plants] insert a thought directly into [Neelay's] limbic system. There will be a game, a billion times richer than anything yet made, to be played by countless people around the world at the same time" (2018: 110). That video game—titled *Mastery*—gains mass following and turns Neelay into one of Santa Clara County's wealthiest individuals: it is a *Civilization*-type game focusing on resource extraction and technological progress; ironically, "Enlightenment" is the name of an "overpowered victory strategy" (2018: 225) in the game. But Neelay slowly comes to realize that, whether the environment is real or computer-simulated, human mastery and the Enlightenment's faith in progress are actually self-defeating strategies. After resigning from the software house he has founded, and after reading Westerford's *The Secret Forest*, the full significance of plant intelligence dawns upon him: "He sees the tree's central aim, the math behind the phloem and xylem, the intermeshed and seething geometries, and that thin layer of living cambium swelling outward. Code—wildly branching code pruned back by failure—builds up this great spiraling column from out of instructions that Vishnu managed to cram into something smaller than a boy's fingernail" (2018: 435). The tree's "math" is the self-organizing complexity of life itself, how it keeps expanding despite being "pruned back by failure" and by the anthropogenic devastation wrought upon the Earth's ecosystems. DNA code—the language of life—is fundamentally similar to the lines of Neelay's computer code, and the two can be yoked together. The seed planted by the tree intelligence after Neelay's dramatic fall germinates into a concrete plan: he must create a computer algorithm that is able to match the complexity of life and help it overcome the ecological crisis.

These algorithms—referred to as "learners" in the novel—are capable of self-organization, self-knowledge, and ethical reasoning, at least if we consider the preservation of life (human *and* nonhuman) as the ultimate ethical value. No longer under Neelay's control, the learners "head off to scout the globe, and the code spreads outward. New theories, new offspring, and more evolving species, all of them sharing a single goal: to find out how big life is, how connected, and what it would take for people to unsuicide" (2018: 482). The scale of this algorithmic vision transcends the human species, even if the fate of humanity and its probable greenhouse gas suicide are deeply entangled in it. There is something mysterious and God-like about this biological force, which resonates deeply with the magic and "productive indeterminacy" of computational cognition. Like Mitchell's Zookeeper, the computational "learners" join forces with nonhuman intelligence; but while Mitchell foregrounds animals, Powers focuses his imagination on plants. Both novels reveal, through their algorithmic endings, a form of nonhuman vitality that is secretly in charge of the planet, despite humanity's delusion of mastery. Thus, the final pages of *The Overstory* not only announce "disastrous setbacks and slaughters" but also add that "life is going someplace. It wants to know itself; it wants the power of choice"; Neelay has only "nudged it along" (2018: 496).

Despite the apparent failure of their activism, the environmentalists also contribute to this "nudge." Neelay's vision of "intermeshed and seething geometries" is prompted by a digital artwork realized by one of the environmentalists, Nick Hoel, who becomes a wandering artist after the group disbands; it is a time-lapse video of a chestnut on Nick's family farm, followed by visual poetry in the shape of the tree, which incorporates Henry David Thoreau's lines:

> The gardener sees only the gardener's garden.
> The eyes were not made
> for such grovelling uses as they
> are now put to and worn out by,
> but to behold beauty now invisible.
> MAY
> WE
> NOT
> SEE
> GOD?
> (Powers 2018: 435)

The divine "beauty now invisible" brings us back to the "cathedral of computation" discussed by Bogost (2015) and Finn (2017) in their critique of contemporary culture's quasi-religious imagination of the algorithm. In the context of Powers's novel, however, that numinous quality of the algorithm is revitalized by being mapped (via the reference to Thoreau's transcendentalism) onto the formal complexity of both nature and art. Nick's creation is discontinuous, abstract, and multifaceted—all features that his digital art shares in common with the patterned strands of biological life and with the lines of computer code written by Neelay. In this way, the story lines of this network narrative come together in the deus ex algorithmo of the ending: Neelay's diegetic role in creating the "learners" is augmented by conceptual input from the environmentalists (through Nick) and Patricia Westerford.

The two remaining characters are also involved in this narrative pattern. They are Ray and Dorothy, a middle-aged couple living in suburban St. Paul—"two people for whom trees mean almost nothing" (2018: 64), states the narrator in "Roots." But, partly through reading Patricia's book, their minds change. Ray suffers a stroke and remains bedridden; in a final scene, he hears about the two life sentences faced by one of the environmentalists after arrest. Ray, a lawyer, imagines arguing in court that the ecoterrorist's actions constitute self-defense, on behalf of humanity, against the capitalist exploitation of the planet. That thought fatally destabilizes Ray's brain and yields the following near-death vision:

> The vessels in his brain give way, the way that earth does when roots no longer hold it together. The flood of blood brings a revelation. ... Their branches rush

> to enclose the house and punch through its windows. At the stand's center, the chestnut folds and unfolds, girthing out, spiraling upward, patting the air for new paths, new places, further possibilities. Great-rooted blossomer. (2018: 498)

On the brink of death, Ray experiences the collapse of the Earth as well as the vital blossoming of the planet, his bursting brain anatomy mirroring—through its complex formal arrangement—the branching structure of a chestnut tree. The insight into Ray's dying brain evokes the entanglement of human subjectivity in the drama of life on Earth—and how that subjectivity itself is eventually superseded by life's ever-growing spirals. This section is thus functionally analogous to the last chapter of Mitchell's novel, with its foregrounding of Quasar's deviant mind: the current Anthropocenic predicament is injected, with devastating consequences, into a character's psychology.

But while Mitchell's final chapters juxtapose the Zookeeper's humor and the nightmarish anxieties of a psychopath, the affect that prevails in Powers's algorithmic ending is the sublime of complex pattern, where—as seen above—religious language infuses art and the deep history of life on Earth. It is by adopting the sublime imagination of the "great-rooted blossomer" that Powers's novel invites the reader to embrace catastrophic change and its possibilities. This is an open ending, the extinction of *Homo sapiens* being far less definite than *Ghostwritten*'s "Zookeeper" chapter presents it: "the Earth—announces the narrator of *The Overstory*—will become another thing, and people will learn it all over again" (2018: 500). Who are these "people," though, and to what extent will they resemble our fellow human beings? We do not, and cannot, know. Yet, paying attention to the quasi-divine magic of formal complexity, whether through art (including Powers's novelistic art), biology, or computer science, evokes the startling possibility that life will survive an anthropogenic cataclysm. For the reader, there is not only consolation to be found in that idea but also increased awareness of the scale on which the current ecological crisis unfolds.

Tempered by concern over the fate of humankind, the sublime of Powers's prose doesn't aggrandize the human or champion technological progress as the only viable solution to the current crisis: even if the learners are a technological device, their intelligence and capacity for ethical decision-making far transcend the human. Instead of merely affirming an individualistic and heroic conception of humanity, as science fiction's technological sublime so frequently does, the learners bring about a profound transformation in humanity as we know it.[15] Thus, Powers's sublime of complexity offers comfort by providing insight into the more-than-human scale of life on Earth—an insight that doesn't downplay humanity's responsibilities toward the nonhuman but rather brings into view the immense ethical stakes of the climate crisis. It is from this position of heightened conceptual and affective understanding that the reader's willing embrace of uncertainty becomes possible.

* * *

In an already quoted passage of *What Algorithms Want*, Finn argues that algorithms involve interactions that are "like flocks of birds from a computational game of life" (2017: 52). We are now in a better position to understand how apt Finn's simile is to characterize the narrative operation performed by both Mitchell and Powers. Finn's reference is to the famous "game of life" devised by mathematician John Horton Conway in the 1970s, a cellular automaton that displays self-organizing behavior—in the form of recurring spatial patterns—on the basis of a simple rule set. None of the game's rules dictates, for instance, the existence of "gliders" (patterns traveling across the board) or stable "still lifes"; these coherent configurations are a product of algorithmic magic.[16]

The flock of birds that soars, unexpectedly, in the endings of *Ghostwritten* and *The Overstory* is a vision of life itself as a creative force that envelops, and at the same time reaches far beyond, the history of *Homo sapiens*. There is nothing fundamentally metaphysical about this vision: life, for both writers, is encoded in genes and shaped by evolutionary pressures; its operations may be mysterious and God-like, but its nature is material, even as the complexity that distinguishes living and cognizing matter from "mere" matter is only partly understood by science.[17] Just as Conway's game necessitated computers for a full-scale implementation, the life imagined by Mitchell and Powers springs up only under the lens of algorithmic intelligence capable of overcoming the intellectual strictures and ethical blind spots of human cognition—a posthuman perspective that leaves our species, perhaps tragically, on the sidelines. This algorithmic logic is active in contemporary culture at large. Mitchell and Powers blend it into the formal workings of narrative, and the genre of the novel in particular, by revisiting the classical device of the deus ex machina.

This final intervention of a computational savior, Mitchell's Zookeeper and Powers's learners, generates significant tension between form and theme: structurally speaking, the deus ex algorithmo is different from the narrative strategies examined in Chapter 1 in that it appears to bring in closure through the coming together of the strands of the network plot. While future-tense narrative and parallel storyworlds reject the gratification of closure, the deus ex algorithmo creates a semblance of formal closure even as it leaves many questions problematically open by shifting the focus away from the human. In that respect, the algorithm is an expression of the uncertainty that the novels had foregrounded at the level of theme—namely, the uncertainty surrounding the fate of the human (including the human mind) in a nonhuman world. This negotiation of the climate crisis helps readers grasp how the uncertainty of the future should not be swept under the rug but rather welcomed as a source of radical change in psychological and political terms. Affectively, though, the two texts come to this idea from significantly different angles: Mitchell's unresolved combination of humor and existential angst gives way, in Powers's work, to a sublime of formal complexity that also remains suspended, but without closing the door on the possibility of human survival as part of a much greater pattern of life. In both novels, acceptance of uncertainty is heralded by a complex affect that moves beyond a merely pessimistic construal of humanity's unstable future.

Algorithmic strategies may be present in contemporary fiction well beyond *Ghostwritten* and *The Overstory*, and they may bring in an even larger affective palette. More importantly, however, that strategy is part of a broader need for calamity forms that allow us to engage with the deep uncertainty of humanity's future in times of ecological crisis. As I have argued in this book's introduction and elsewhere, imagining the ecological crisis is, fundamentally, a *formal problem*. The next chapter pursues this investigation by focusing on digital narratives that are in a literal sense algorithmic. Because of the nonlinearity of digital narrative, that medium is particularly well suited to complicate the form of human–nonhuman relations beyond a fundamentally hierarchical—and therefore linear—conception that frames human beings as masters of the natural world.[18] The device of the deus ex algorithmo, discussed in this chapter, should be seen as part of a broader endeavor to question that assumption and shed light on humanity's participation in a game of life on a planetary scale.

Notes

1 See also Cooper (2010) and Chapter 1 on how the climate crisis is also a crisis of scientific predictability.

2 See Golumbia: "It seems problematic to put too much emphasis on computers in projects of social resistance, especially that kind of resistance that tries to raise questions about the nature of neoliberalism and what is (too often, disingenuously) referred to as free-market capitalism" (2009: 5).

3 Finn is referring here to the famous "game of life" invented by British mathematician John Horton Conway in the 1970s. I will return to this game in the chapter's conclusion.
4 This idea has been discussed extensively in the mind sciences in the context of "distributed" (Hutchins 1995) or "extended" (A. Clark and Chalmers 1998) cognition.
5 For discussion of the computational theory of mind, see Horst (2011); for an influential critique, see Lakoff and Johnson (1980), who introduce the distinction between first-generation (computational) and second-generation (embodied) cognitive science.
6 David Chalmers (1995) calls this the "hard problem" of the conscious mind, to distinguish it from the less thorny problem of understanding mind in a functionalist sense, as a system regulating action and behavior.
7 For more on the anthropocentric bias of narrative, see Caracciolo (2018).
8 See also Schmitt's (2014) distinction, discussed in the previous chapter, between "knots" (a diegetic convergence of story lines, for instance, when characters meet) and "connectors" (merely thematic links and resonances across story lines).
9 Rita Barnard (2009) reads the network narrative of *Ghostwritten* as a prime example of contemporary fiction's engagement with globalization. For more on the network as a productive aesthetic form in the contemporary moment, see Jagoda (2016) and Caracciolo (2021: chap. 1). In the latter, I focus on the network as a narrative form that is particularly suited to capture human–nonhuman entanglement in times of ecological crisis.
10 See also Lynn White's (1967) influential argument on the Christian roots of the ecological crisis, as already mentioned in my introduction, as well as the previous chapter's discussion of the transmigration of souls in *Cloud Atlas*. For more on Mitchell and Buddhist thought, see Harris-Birtill (2019).
11 Of course, this strategy also resonates with the unreadable animal minds we have examined in Chapter 3. Although Mitchell's crane, locust, and bat are not completely opaque, they are certainly mysterious creatures (with the mystery reflecting the spiritual inspiration of Mitchell's plot device).
12 For discussion of this (mis)reading of the Anthropocene, see Crist (2013) and Caracciolo (2020b).
13 See Lambert (2021a, 2021b: chap. 3) for a comprehensive discussion of the analogy between plant systems and narrative structure in *The Overstory*.
14 Powers's novel ties in with a recent wave of interest in plant cognition and intelligence in biology; for an overview and discussion from a humanities perspective, see Gagliano, Ryan, and Vieira (2017). See also Wohlleben (2017) for a popular account of mycorrhizal networks that overlaps significantly with Patricia Westerford's ideas in *The Overstory*.

15 See Istvan Csicsery-Ronay's (2008: chap. 5) discussion of the "technoscientific sublime" and its ideological underpinnings.
16 For more on Conway's game of life, see Gardner (1970).
17 Cf. also Caracciolo (2016a), where I explore contemporary fiction's confrontation with the seemingly insoluble "hard problem of consciousness"—or how subjectivity can exist in a material world—with a focus on *Ghostwritten*.
18 See also Caracciolo (2021) for more on nonlinear narrative forms and their role in imagining climate change.

6

Ecologies of Interactive Narrative

The previous chapter examined the way in which computational intelligence has become a conceptual resource for negotiating uncertain futurity in contemporary culture. This chapter retains many of the same conceptual coordinates, particularly Finn's argument on the close connection between cultural engagements with the algorithm and a quasi-magical understanding of uncertainty; however, my emphasis shifts from remediations of the algorithm in a print-based genre (the novel) to the inherently computational medium of the video game.

Consider, for example, *Outer Wilds* (Mobius Digital 2019), a time loop video game in which the player has twenty-two minutes to explore a small solar system before the sun, turned into a supernova, obliterates everything and everyone in its vicinity (including the player). After this catastrophic event, the game restarts, sending the player back to their home planet. This world brims with history and lore, which can be uncovered by visiting—in twenty-two-minute bursts—the archeological sites dispersed over the five planets of the solar system. As players collect artifacts and read inscriptions, they become acquainted with this world's extinct civilization and obtain key information on the time loop and how it can be broken. This plot emerges nonlinearly as the player unlocks, loop after loop, the mysteries of the solar system. The framing of *Outer Wilds* is explicitly apocalyptic and closely reminiscent of the ending of Mitchell's *Ghostwritten*, with the Zookeeper's decision not to prevent the Earth's collision with a comet that threatens to wipe out humanity.

In *Outer Wilds*, the narrative's interactivity derives from the relative lack of constraints on the player's exploration: the game does not dictate the order in which players can visit the five planets and investigate their various sites. Instead, the logic of the plot's unfolding is *environmental* in the sense of Henry Jenkins's (2004) "environmental storytelling": story-advancing cues are distributed across multiple locations, and it is up to the player to collect those spatially embedded elements and thus piece together the plot. Environmental storytelling is widely seen as a more effective narrative strategy in games than delivering a plot through cinematic "cutscenes" that break the flow of the player's interactions. Because it employs spatial elements that the player can manipulate within the game world, environmental storytelling enables a closer integration between narrative and the player's interactions than cutscenes: the plot unfolds as we act within the game world, for instance, by unlocking doors and reading documents left behind by the characters, rather than via scripted sequences.

Outer Wilds foregrounds computational intelligence in that—while everyone seems unaware of the time loop—the onboard computer of the player's spaceship "remembers" the information collected in the course of previous loops. The computer thus supports the game's environmental storytelling, helping the player make key inferences about this world's past. The game's nonlinear narrative is thus computationally enabled at two levels: first, the player uncovers the plot by interacting with the physical computer on which the game is running and, second, the work of reconstructing the plot is facilitated, within the game world, by the maps and summaries created by the spaceship's computer. Even though the game may seem to cast the player in the role of the savior of the solar system, all we can do is break the time loop, allowing the supernova to run its course. As we find out in the game's ending, life will need 14.3 billion years to recover after this catastrophic event. This twist is not without irony: the player's narrative-advancing efforts turn out to be directed toward making possible, rather than avoiding, the end of the world. Again, the comparison with Mitchell's Zookeeper is apt: computational intelligence works against the grain of an anthropocentric narrative template whereby the world is saved by the human hero's actions; instead, the plot achieves closure only when human extinction is embraced.[1]

The mysterious time loop of *Outer Wilds* serves as a bridge toward imagining the precarity of humanity's ecological predicament. Because the player's actions have no consequence on the game world other than enabling the catastrophe to happen, the circular temporality of *Outer Wilds* severs the usual link between action and consequence: this world has a rich history but no future. Seen in this light, the loop is a calamity form that channels humanity's current delusion of living in an eternal present, one in which the Earth is able to support unlimited growth and extraction of its resources.[2] The future, from this misguided perspective, is not contingent on the consequences of collective actions in the present (e.g., burning increasing amount of fossil fuels, ignoring the signs of impending ecosystemic collapse). The looping temporality thus goes hand in hand with deep uncertainty in human–nonhuman relations—an uncertainty that is overcome only when the loop gives way to a dizzying expansion in the scale of the plot (from the twenty-two-minute intervals of the player's travels to the 14.3 billion years needed for life's reemergence after the supernova). Crucially, this negotiation of uncertainty takes a profoundly different form from the solutions I examined in previous chapters of this book, through the active involvement of the player—even as their engagement with the game is eventually revealed to lead to a different outcome than the one we may have assumed (not saving the world, but terminating it).

This is, then, the starting point for this chapter: not only does interactive narrative in video games foreground the player's agency, but it also problematizes it, as *Outer Wilds* does by undercutting our hopes of saving the world. This strategy fosters players' emotional as well as ethical investment in their interactions with the game system. Many games even encourage multiple "traversals" of the plot to explore alternative lines of action and their consequences. These distinctive features of interactive narrative are well known to game designers and scholars, who have developed sophisticated accounts of how, in video games, the meanings of narrative can intersect with the rules and objectives that define ludic engagements.[3] The encounter of narrative and gameplay also offers unique possibilities for staging the uncertainty of our ecological predicament, as I argue in the following pages. This does not mean that we won't find continuities between the literary examples examined so far and contemporary video game narratives. However, the interactivity of the latter does create new opportunities: it offers a powerful form for capturing the complexity and multilinearity of the ecological crisis. Of course, not all games leverage the potential of interactive storytelling to the same degree, and only a few do so while raising or explicitly addressing ecological questions. *Outer Wilds* is certainly one of them. My two case studies in this chapter—*Heaven's Vault* (Inkle 2019) and *Kentucky Route Zero* (Cardboard Computer 2020)—are also representative of this trend. They are both "literary games," in Astrid Ensslin's (2014) phrase, in that they feature highly evocative writing and use stylistic strategies typical of literary fiction to engage the player and bring out the ethical depth of the choices they are asked to make. Before discussing those games in detail, I will turn to the challenges and potentialities involved in the intersection of narrative and the ludic logic of video games, and I will also expand on the role that uncertainty plays in game experiences.

Video Game Narrative and Its Compromises

In the early 2000s, game studies entered the scholarly stage with a debate that proved, in many ways, foundational to this emerging field. The debate opposed narratologically inclined theorists to so-called "ludologists": while the former (the already mentioned Jenkins was one of them) tended to emphasize the narrative dimension of video games and build on existing theoretical tools from the literary study of narrative, scholars in the latter camp—including Markku Eskelinen (2001) and Gonzalo Frasca (2003)—insisted on the specificity of video games *as* games, cultural artifacts that are primarily designed around rules and competitive objectives. The debate fizzled out within a few years, but it left a deep mark on game studies: if we look at one of the most influential introductions to the field to date, *Rules of Play* by Katie Salen and Eric Zimmerman (2004), there can be little doubt that ludological positions have had the upper hand, with game scholars developing a vocabulary distinct from literary theory and examining narrative as one of the many dimensions of game experiences (and not a particularly central or indispensable dimension at that). Video games, like games in general, involve rules and foreground competition, strategy, and the open-ended interactions that are discussed in game studies under the elusive rubric of "gameplay." Narrative is frequently accessory to gameplay, which offers its own ludic challenges and rewards regardless of narrative framing: clearing a level in a first-person shooter, for example, calls for fast reflexes and extensive knowledge of game mechanics (such as the possibilities and limitations of various weapons, etc.). These challenges are independent from knowing that (for example) the thugs we are facing kidnapped the protagonist's daughter, which is what the narrative frame tells us. Yet that backstory may deepen the player's emotional investment in the protagonist's situation, thus enhancing the ludic interests of gameplay. "[Computer] games are an art of compromise between narrative and gameplay," writes Marie-Laure Ryan (2006a: 198) in one of the most thorough discussions of narrative and interactivity in digital media. In most mainstream games, the compromise strongly favors gameplay: the plot may play a supporting role, but ultimately it is the gameplay that engages players and inspires them to devote countless hours to the game.

Not all video games assign an equally important value to narrative, then. But some games do tilt the balance toward storytelling, by tying the ludic challenges to the progression of the narrative itself (as opposed to using the story as a mere "hook," as in my hypothetical kidnapped daughter scenario): in these story-focused games the main ludic objective is to advance, or alternatively uncover, a story, and the main challenge involves finding out how to do so.[4] *Outer Wilds*, discussed above, is an excellent example of this category, because it directly maps the exploration of a miniature solar system onto the plot: as the player investigates the game world's locations, the story of the alien civilization that had inhabited them emerges from spatially distributed artifacts of various kinds. Piecing together the backstory of this world is the game's primary objective.

The environmental storytelling of *Outer Wilds* is only one possibility in the repertoire of story-focused games, however. In Ryan's (2006a: 108) terminology, *Outer Wilds* integrates narrative and gameplay by way of "exploratory interactivity." In this exploratory mode the player's role is primarily epistemological rather than ontological: the game encourages the player to discover what happened prior to the time loops we are currently experiencing. Only with the game's ending, in which the player-controlled character uses the information they have gained to *end* the loop, we transition to what Ryan calls "ontological interactivity"—that is, the player actively shapes the game world.

Other narrative-focused games privilege ontological interventions over exploratory interactivity (even if it is sometimes impossible to fully differentiate them). The narrative setup of these games is perhaps more closely indebted to hypertext fiction than exploration-based games like *Outer Wilds*.[5] Here most of the strategic decisions made by the player involve text-based prompts. For example, at the end of season 1 of *The Walking Dead* game (Telltale Games 2012) we are asked to choose between killing Lee (the season's protagonist, who has just been bitten by a zombie) and watching him turn into a zombie. The choice comes in the form of a dialogue option (see Figure 6.1): in an interaction with Clementine, the child who accompanied Lee throughout the season's five episodes, the player can choose on Lee's behalf between saying "Leave me" or "You have to shoot me." The decision is an ethically fraught one given that the season centers on Lee and Clementine's budding relationship. It also frames the player's relationship with the game world in ontological terms, since the player is put in a position to shape the development of the plot at a critical juncture: although Lee's death is inevitable, it is up to the player to make the morally complex choice between letting the season's protagonist become a zombie and having a child, Clementine, deliver the coup de grâce. A dialogue-based prompt asks players to make the call, restricting the scope of their interactions with the game and at the same time flagging this as a plot-advancing moment.

Figure 6.1 A key moment of ontological interactivity at the end of season 1 of *The Walking Dead* (Telltale Games 2012).

In ontological interactivity, choices like the one presented by *The Walking Dead* are strung together to create a branching structure of diverging story lines that lead to multiple endings.[6] Typically, however, the necessity of retaining a degree of authorial control over the narrative (as well as the pragmatic constraints of game development) reduces the range of possibilities, with most story-focused games limiting themselves to two or three endings; other decisions made by the player may impact the immediate situation or episode while having no repercussions on the story's long-term progression.

In playing *The Walking Dead*, the bulk of the narrative interest lies in the here and now of the survivors' predicament—hence the focus on ontological interactivity. *Outer Wilds*, by contrast, presents us with an entirely predetermined narrative that we reconstruct on the basis of our exploration of the game world. The nonlinearity of *The Walking Dead* reflects the numerous possibilities brought in by dialogue options; in *Outer Wilds*, by contrast, nonlinearity has to do with the player's exploratory freedom in uncovering and piecing together environmental cues that tell a prescribed narrative. The distinction between exploratory and ontological interactivity is not always clear-cut, however. Other story-focused games seek a middle ground between these possibilities. This, as we will see, is what happens in both *Kentucky Route Zero* and *Heaven's Vault*, which either blur the boundary between ontological and exploratory interactivity (in the former case) or achieve a high degree of integration between them. The next section turns to uncertainty as an experience made more conceptually and affectively salient by the interaction of narrative and gameplay.

More on Types of Uncertainty

Bradley and Drechsler's (2014) taxonomy of uncertainty, discussed in the introduction, distinguishes between four types of uncertainty in decision-making: empirical or "state" uncertainty, which refers to what we simply do not know about the world; ethical uncertainty, which denotes lack of clarity concerning the desirability of an action's predicted outcome; option uncertainty, which means that, when faced with a particularly difficult situation, we cannot fully predict the consequences of our actions; and finally state space uncertainty, which involves awareness that there might be possibilities or options we are not considering. While traditional, noninteractive narrative favors the first two types of uncertainty and can stage them in culturally transformative ways, option and state space uncertainty tend to play a more significant role in the kind of digital fiction I will discuss in this chapter. Of course, empirical and ethical uncertainty are also implicated in sophisticated video games like *Heaven's Vault* and *Kentucky Route Zero*, but the staging of the other two types of uncertainty accounts for the distinctiveness of video games' engagement with ecologically unstable futures. This distinctiveness reflects the complexity of the encounter between narrative and ludic challenges in the game medium. In particular, the player's decision-making and experience of agency have a major impact on the negotiation of uncertainty in story-focused video games.

Video game critic and designer Greg Costikyan (2013) has offered a nuanced discussion of uncertainty in games. Much of the thrill of games—and of playful activities in general—has to do with the management of uncertainty in a safe environment, one in which we can experiment with a wide range of experiential possibilities, because the stakes of the situation are low. Compare the uncertainty of encountering a real bear in a forest and the make-believe scenario, famously discussed by Kendall Walton (1990: 38), in which children imagine a tree stump to be a bear: both situations involve uncertainty, but in the latter it is only the result of the children's deliberate make-believe. The playful context is what makes the uncertainty manageable and enjoyable; thus, play opens a safe space to probe the uncertainty that comes with many high-stakes interactions in the real world.[7]

In games, uncertainty can take many forms, ranging from the randomness of a die roll in nondigital games to the erratic behavior of our opponents in a multiplayer online shooter. Lastly, uncertainty can be generated by what Costikyan calls "algorithmic complexity," which is closely related to Bradley and Drechsler's (2014) option uncertainty: when a game has "sufficient algorithmic complexity ... the consequences of a player's actions are uncertain, because the player cannot grasp all potential ramifications of an action" (2013: 41). With algorithmic complexity we begin moving toward what is unique about uncertainty in video games. Decisions are central to the experience of gameplay and an integral element of the ludic challenges discussed by game scholars. But video games can present us with decisions whose stakes and outcomes are hard to predict even if we are closely familiar with the game, its genre, and its specific mechanics. Option uncertainty thus comes to the fore in the player's experience of the game, and it may complicate the ethical uncertainty of their actions. Consider the already mentioned case of *The Walking Dead*, which asks us to choose between killing Lee or letting him turn into a zombie: we may wonder, for example, whether letting Lee live may not jeopardize Clementine's own survival; once turned into a zombie, Lee may break free and attack her. This kind of option uncertainty, which is a function of the game's algorithmic complexity, muddles the ethical calculus involved in killing the man who has served as Clementine's father figure for the entire first season of the game.[8]

State space uncertainty may inflect game experiences, too. Although this is not the case for this episode of *The Walking Dead* (in which Lee's death is, as I mentioned above, inevitable), it is at least theoretically possible to wonder whether making different choices before this juncture couldn't have led to a dramatically different outcome, such as Lee not being bitten by a zombie. State space uncertainty involves awareness of the roads not taken, unrealized possibilities that are too cloudy to be fully understood: commonly in interactive fiction, these options hover around our experience, holding out the promise of an ethically more desirable outcome (e.g., one in which we don't have to choose whether to shoot Lee) and thus inspiring multiple playthroughs.

In story-focused games, the uncertainty of playful activities is compounded by the epistemic gaps that drive the experience of plot in general (see Chapter 1). Sternberg's (2001) "narrative universals" of suspense and curiosity are emotional interests that arise from uncertainty: in suspense, the uncertainty concerns a future state of affairs (e.g., Is Clementine going to survive after Lee's death?), while it is directed at the story's past in curiosity (e.g., What happened to Clementine's family?).[9] In a story-focused game, the empirical uncertainty that comes with narrative suspense and curiosity is likely to be enriched by the player's sense of agency in shaping the story's future (Ryan's ontological interactivity) and/or uncovering the story's past (in exploratory interactivity). But narrative may implicate uncertainty well beyond these basic emotional responses. Some stories revolve around a sense of stubborn mystery or an "egregious gap" that cannot be filled in by way of plot progression, as we know from Porter Abbott's *Real Mysteries* (2013; see also Chapter 3). Moreover, stories can integrate and engage with the culturally specific horizon of uncertainty that defines the audience's real-world experiences. This kind of extrinsic uncertainty doesn't derive from epistemic gaps in the narrative but from existential queries and anxieties that originate extratextually from cultural debates and historical contingencies. As I have discussed in the introduction, climate change doesn't need to be explicitly referenced to become a shared concern in the triangulation between the storyteller, the audience, and a story.[10] Any narrative that foregrounds ecological relations or experiments with a collective future has potential for implicating climate change–related anxieties in the audience's experience—and thus for arriving at a meaningful negotiation of uncertainty.

The hazy futurity of climate change presents itself as an empirical uncertainty (What will the future be like in times of rapidly shifting and deteriorating human–nonhuman relations?); it is rich in ethical implications (What does it mean to be ecologically responsible as our own species and numerous other species are being jeopardized by anthropogenic climate change?); and it may also involve option and state space uncertainty—for instance, when we start realizing that we are running out of time and options in mitigating the most catastrophic consequences of climate change. If we consider all these dimensions, the landscape of climate change uncertainty starts looking very complex indeed. But, as I hope to have shown in this book, the multiple ways in which stories channel uncertainty can match this complexity. Further, those narrative approximations to uncertainty are greatly enriched by the encounter between narrative form and the interactivity of the video game medium. My case studies are representative of engagements with uncertainty in contemporary interactive narrative; without using climate change as a central plot or gameplay element, they resonate with a culturally pervasive sense of uncertain futurity by integrating the temporality of catastrophe. Yet, in the landscape of story-focused gaming, *Kentucky Route Zero* and *Heaven's Vault* are also unique for their formal innovations and for the lucidity with which they weave human–nonhuman relations into the fabric of both narrative and gameplay.

Mold Computers and Mushroom Pickers

Through discussion of multiple works by Jeff VanderMeer, I have already introduced weird fiction as a literary mode that is especially attuned to the negotiation of climate uncertainty. While related to established genres such as horror and science fiction or the fantastic, the weird is a label that cuts across generic divides. A fundamentally hybrid mode, the weird builds on a sense of elusive oscillation or disruption in the readers' imagination of the storyworld (see Chapter 2 and Hegglund 2020). For Luckhurst, weird fiction creates "an expansive borderzone of uncertain limits, where natural law and meaningful human structures of authority are subtly undermined" (2017: 1056). Area X in VanderMeer's Southern Reach trilogy and the split but coextensive cities of Miéville's *The City & the City* (both discussed in Chapter 2) are two excellent examples of these weird "borderzones" where ontological boundaries are constantly troubled and renegotiated: the boundary between human and nonhuman life, in Area X, and between two distinct but spatially overlapping cities, in Miéville's novel. The titular route of *Kentucky Route Zero* is one of such spaces. The Zero is a mysterious highway traversing the state: its access points are constantly shifting, its geography is indeterminate and can be navigated only via ghostly landmarks that keep appearing and disappearing as the player drives in circles.

The narrative of *Kentucky Route Zero* unfolds in five acts and four interludes. The latter explore side characters or offer new perspectives on the locations visited by the protagonists but without featuring the protagonists themselves. The game's release was spread out over seven years, with the first act appearing in 2013, the fifth and final one in 2020. In the first act, a truck driver named Conway is on his way to Dogwood Drive for a delivery; unable to find his destination, he stops at a gas station, where he learns that Dogwood Drive can be accessed via the mysterious Route Zero. This quest sets off a series of encounters with characters who end up joining Conway: first, Shannon Márquez, a TV repair technician; then (in act II) a boy abandoned by his parents, Ezra; the robotic musicians Johnny and Junebug in act III; and so on. As the cast of characters expands, the narrative becomes more convoluted and explicitly nonlinear: for instance, in act III we see Conway and Shannon enter a church to recover a password necessary to operate a "mold computer" named XANADU (the computer supposedly contains information on how to reach the Zero). The player first experiences this scene while controlling Ezra, who remains in the courtyard: we see Conway and Shannon enter the building and reappear with the password in the space of a few minutes. Later in the same act, a flashback shows what happened inside the church: Conway and Shannon are led into an underground facility, which turns out to be a whiskey distillery run by a crew of skeletons. (The plot of *Kentucky Route Zero* calls for a significant effort to suspend disbelief.) Once inside the distillery, a new player-controlled character (also known as the "avatar" in game studies) enters the stage: instead of Conway, we control Conway and Shannon's skeletal guide, who hires Conway as a distillery worker in exchange for the XANADU password.[11] The scene is, of course, a flashback filling in the blank left by the Ezra-focused scene in the church courtyard. Together with the flashback, the constant fluctuations in point of view and avatar illustrate the nonlinearity of the game's narrative. At the same time, the incongruity of the setting and of the causal links foregrounded by this narrative sequence (underground distillery, skeletons, password, etc.) offers a taste of the game's weirdness, how it shifts constantly between a realistic portrayal of quintessentially American locations (the gas station, the highway, a dive bar in act II, the small-town setting of act V, etc.) and fantastic elements. The game designers' own label of "magical realist adventure game" seems completely on target.[12]

This sense of weirdness is greatly enhanced by the game's implementation of interactive storytelling. I have introduced above Ryan's distinction between ontological and exploratory interactivity: in the former, the player makes choices that shape the plot qua the game world's future; in the latter, the player functions as a detective uncovering a preexisting narrative (reflecting the game world's past). *Kentucky Route Zero* consistently blurs the boundary between those two types of interactivity. This feature is neatly illustrated by the first scene of act I, in which Conway has to locate another computer password—this time, to access Weaver Márquez's address (Weaver, Shannon's sister, is said to know how to reach the Zero). The owner of the computer tells Conway that he has forgotten the password, although it's "kinda long, kinda like a short poem": his advice is to "feel it out." When Conway switches on the computer, he composes a poem by choosing one of three possible lines, three times (e.g., "Wheels slide loose / Nobody saw the accident / You just breathe road"; the alternatives for the first line include "The stars drop away" and "I talk and listen to him talking"). Regardless of what combination the player chooses, the password turns out to be correct. This puzzling sequence blurs the line between detective-style, exploratory interactivity (finding out what the password is) and ontological interactivity (shaping the game world by creating a new password). Likewise, *Kentucky Route Zero*'s dialogue constantly asks players to determine the protagonists' past, identities, and personalities as the plot unfolds: we are—paradoxically—learning about the characters and fashioning their personas in the same breath. This ambivalence creates a particular kind of state space uncertainty, which mirrors the widely divergent possibilities of the game's dialogue system: had we chosen a different dialogue line, we could have shaped or uncovered new aspects of this mysterious game world—and that, of course, encourages multiple traversals of *Kentucky Route Zero*.

Through this peculiar dialogue system, the game uses its algorithmic complexity to maximize the uncertainty typical of writing in the weird mode. That uncertainty is framed in explicitly ecological terms in act IV, and again through the catastrophic dimension of the game's final act. Before discussing those episodes, though, it is worth examining another scene (from act III) that explicitly stages the uncertainty at the heart of computational intelligence. After obtaining the password for XANADU, Conway and his companions can finally access the computer, which is named after the mythical city that inspired Samuel Taylor Coleridge's poem *Kubla Khan*. Another reference is to the first hypertext system, Project Xanadu, a forerunner of the World Wide Web conceived by Ted Nelson in the 1960s.[13] In *Kentucky Route Zero*, XANADU's programmer, a character named Donald, describes himself as a "hypertext enthusiast," and he may well be a fictional stand-in for Nelson himself. But Donald's creation is even more experimental than Nelson's project, and it troubles the dividing line between a human tool and a natural entity, mold: "As the mold accumulated on the circuitry, XANADU blossomed for a moment into something holy and enchanted … then all the charm was broken." Having recovered the password at the distillery, Conway and the other protagonists manage to restore XANADU's "charm," which represents another instance of the algorithmic magic discussed by Ed Finn (2017): a sense of mystery that drives the cultural and narrative imagination of computer technology (see Chapter 5). The computer's interface harks back to the early days of adventure gaming, with simple vector graphics and text-based commands. XANADU lets us explore an extensive cave system and even talk to some of the characters we had encountered in the main storyworld of *Kentucky Route Zero*. Technically, this is an instance of what Jeff Thoss (2015: 24–8) would call a "Storyworld-Imaginary World Metalepsis," a disruption of the assumed ontological divide between the primary game and XANADU, the game-within-the-game (see Chapter 4). Players think they are interacting with a fictional adventure game, but in fact they are talking to and learning about some of the characters (including Donald) who are featured in the baseline reality of *Kentucky Route Zero*.

The uncertainty here is empirical (How is XANADU positioned vis-à-vis the world of *Kentucky Route Zero*?), but it also mirrors and heightens the uncertainty involved in our dialogue-based decisions as we make our way through *Kentucky Route Zero* and get to shape, simultaneously and counterintuitively, the characters' past, present, and future. The thematization of computational intelligence via

XANADU thus amplifies the option and state space uncertainty of the player's engagement with the game: we don't fully understand the ramifications of the choices we are making (option uncertainty), and we don't know what possibilities would have been unlocked by making different choices (state space uncertainty). The more-than-human nature of this "mold computer" begins steering this uncertainty toward the ecological issues that are staged by two key episodes.

In act IV, the protagonists sail along an underground river, the Echo, as they attempt to locate the Zero and Dogwood Drive (the address of Conway's delivery). The players can learn more about the river's whimsical geography and ecology in an interlude titled "Here and There Along the Echo," where they interact with an automated phone system maintained by the "Bureau of Secret Tourism." As they navigate the Echo river in act IV, the protagonists stop at a number of locations mentioned in the interlude, including a bat sanctuary where a sign warns visitors that they should "take extra precautions in order to prevent the introduction of foreign fungal contaminants and the spread of *white nose syndrome*." The sign continues: "Will honey bees and the Nomadic River Bat be two more lost species, wiped out in the geological blink and forgotten to natural history?" Like the bats, the ecological landscape of the river is fragile and heavily impacted by human activities (the characters repeatedly comment on the waste floating past the ship).[14] The river thus serves as a material stand-in for the fragility of human–nonhuman interconnection in times of climate change, which even receives an explicit mention in one of the scenes: when Shannon visits the Rum Colony, a riverside bar, one of the patrons expresses concerns over melting polar ice caps.

Crucially, the ecological questions that emerge in this act are deeply inflected by the weirdness of the game's atmosphere and mechanics. The fragility of the nonhuman environment goes hand in hand with a sense of uncertain futurity, which is mirrored by the ontological hesitations introduced by the dialogue system and by metaleptic devices such as the XANADU computer. But in *Kentucky Route Zero*, uncertainty also takes a spiritual tone as it is elevated to a metaphysical mystery that pervades the storyworld (again, tying in with what Finn calls the "productive indeterminacy" of the algorithm). From the player's perspective, experiencing this mystery serves as a negotiation of ecological anxieties through an acknowledgment that fragility and vulnerability are not just features of the nonhuman environment but shared widely across the human–nonhuman divide.[15]

As I explained in the introduction, this negotiation starts at the level of characters' mental processes: uncertainty, conjugated as mystery, colors the protagonists' relations with this bizarre environment. But this mystery gradually begins affecting the form of the game through the dialogue-based decisions and ultimately reaches players' experience, facing them with the limitations and breakdowns of human knowledge. This is what emerges from a scene set in a "memorial grove" where Ezra, the boy, and Cate, the captain of the boat, go mushroom picking. Formally, the episode presents us with two columns of interactive text, each focusing on one of the characters (see Figure 6.2). In yet another instance of the game's play with multiple perspectives, not only can we choose what Ezra and Cate do and say to each other, but we are also in control of their memories and inner experiences. We advance the scene by making choices within each column, with the text scrolling in parallel, as if we were offered a simultaneous glimpse into two minds in interaction.

As they engage in close observation of the grove and its nonhuman inhabitants (the mushrooms, the trees, a caterpillar, and so on), Ezra and Cate keep wondering about the memorial function of this place. "I guess I don't know much about this place, really. It's supposed to be some kind of memorial? To something? … Sorry, it's a mystery," Cate remarks. Later in the same scene, a ghost ship named the "Iron Pariah" makes an appearance in front of the grove. Cate reflects on the inevitable presence of nonhuman life onboard: "I mean, there must be *something* on there. Life is everywhere. Rats, insect, some kind of hardy mold … Part of it could be flooded, and host to some of the eyeless fish

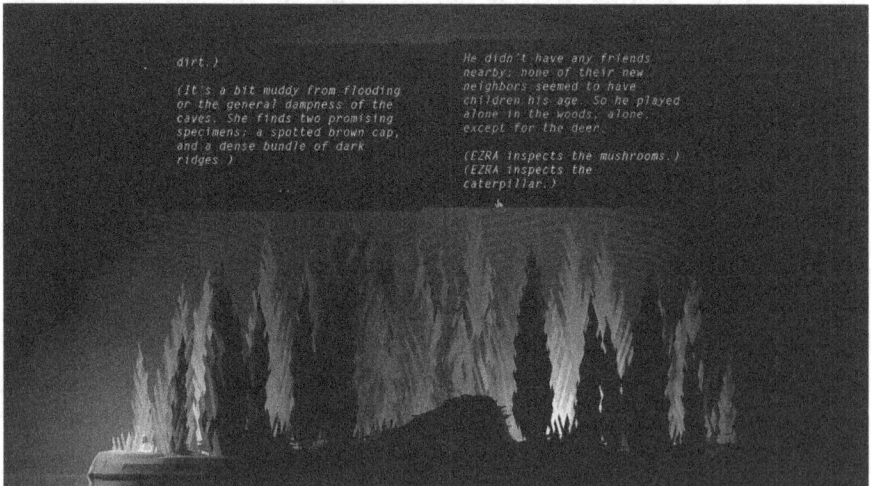

Figure 6.2 The layout of the grove scene in Act IV of *Kentucky Route Zero* (Cardboard Computer 2020), with two columns of text unfolding in parallel and reflecting the perspectives of Cate (left-hand column) and Ezra (right-hand column).

that live in the Echo." Cate adds, "More mysteries. They do pile up, over time, as people forget the details."

People's forgetfulness hints at the fragility not just of human life but of human knowledge, which gradually slides into oblivion (just as everyone seems to have forgotten, or ignore, what this memorial grove is supposed to commemorate). Nonhuman life, by contrast, is seen as deeply resilient and able to occupy spaces—like the Iron Pariah itself—that have been abandoned by human communities. It is no coincidence that the protagonists are picking mushrooms in this scene, and that Cate shares how she started finding solace in mushrooms after a traumatic miscarriage. In *The Mushroom at the End of the World*, Anna Tsing develops an anthropological theory of precarity in times of climate crisis, when large-scale industrialization is upsetting the balance of human–nonhuman relations. Tsing's conceptual gambit is to reframe this precarity as a valuable, and even essential, resource for life to flourish: "Indeterminacy, the unplanned nature of time, is frightening, but thinking through precarity makes it evident that indeterminacy also makes life possible" (2015: 20). Tsing's titular mushroom, the matsutake, which tends to grow in areas ravaged by bushfires, becomes a symbol for life's "willingness to emerge in blasted landscapes" (2015: 3). This willingness suggests that the violence of human interventions in ecosystems—and the uncertainty that results from it—can be reabsorbed into the transformative, if indeterminate, vitality of the more-than-human.

Also through dialogue with mushrooms, *Kentucky Route Zero*'s grove scene attempts a similar operation by staging a gap in knowledge—the paradoxical forgetfulness that surrounds this memorial—that opens onto a metaphysical mystery. While the experience of nescience (or not knowing) can be seen as debilitating, the mystery conveyed to the player is existentially productive: it hints at an embrace of the limits of human knowledge and agency, and it evokes confidence in the nonhuman world's ability to regenerate, like Tsing's mushrooms, despite the catastrophic impact of human activities (the polluted fragility of the Echo River's environment). The scene channels all this in a sophisticated and suggestive fashion: as players shape Ezra and Cate's interactions and mental life, they gradually become privy to a higher mystery, which transcends the two characters' individual memories even as it pervades the physical space they (and the players) are exploring. This memorial whose very memorial function is unknown becomes a probe into a different way of being human, one attuned to the empirical and ethical uncertainties of our ecological predicament, and one that has learned how to value those uncertainties instead of rejecting them.

This theme of honoring precarity comes to the fore again in the game's epilogue, which is set in a town devastated by severe flooding. The final interlude ("Un pueblo de nada") places the player inside the office of the local TV station, during the catastrophic rainstorm that preceded the flooding. In act V, the TV station building has collapsed, but a new building has sprung up nearby: it is, as we soon find out, the Dogwood Drive home that the game's protagonists had been attempting to locate from the outset. The act begins with the protagonists emerging from a hole in the ground, where a long spiral staircase connects the town to the Echo river. Unlike the previous acts, this episode is not subdivided into scenes: it all takes place in this town, which serves as a sort of theatrical stage for numerous events and conversations involving the local residents and the protagonists from the previous acts (minus Conway, who has now joined the skeletal distillery workers). The game adopts a nonhuman perspective on these happenings: to navigate the episode, the player controls a cat, who chases a dragonfly-like projection at every click of the mouse.

As the cat scampers from one scene to another, the world around it appears to slowly come back to life; most of the locals decide to abandon the town, rendered uninhabitable by the flood. The atmosphere is one of melancholic acceptance of the reality and consequences of the disaster. What emerges from the conversations we overhear from the cat's perspective is a subdued, humbled humanity that knows its limits and welcomes the uncertainty of the future.[16] This image is very much in line with the memorial grove scene, but the object of the characters' collective memory—which was indeterminate in the grove—becomes much more concrete and tangible: the town gathers to commemorate two horses that died in the flood. The epilogue thus sees the characters assembled around the grave that has been dug for the two animals (see Figure 6.3). If the grove scene elevated the fragility of human–nonhuman connection to a sense of mystery, this burial ceremony amplifies the affective dimension of that mystery: acknowledging human–nonhuman connection is not a purely conceptual gesture but calls for the honoring of uncertainty, vulnerability, and mortality as ethical and existential horizons that bring together human and nonhuman life.

Community emerges in this conclusion as an essential dimension in encountering uncertainty as mystery. The game evokes community in an enlarged sense, encompassing human beings and nonhuman creatures (the horses, the player-controlled cat), as well as shadowy anthropomorphic presences that also gather around the horses' grave. These are perhaps the ghosts of the first inhabitants of this place, the "pueblo" that—as one of the characters,

Rita, remarks during the burial ceremony—brought the horses from Central America. This final emphasis on community explains the game's stubborn refusal to ground the player's experience in a single character or perspective: by controlling multiple characters in the course of the game's five acts, the player's agency is linked to an expanding sense of collectivity that, eventually, transcends the boundaries of the human.

The epilogue, just like the game's first scene, also lets the player compose a poem to commemorate the dead horses. Nikki, one of the town's inhabitants, steps forward to recite a poem that players can assemble themselves, stanza by stanza. This device foregrounds, again, the algorithmic complexity of the game and how uncertainty is central to the ludic logic of choice (which is also what the player's interactions with XANADU had suggested, through the blurring of the ontological distinction between game and game-within-the-game). But if algorithms and computational intelligence tend to be seen as inherently magical in contemporary culture, *Kentucky Route Zero* uses its formal innovations and weird aesthetics to revitalize that magic and push it in culturally transformative directions: algorithmic magic opens a window onto the deep uncertainty of human–nonhuman relations and highlights the need to appreciate the shared fragility of human and nonhuman life. For willing players, that appreciation is a necessary step toward a more resilient humanity that is truly attuned to the strange wonders of the nonhuman world.

Figure 6.3 The game's characters commemorate the death of two horses in the flood, in the final act of *Kentucky Route Zero* (Cardboard Computer 2020).

Sailing the Nebula

If *Kentucky Route Zero* blurs the boundary between ontological and exploratory interactivity, *Heaven's Vault* works toward integrating them. The game is set in a science fiction universe—a "nebula," as the characters call it—with clear Middle Eastern influences at the level of architectural style and clothing. While *Kentucky Route Zero* builds on a large and diverse cast of player-controlled characters, as we've seen, *Heaven's Vault* has a more traditional setup: the player is placed in the shoes of a single protagonist, Aliya, an archeology PhD student at the University of Iox (one of the planets or "moons" in the nebula). The game begins with Aliya's supervisor, professor Myari, sending her on a mission to locate a missing colleague, a roboticist named Janniqi Renba. We then find out that Renba's ship has crashed on an uninhabited moon, in a remote part of the nebula. The artifacts we recover near Renba's ship reveal a series of previously unknown archeological sites, which provide fresh evidence on the history of this universe: the current Iox Protectorate was preceded by an Empire, and before that by an elusive period known simply as "Ancient times." With her robot companion, Six, Aliya is free to roam the nebula by navigating the currents—or "rivers"—that connect the various moons. During her travels, Aliya discovers that a catastrophic "darkness" is about to envelop the nebula. Ultimately, the clues she collects point to a mysterious place, the "Heaven's Vault," on which hangs the fate of the whole universe.

As in *Kentucky Route Zero*, we are asked to make a large number of choices within the game's dialogue system. Some of these choices involve interactions with other characters and can be variously consequential at the ontological level (i.e., in terms of shaping the trajectory of Aliya's narrative and the world around her). We can, for example, disclose all our discoveries to Myari, or we can keep them from her based on her suspected implication in Renba's death. Other choices are—to use again Ryan's category—exploratory in nature, particularly those prompted by the game's unique translation mechanic. As she travels the nebula, Aliya comes across numerous objects and buildings bearing inscriptions. This text is written in the language known as "Ancient," which predates the Empire and has been forgotten over the millennia of the nebula's history: as we play the game, we have to build Aliya's knowledge of Ancient from the ground up, which involves constant guesswork and attention to the iconic shape of the signs as well as contextual elements (see Figure 6.4 for an example of the text decoding interface). After encountering the same word a number of times, Aliya and Six will tell the player whether they think their guess is correct or not.

Remarkably, *Heaven's Vault* has been programmed to increase the difficulty and length of the Ancient inscriptions over time, based on the player's previously acquired knowledge: the result is a system of high algorithmic complexity, where we may reach profoundly different conclusions about the same inscription depending on previous hypotheses and inferences. Because these inscriptions are the main vehicle of environmental storytelling in the game, making a decision about their meaning has an enormous impact on the player's understanding of the game world and its history. This investigative work is an instance of exploratory interactivity in the game, in that each text has a correct interpretation that we are recovering rather than creating. But the process of arriving at an accurate reading of a passage is fraught with uncertainty, and indeed most players are likely to finish the game without having established the meaning of certain key words or phrases (and therefore without having a complete picture of the nebula's history).

Further complicating the exploratory interactivity of *Heaven's Vault* is the navigation of the nebula: this is plainly exploratory work in that the goal is uncovering the nebula's past.[17] There are multiple moons that Aliya and Six can decide to visit at any point in the game: the sequence of the plot is not as fixed as it is in *Kentucky Route Zero*. After discovering Renba's wrecked ship, for instance, players can travel back to Iox immediately and inform Myari, or they can decide to keep exploring a nearby site. This choice has repercussions on the protagonist's relationship with Myari and also on the possibilities that the game will make available to the player later. The information obtained by decoding Ancient inscriptions also inflects players' understanding of the moons

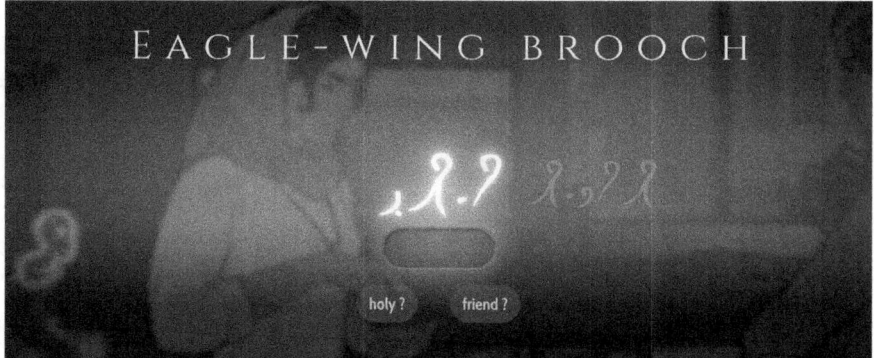

Figure 6.4 Decoding the Ancient language in *Heaven's Vault* (Inkle 2019).

they visit: the same site may be labeled "Domed Market Moon," "Pre-Empire Site," or "Serpent's City" in different traversals of the game, depending on earlier interactions.

The exploratory openness of the game world is supported by an incredibly robust and sophisticated storytelling algorithm: the plot adapts dynamically to the player's choices, of which there are so many that every playthrough is, in some way, unique. Empirical uncertainty (What does this inscription mean? What was the function of this site?) is maximized by the flexibility of the game's plot, which keeps reminding Aliya—and the player—of the many unknowns in their understanding of this world. For instance, when visiting a site known as the "Cratered Moon," Aliya and Six come across an observatory and a massive landing pad, but the function of these structures remains unclear. The observatory could be the one mentioned earlier in the game by a ghostly apparition of Renba (the dead roboticist). Yet, after searching the site thoroughly, Aliya's comments evoke a nagging feeling of having missed something, which is likely to reflect the player's own frustration at this point: "I hope this isn't Renba's observatory. If it is, I'm definitely missing something. There's *nothing* here!" When Six asks us if we are ready to leave, one dialogue option is to reply that before leaving we would like to get to the bottom of the landing pad and open the hatch there. It is possible to climb down the ruined landing pad, but it is rather tricky given the absence of a visible path; many players will move on without having opened the hatch (and even if they do get there, what Aliya discovers inside the hatch does not explain much about this place).

Through these rhetorical and gameplay tricks, the game teases the player into thinking that there is always more to the story than what they have been able to experience. Put otherwise, the game attempts to convince the players that, if they are "missing something," it is not because the plot is incomplete or inherently vague but because they haven't been thorough enough in their searches. This kind of uncertainty is compounded by state space uncertainty, particularly when decoding Ancient text: so much of our understanding of the nebula's history is a matter of guesswork, and while some of these guesses are eventually sanctioned by the game, others remain mere question marks—and the feeling that a key text could have meant something completely different lingers (hence our state space uncertainty about choices we made earlier in the course of the game).

One of the most intriguing features of the interface is a timeline that fills up *both* with choices made by the player during actual game time (e.g., visiting a moon at a particular time) and with historical events we have inferred or hypothesized in the course of our explorations. Our interactions with the game are thus put on a continuum with the history of the nebula, which foregrounds players' agency in constructing the past through their interpretive choices in the present. This focus on historicity at the level of the game's mechanics is augmented by the religious doctrine of the "Great Loop," which enjoys wide popularity on Iox. For believers in the loop (Professor Myari is one of them), history is fundamentally circular: everything that happens has happened before and will happen again in the future. The startling implication is that, as Myari puts it in a conversation with Aliya, "You think you're studying the past, but you're actually studying the future." Aliya, however, remains skeptical and believes that her archeological discoveries support a linear conception of time. The apocalyptic framework introduced by the impending "darkness" enriches the tension between these philosophies of history: clearly, the nebula is facing a fundamental crisis, which is at the same time environmental (the rivers are drying up) and economic (Iox is thriving at the expense of the other moons, including Aliya's home planet, Elboreth, which has a quasi-colonial relationship with Iox). The apocalyptic prospect amplifies the ambivalence of history, since the catastrophe could be read as a sign that time is irreversible and that the circular conception of history is profoundly misguided or, on the contrary, it could mark the beginning of a new cycle.[18]

The game doesn't fully resolve this tension, and the ending further implicates the players in that ambiguity by asking them to choose between two courses of action that seem to support alternative conceptions of history. Aliya finally arrives at the Heaven's Vault, which turns out to be a Noah's Ark–like ship that was programmed by an alien civilization to release the rivers and thus render the nebula inhabitable. The player has to choose between "vaulting" (jumping to another part of the universe to escape the looming "darkness") and shutting down the ship's systems in the hope that this action will somehow prevent the nebula's rivers from running dry (see Figure 6.5). This choice—an instance of ontological interactivity on a cosmic scale—creates ethical and option uncertainty, given how little we can discern about the consequences of Aliya's decision for life in the nebula. The two possible endings also carry ramifications for the empirical uncertainty that surrounds this world's history: if Aliya decides to vault, then the nebula is doomed and its history cannot repeat itself ("entropy is inescapable," remarks Six in this final scene, which implies that the arrow of time cannot be reversed); if, on the other hand, Aliya decides to stay in a desperate attempt to save the world, then the possibility of restarting the cycle of history is at least not ruled out completely. Either way, the final choice that the player faces feeds into the larger undecidability of the nebula's history, which derives from both the plot gaps that the game does not fill and from the algorithmic complexity introduced by the game's interactive storytelling and by the Ancient language.

Importantly, that algorithmic complexity is doubled by the way in which *Heaven's Vault* directly stages artificial intelligence. *Kentucky Route Zero* uses the XANADU computer system in act III to a similar end, but in *Heaven's Vault* artificial intelligence—in the form of robots like Aliya's companion, Six—is structurally part of the game world. Despite players' best attempts to piece together the past of the nebula, their reconstruction of the events is bound to remain incomplete, as I pointed out above. The game repeatedly hints that robots are key to this mystery, that deep down they know what really happened in Ancient times, even though they have been forced to forget it. Thus, when we visit a location named "Withering Palace," Six has a déja vu, he remembers having been there before—possibly, in human form. The Withering Palace, Aliya and Six speculate, could be a place of execution, one where human beings were killed and their minds trapped (or "bottled," as Six puts it) within the robots' computational hardware. This scene raises questions on the relationship between artificial and biological intelligence. It also conjures up the problem of locating the conscious mind (human or otherwise) within a fundamentally physical world—a version of what philosopher David

Figure 6.5 Aliya chooses between vaulting and staying in the nebula, in the final scene of *Heaven's Vault* (Inkle 2019).

Chalmers (1995) famously called "the hard problem of consciousness."[19] In the game, the evocation of these dilemmas contributes to an atmosphere of persistent uncertainty.

In many ways, the ending of *Heaven's Vault* is a "deus ex algorithmo" as I have discussed that concept in the previous chapter. Aliya's decision to vault or not to vault is implemented by her robot, Six, and the vault-ship itself was built by a civilization of which robots were an essential (and perhaps the only) part. Because of this computational intervention, the ending also comes across as a "trick" that wraps up the plot without fully resolving its many ambiguities.[20] The many tensions that underlie the nebula—between a colonialist Iox and the destitute moons, between robots and humans, between cyclical and linear time—are left unaddressed. The empirical and ethical uncertainty of the computational ending is further complicated by the state space uncertainty that players are bound to experience as they wonder if different choices made in the course of the game couldn't have led to a more satisfying, enlightening outcome. We can, of course, replay the game to achieve a clearer picture: *Heaven's Vault* even offers a "Game Plus" mode that allows the player to retain the Ancient words successfully decoded in the previous traversal of the game. Yet, no matter how many times we play the game, some of the fundamental questions concerning the past and future of the nebula remain unanswered. That ambiguity is built into the game's systems and writing, and it furthers the game's interest in forms of complexity and nonlinearity that don't admit of easy solutions. "Stories don't have tidy beginnings, the past is always present," reflects Aliya; the same could be said about endings and their engagement with a future that is both intrinsic (the future of the nebula) and extrinsic (the real-world ecological crisis that *Heaven's Vault* evokes through the "darkness" looming over the game world).

The game's ending is as potentially frustrating as it is algorithmic, as I showed above. "Algorithmic" here denotes both the central role that robots have in the plot and the deeply algorithmic nature of a game whose storytelling adapts so deftly to the player's choices. Importantly, *Heaven's Vault* asks players to live with, and appreciate, the uncertainty of this algorithmic setup, including the lack of straightforward answers. The stakes of this uncertainty are extremely high, involving the future of the nebula with all that it contains, human life and nonhuman entities (such as the rivers and the robots). The Heaven's Vault can only offer partial and imperfect salvation: nevertheless, we must embrace the sense of ethical responsibility that comes with our choices in the face of impending disaster, rather than ignoring the coming darkness or believing in an improbable Great Loop. That conclusion, which can only be arrived at in a storytelling medium that weaves the player into the murkiness of choices, resonates strongly with the ethical quandaries of the climate crisis. There is, simply put, no technological Heaven's Vault that could rescue humanity—and the other species we are ecologically bound up with—from our self-inflicted environmental catastrophe. Instead, there are extremely complicated choices to be made and collective responsibilities to be taken on to mitigate the consequences of the crisis. *Heaven's Vault* seeks to attune the player to the intricacies of decision-making on a planetary scale, in the absence of absolute empirical or ethical certainties.

***

Kentucky Route Zero and *Heaven's Vault* are games that require a great deal of patience of the player. In *Kentucky Route Zero*, ludic challenges are limited, the progression is mostly linear, the vast majority of interactions unfold within long dialogues whose main appeal is the thoughtful, atmospheric writing. Even straightforward identification with a character is frustrated, because the point of view keeps shifting, sometimes within the same scene, and the game's quasi-protagonist—the delivery man Conway—vanishes before the final act. *Heaven's Vault*, for its part, revolves around a decision of cosmic proportions (vaulting or staying in the nebula?) while withholding decisive elements of the world's history: even the conceptual shape of this history (line or loop?) remains indeterminate. What emerges is an image of the past as a factual and ethical work-in-progress whose ramifications into the present and future are profound but inherently elusive. The writing, more concise than in *Kentucky Route Zero* but equally evocative, only deepens the plot's perplexities.

The uncertainty brought into view by these games' literary and narrative strategies is amplified by the interactivity uniquely afforded by the game medium. Players are immersed in a setting and narrative whose many ambiguities do not only preexist but flow from the choices they make as they attempt to shed light on the games' mysteries. Through this ludic implication, players experience uncertainty at an uncomfortably close range. Yet mystery is revealed to be a positive force rather than merely a source of frustration. Remember the observation, quoted in Chapter 1 from Ali Smith's *How to Be Both*, that "we live in a time and in a culture when mystery tends to mean something more answerable, it means a crime novel, a thriller, a drama on TV, usually one where we'll probably find out—and where the whole point of reading it or watching it will be that we *will* find out—what happened" (2015: 72). Video games, contemporary culture's youngest storytelling medium, are certainly complicit in this narrow sense of mystery as a gap that calls for immediate closure. That is particularly true for mainstream games, whose narratives tend to be formally derivative and unimaginative; they are delivered by way of cutscenes and subordinate to the challenges of gameplay. Story-focused games by independent developers like *Kentucky Route Zero*'s Cardboard Computer and *Heaven's Vault*'s Inkle reject ludic challenges and strategy in favor of affectively resonant storytelling. This chapter's case studies demonstrate how the game medium has achieved a remarkable level of narrative sophistication, how it can reach toward a higher sense of mystery, which does not sit well with linear plots and perfectly satisfying outcomes.

This mystery is bound up, in both games (albeit in profoundly different ways), with catastrophic anxieties and questions surrounding human societies' relationship with the nonhuman world. The nonhuman is presented in both ecological and computational terms: think about the Echo and XANADU in *Kentucky Route Zero*, the rivers running dry across the nebula, and the robots that form an essential part of the storyworld's murky history in *Heaven's Vault*. The player becomes responsible, through ludic decision-making, for the fate of human–nonhuman relations, even though answers are not forthcoming and responsibility does not imply immediate solutions—perhaps it implies no solutions at all. It is the player's experience of deep involvement in a logic of choice that sets these games apart from the novelistic engagements with uncertainty I examined in the previous chapters. Ultimately, *Kentucky Route Zero* and *Heaven's Vault* are explorations into the ethics of uncertain decision-making, which is an essential skill to hone in the face of today's ecological crisis. Through dialogue with established literary genres (magical realism, science fiction, the weird), these games promote an embrace of mystery and enchantment as pathways for grasping human entanglement with nonhuman life and intelligence—an entanglement that may be partly revealed and probed by scientific models of the natural world but whose significance resists capture in the descriptive language of science. Facing up to climate change means honoring the complexity of the human–nonhuman assemblage, but it also means accepting, and welcoming, the absence of easy choices or measures against the crisis. Yet that does not imply indifference or nihilism, or a sense that all choices are equally undesirable. Intellectually and affectively, story-focused video games can negotiate uncertainty by fostering an embrace of precarious decision-making in times of rapidly shifting human–nonhuman relations.

Notes

1. I am taking some liberty with the idea of "human extinction" in this reading of *Outer Wilds*, since the character controlled by the player is anthropomorphic but not strictly human.
2. For more on this sense of presentness that erases historicity and futurity, see the discussion of temporality in Chapter 1 (via Currie's work) and also Gumbrecht (2014).
3. See, for example, the approach to game criticism outlined by Ian Bogost in *Unit Operations* (2006).
4. For more on the player's experience of story-focused games, see Caracciolo (2015).
5. Ryan discusses hypertext fiction extensively in chapter 6 of *Avatars of Story* (2006a). See also Espen Aarseth's (1997) authoritative treatment of this genre, which played a crucial role in the development of game studies.
6. See the helpful distinctions introduced by Ryan (2006a: 100–7) to visualize various interactive architectures at the level of story and discourse.
7. See also the account of play in Di Paolo, Rohde, and De Jaegher (2010), which doesn't highlight uncertainty per se but is very much in line with Costikyan's discussion.
8. See also Smethurst and Craps (2015) on the high ethical and emotional stakes of the player's decision-making in *The Walking Dead*.
9. Sternberg's third narrative universal, surprise, also derives from an epistemic gap, but less straightforwardly than in the case of suspense and curiosity. An example of surprise is the revelation that the suspected murderer was already dead at the time of the murder; when something like this occurs, readers update their understanding of the situation in light of new information, which may deepen uncertainty by eliciting suspense or curiosity (in my example, concerning the identity of the murderer).
10. For an account of this triangulation in terms of "joint attention," see Herman (2008).
11. I refer to Vella (2013) for more on player-controlled characters and how the choice of an avatar intersects with game narrative.
12. See http://kentuckyroutezero.com/.
13. See the extensive discussion of Nelson's Project Xanadu at this link: http://www2.iath.virginia.edu/elab/hfl0155.html.
14. See, for instance, this exchange: "See that? Just looks like a swirling mess of garbage, doesn't it? Well that's what it is."
15. See Anat Pick's *Creaturely Poetics* (2011) for a contribution to critical animal studies that focuses on that shared sense of vulnerability. The same concept of vulnerability plays a central role in Johns-Putra's (2019: 45) discussion of the ethics of reading climate fiction.

16 For more on this diminished humanity, see also Jon Hegglund's (2021) discussion of the "partially human" in Richard McGuire's comic book *Here* and Don Hertzfeldt's animated film *World of Tomorrow*.
17 The twist, though, is that according to the "Loop" interpretation of this universe, the past is also its future—I will return to this point soon.
18 The ambivalence of the temporal setup of *Heaven's Vault* is closely reminiscent of Mitchell's *Cloud Atlas* and how that work also builds on conflicting conceptions of temporality (see Chapter 4).
19 "Surely, the neural mesh must be physical," observes Aliya, disputing Six's theory that in the Withering Palace the mind was dualistically separated from its material basis, the body. For more on the problem of integrating the conscious mind within a materialist view of the universe, see Joseph Levine's (1983) influential article on the "explanatory gap." See also the discussion in Chapter 5 and Caracciolo (2016a).
20 Several reviewers of the game express frustration over this lack of real closure. See, for instance, Samuel Horti's (2019) critical comment: "You're always learning about the world, but *Heaven's Vault* never pieces it all together into a single story that drives you forward, and jumping between themes meant I often forgot key information I'd found out earlier. It made the ending far less impactful than I'd hoped."

Coda: Weathering Uncertainty, with Jenny Offill

I have argued in this book that literary storytelling is uniquely equipped to confront humanity's climate predicament, textually (through the manipulation of form) as well as experientially (by inspiring an interpretive negotiation of uncertainty in audiences). My six chapters have charted various formal configurations that evoke and negotiate uncertainty in contemporary fiction, from the basic parameters of storytelling (time in Chapter 1, space in Chapter 2, characters in Chapter 3) to more particularized—but still recognizably formal rather than merely thematic—engagements with an unstable future: metafiction (Chapter 4), the uneasy closure provided by the ending (Chapter 5), and the nonlinear setup of interactive narrative (Chapter 6). These formal devices mirror the experience of climate uncertainty and afford readers insight into their own personal and collective teetering on the brink of environmental catastrophe. This insight can result in a shift from a primarily negative understanding of uncertainty—as something to be avoided at all costs—to a more complex construal of this experience, involving both positive and negative affect, hope and concern.[1] "Embracing" uncertainty in this sense means abandoning presumptions of human exceptionalism and respecting the inscrutable complexity of human–nonhuman interconnection, including the intricacies of our moral responsibility toward more-than-human ecologies. By embracing uncertainty, we let go of our culturally ingrained faith in metanarratives of scientific and technological progress and unlimited economic growth—metanarratives that have largely shaped the ecological crisis we are facing.[2] Instead, we start entertaining the real possibility that everyday life, as we know it in the Western world, could change dramatically as global temperatures rise. When radical change does knock at our door, appreciating the open-endedness of our future and being able to harness it creatively might prove essential—perhaps as important as practical survival skills.

That welcoming of uncertainty recalls the strategy that Jem Bendell (2018) has discussed under the heading of "deep adaptation." In a thoroughgoing critique of the field of sustainability management, Bendell argues that sustainability discourse is based on the false premise that society as the Western world knows it can be maintained in the aftermath of climate catastrophe. Instead, Bendell argues provocatively that collapse is inevitable, and that the focus of academic debates should shift from sustainability to deep adaptation. As a coping strategy, deep adaptation involves psychological resilience and what Bendell calls "relinquishment." While resilience refers to the tendency to spring back after a traumatic event and adapt to new circumstances, relinquishment denotes an ability to let go of societal structures and material comforts that cannot be salvaged from ecological devastation. Both resilience and relinquishment go hand in hand with the embrace of uncertainty I have theorized in this book as a particularly desirable outcome of narrative experience and negotiation. If Bendell is right, to cope with the existential threat of climate change we need to achieve acceptance of uncertainty on a society-wide scale. In this book, I have suggested that, through its imaginative negotiation of uncertainty, narrative has an essential role to play in cultivating that response and creating the conditions for psychological and societal resilience.

Yet embracing uncertainty in and through narrative form is harder than it looks. It requires, first, sophisticated narratives that can deviate from established templates to channel a sense of profoundly disrupted futurity—narratives, in other words, that fully rise up to the existential challenge posed by climate change. Such formally innovative works, as I have demonstrated in this book and elsewhere (Caracciolo 2021, 2022), are not in short supply. But embracing uncertainty also calls for sophisticated reading strategies and audiences that can value ambiguity and open-endedness rather than dismissing them as frustrating or problematically unsettling. Clearly, there is much more work to do to refine audiences' sensitivity to the shifting forms and ambiguous affects of literary narrative.

Joshua Landy (2012) has offered an insightful discussion of what he calls "formative fictions," narratives that hone readers' skills—not by imparting a prefabricated message but by cultivating their affective and ethical meaning-making. Landy sees this exercise as a slow process that requires repeated exposure to formative fictions over the years. Although Landy doesn't foreground this element, the effects of formative fiction can be amplified by the teaching of literature, including training in the kind of formal analyses I have delivered in this book—provided, of course, that form be seen as fundamentally bound up with culturally shared issues (see introduction and Caracciolo 2021). All the narratives I have discussed in the previous chapters are potentially "formative," but that doesn't mean that engaging with them is sufficient to reshape readers' outlook on the ecological crisis. Literature's impact on audiences is anything but straightforward and linear, despite a number of well-meaning arguments on how climate change fiction could contribute to promoting pro-environmental views (see introduction). The effects of formative fiction are mediated by collective practices, which are responsible for focusing readers' attention on the way in which literature is entangled with the imagination of human–nonhuman relations.[3] Without these contextual practices, the impact of climate fiction or environmentally engaged narrative is likely to be negligible.

Literary studies departments—as well as the teaching and the critical discussion of literature more broadly—have an important role to play in fostering this kind of attunement to the nonhuman. On the one hand, educational institutions present readers with tools to appreciate formal complexity and its cultural stakes. On the other hand, the collective discussion of narrative in schools and universities (but also in settings like book clubs and online forums) confronts readers with significant interpersonal differences in literary interpretation and cultural evaluation. Readers are thus made aware that narrative itself is an unstable and uncertain object, infinitely refracted by individual psychology and personal experiences. This training in both formal complexity and interpretive difference prepares readers for coexistence with uncertainty. If that formative experience is framed and channeled in ways that speak directly to our ecological crisis, it can lead to an affectively empowering embrace of our uncertain climate future, one that marries concern and hopefulness. However, because that training is a slow, gradual, and intersubjectively guided process, achieving a genuine embrace of uncertainty is anything but self-evident.

Circling back to the beginning of this book, with its commentary on the Covid-19 pandemic, one could perhaps see the uncertainty that surrounds (or, hopefully, surrounded, at the time of reading) the outbreak as a dress rehearsal: the devastating impact of the virus enfolding the global economy—and scuttling fantasies of hyperconnected, borderless living in the Western world—foreshadows the even more dramatic and large-scale destabilization that the climate-changed future could have in store for us. Against this backdrop, I will conclude by discussing a number of online reviews of Jenny Offill's climate change–focused novel *Weather*, which came out in February 2020, a mere few weeks before the

Covid-19 outbreak was declared a pandemic by the World Health Organization. This discussion is not meant to be exhaustive, but it hints at the possibility of extending this book's argument in more empirical directions—in dialogue with actual readers rather than an implied audience. Over thirty reviews of Offill's novel published on Goodreads.com in March 2020 draw an explicit link between Covid-19 and the acute climate anxiety experienced by the protagonist of *Weather*. However, only one of them expresses an attitude toward uncertainty that chimes in with what I have been calling "embracing uncertainty."[4] Before elaborating on the difference between that negotiation of uncertainty and those emerging from the other reviews, a few words on Offill's novel are in order.

Formally, the most striking feature of *Weather* is its highly fragmentary, disjointed presentation. The narrator, a librarian named Lizzie, becomes more and more obsessed with climate change while working for her former thesis advisor, who hosts a podcast on the ecological crisis. Climate anxieties start seeping into Lizzie's private life, which is reconstructed by way of paragraph-long sketches focusing on her marriage, her concerns over her young son's future, and her relationship with her brother, who is recovering from drug addiction. The events told by Lizzie in the present tense are largely mundane, but Offill's point-blank brevity and wit transform them into illuminating insights into the entanglement of everyday life and the troubled futurity of climate change. In this way, the novella becomes a study in existential angst vis-à-vis the climate crisis, as many of the book's reviewers point out. In a *New York Times* review, for instance, Leslie Jamison states,

> *Weather* is a novel reckoning with the simultaneity of daily life and global crisis, what it means for a woman to be all of these things: a mother packing her son's backpack and putting away the dog's "slobber frog," a sister helping her recovering-addict brother take care of his infant daughter, and a citizen of a possibly doomed planet that might be a very different place for the son whose backpack she is packing. (Jamison 2020)

To prepare for this "very different place," Lizzie keeps sharing with her reader tips on how to turn canned tuna into an oil lamp or how to make toothpaste from scratch—practical advice on survival after societal collapse.

Weather is also a novel that doesn't flinch from uncertainty, with its telegraphic paragraphs that leave so much unsaid. Nowhere is uncertainty more tangible than in the novel's highly ambiguous ending, with Lizzie and her husband lying in bed: "He turns out the light, arranges the blankets so we'll stay warm. The dog twitches her paws softly against the bed. Dreams of running, of other animals.

I wake to the sound of gunshots. Walnuts on the roof, Ben says. The core delusion is that I am here and you are there" (2020: Kindle Location 1614). The sound of gunshots—a prefiguration of the threat impinging on Lizzie's family—might be as fanciful as the dog's dreams, a mere patter of falling walnuts. The uncertainty of perception is augmented by what Lizzie calls the "core delusion" of subjectivity: a delusion of distance and separation, and therefore of individual autonomy, in a world that so desperately needs collective action instead of individualistic thinking. The indeterminacy of the second-person pronoun ("you are there") complicates the ambiguity even further: at one level, the addressee could be Lizzie's husband, who is next to her in bed; however, given that this is the novel's final sentence—the place where the text opens onto the real world—the reader also becomes implicated in the "you."[5]

There is something distinctly hopeful about this final image, which evokes the possibility that individuality might be a "core delusion"—an idea that resonates with the Buddhist references scattered throughout Offill's novel—and that this delusion may be overcome through intimacy (between long-time partners, between the narrator and the implied reader). Yet this vague hope flies in the face of many conspicuous comments in the novel. Lizzie's employer, Sylvia, a climate change expert, states, "I'm about to send off this article, but I have to come up with the obligatory note of hope" (2020: Kindle Location 590). A few pages later, we read that Sylvia "quit the foundation last week; there's no hope anymore, only witness, she thinks" (2020: Kindle Location 1093).

The novel's ending keeps the door open for hope, however. This is signaled not only by the prospect of doing away with the "core delusion" of subjectivity but also by an internet link on the final page (right after the passage I have been discussing). It points to www.obligatorynoteofhope.com, a website that, while anonymous, was clearly curated by Offill herself. The page contains inspirational quotes—labeled "tips for trying times"—as well as information on environmental organizations like Extinction Rebellion. On the main page of the website, an anonymous "I" states, "Slowly, I began to see collective action as the antidote to my dithering and despair. There's a way in for everyone. Aren't you tired of all this fear and dread?" Like the "you" of the final paragraph of *Weather*, the "I" hovers between two referents, the narrator of the novel we have just finished reading and Offill herself. The ambiguity of the I blurs the distinction between author and narrator, a strategy reminiscent of the metafictional play of Coetzee's *Diary of a Bad Year* (discussed in Chapter 4). It remains unclear whether this "note of hope" and the call to collective action are really as "obligatory" and superfluous as Sylvia seems to think in the novel. Overall, in conjunction with the novel's ending, the rhetoric deployed by the website suggests that there might still be an opening, a space for steering the uncertainty of the future in a less catastrophic direction.

Weather negotiates uncertainty at all levels of the spectrum discussed in the introduction, from the future-oriented anxiety experienced by the protagonist to the reader's own affective experience, via the elusiveness of the novel's fragmentary form and ending. Ultimately, Offill's goal is to implicate readers, encouraging them to confront the challenge of a deeply uncertain future and turn it into an engine of personal and cultural change. But not all readers are equally receptive to the challenge and prepared to embrace uncertainty. This, at least, is what my survey of Goodreads.com reviews published in March 2020 suggests.

Many readers comment on the relevance of Offill's vision during Covid-19. Although the threat comes from an outbreak and not from melting ice caps, the experience of an ominous but hazy future is strikingly similar: "Odd to read [Offill's novel] in the midst of corona virus anxiety; lots of parallels about how to cope with distant/ill-defined/unpredictable threats on a daily basis without losing your mind" (Brassard 2020); "in these early days of the Corona virus pandemic [the novel] had a resonance and a scary warning behind it" (Deedee 2020). As I have argued in the introduction, relevance stimulates interpretation and therefore the negotiation of cultural topics. But readers appear to respond in vastly different ways to the ambiguity of *Weather*. In many if not most cases, it is the novel's bleakness that prevails: "*Weather* filled me with dread and deep sadness for ourselves and our limited choices, and for the generations to follow" (Maria 2020). This emotional evaluation even leads some reviewers to recommend reading the novel only when the pandemic is over: "I strongly recommend this one, though for those with anxiety, this may not be the moment you want to jump in. Hopefully this pandemic will be ebbing by late summer, and this will be the perfect read" (Bonnie 2020). Only few readers pick up on the ambiguity of Offill's ending, how it speaks to the uncertainty of the pandemic in a more nuanced way than through mere apocalyptic bleakness. Surely, the novel is a "scary warning," and it mirrors the short- and long-term anxieties experienced by many of Offill's readers. But the ending of *Weather* does much more than that, and the "note of hope" it strikes isn't entirely hollow. One of the reviewers puts this point as follows:

> When there is much uncertainty, we feel a lack of control and our brains go into overtime trying to find a way to get in control of the situation. Sometimes though, we just have to accept that there are things beyond our control. We

can't save everyone. We can't plan for every contingency. That is frustrating and frightening, especially for those of us who are control freaks. However, accepting our limitations can bring about a calmer state of mind and thus a healthier state of being. I'm glad I read this book now instead of pre-pandemic times (is it just me or does it seem like that was years instead of months ago?!). It reminded me to take a breath and let go of trying to change the things I cannot change. (Jenna 2020)

This is the closest the Goodreads.com reviews come to articulating what I described in this book as an embrace of uncertainty. The passage from Jenna's review starts with an acknowledgment that "there are things beyond our control"—uncertainty is an inevitable dimension of the experience of the present, vis-à-vis Covid-19 or the seemingly more distant threat of climate change. Letting go of the presumption of control means freeing up mental space for the possibilities of thought and action that Offill's book does afford, through the openness of the final paragraphs and the "tips for trying times" offered by the website. Likewise, although Jenna's review is not explicit in that respect, facing up to the limitations of our knowledge represents a form of intellectual modesty that dovetails with a radical critique of anthropocentrism and human mastery as Western culture has been practicing them for millennia. Many of the narratives discussed in this book have framed this breakdown of knowledge through a sense of mystery that calls for acceptance rather than resolution. Arguably, with its Buddhist allusions *Weather* is not extraneous to that sense of mystery. In Offill's novel, and in most of the works I have commented upon in these pages, human knowledge falls short so as to reveal the vulnerability and mortality that we share with nonhuman life forms. Mystery thus prompts readers to take an egalitarian position within a broader more-than-human community.

Read along the lines of Jenna's review, *Weather* holds a mirror up to our existential precarity in order to highlight what we may consider a way forward, an embrace of uncertainty where concern and hope coexist—uneasily, perhaps, but productively. That approach to fiction is not a simple one, as can be inferred from its extremely low frequency in this set of online reviews. But, if the argument advanced by this book is on the right track, fostering appreciation of ambiguous and unstable patterns is the most significant way in which narrative can contribute to the cultural negotiation of climate uncertainty. That formative effect is necessarily mediated and amplified by educational institutions, which have an essential part to play in bridging the gap between literary form, affect, and the looming crises of the present. If the Covid-19 pandemic is a practice run for the even more unsettling unknowns of the ecological crisis, it is also an opportunity to recognize the value of formally complex stories as aids for navigating uncertainty.

Notes

1 I draw inspiration here from communication researchers Marlon et al.'s (2019) discussion of an amalgam of "constructive doubt" and "constructive hope" as the most effective tone to adopt in public messages about climate change; this amalgam, they argue, is able to avoid the pitfalls of both fatalism and complacent optimism.
2 I lift the term "metanarrative" from Jean-François Lyotard's (1984: xxiv) account of the postmodern condition, where it refers to culturally influential narrative framings (concerning, for instance, science or religion). See the discussion in Chapter 1.
3 See also Suzanne Keen on the benefits of narrative empathy: "Reading alone (without accompanying discussion, writing, or teacherly direction) may not produce the same results as the enhanced reading that involves the subsequent discussion" (2007: 91).
4 I collected these reviews using Goodreads.com's built-in search function and the words "virus," "pandemic," "epidemic," "Covid," and "corona" as search terms.
  I limited my analysis to reviews posted in March 2020. For a stimulating discussion of reading practices on Goodreads.com, see Stinson and Driscoll (2020).
5 David Herman (2002: 352–3) would call this an instance of "doubly deictic you."

References

Aarseth, E. (1997), *Cybertext*, Baltimore, MD: Johns Hopkins University Press.
Abbott, H. P. (2011), "Time, Narrative, Life, Death, and Text-Type Distinctions: The Example of Coetzee's *Diary of a Bad Year*," *Narrative* 19 (2): 187–200.
Abbott, H. P. (2013), *Real Mysteries: Narrative and the Unknowable*, Columbus: Ohio State University Press.
Adam (2018), "Review of *The Strange Bird*," Goodreads website. https://www.goodreads.com/review/show/2322501432 (accessed June 25, 2021).
Alber, J. (2009), "Impossible Storyworlds—and What to Do with Them," *Storyworlds* 1: 79–96.
Alber, J. (2016), *Unnatural Narrative: Impossible Worlds in Fiction and Drama*, Lincoln: University of Nebraska Press.
Alber, J., S. Iversen, H. S. Nielsen, and B. Richardson (2010), "Unnatural Narratives, Unnatural Narratology: Beyond Mimetic Models," *Narrative* 18 (2): 113–36.
Ameel, L., and M. Caracciolo (2021), "Uncertain Ontologies in Twenty-First-Century Storyworlds" (special issue), *Style* 55 (3).
Armstrong, N. (2014), "The Affective Turn in Contemporary Fiction," *Contemporary Literature* 55 (3): 441–65.
Atterton, P. (2011), "Levinas and Our Moral Responsibility toward Other Animals," *Inquiry* 54 (6): 633–49.
Attridge, D. (2005), *J. M. Coetzee and the Ethics of Reading: Literature in the Event*, Chicago: University of Chicago Press.
Barad, K. (2007), *Meeting the Universe Halfway: Quantum Physics and the Entanglement of Matter and Meaning*, Durham, NC: Duke University Press.
Barnard, R. (2009), "Fictions of the Global," *Novel* 42 (2): 207–15.
Bayer, G. (2015), "Perpetual Apocalypses: David Mitchell's *Cloud Atlas* and the Absence of Time," *Critique: Studies in Contemporary Fiction* 56 (4): 345–54.
Beck, U. (1992), *Risk Society: Towards a New Modernity*, trans. M. Ritter, London: SAGE.
Bell, A., and J. Alber (2012), "Ontological Metalepsis and Unnatural Narratology," *Journal of Narrative Theory* 42 (2): 166–92.
Bellamy, B., and I. Szeman (2014), "Life after People: Science Faction and Ecological Futures," in G. Canavan and K. Stanley Robinson (eds.), *Green Planets: Ecology and Science Fiction*, 192–205, Middletown, CT: Wesleyan University Press.
Bendell, J. (2018), *Deep Adaptation: A Map for Navigating Climate Tragedy*. http://www.lifeworth.com/deepadaptation.pdf (accessed June 25, 2021).

Bennett, J. (2010), *Vibrant Matter: A Political Ecology of Things*, Durham, NC: Duke University Press.

Bernaerts, L., M. Caracciolo, L. Herman, and B. Vervaeck (2014), "The Storied Lives of Non-Human Narrators," *Narrative* 22 (1): 68–93.

Birns, N. (2015), *Contemporary Australian Literature: A World Not Yet Dead*, Sydney: Sydney University Press.

Bladow, K., and J. Ladino (eds.) (2018), *Affective Ecocriticism: Emotion, Embodiment, Environment*, Lincoln: University of Nebraska Press.

Bogost, I. (2006), *Unit Operations: An Approach to Videogame Criticism*, Cambridge, MA: MIT Press.

Bogost, I. (2015), "The Cathedral of Computation," *The Atlantic* website. https://www.theatlantic.com/technology/archive/2015/01/the-cathedral-of-computation/384300/ (accessed June 25, 2021).

Bolter, J. D., and R. Grusin (1999), *Remediation: Understanding New Media*, Cambridge, MA: MIT Press.

Bonnie G. (2020), "Review of *Weather*, by Jenny Offill," Goodreads website. https://www.goodreads.com/review/show/3184988119 (accessed June 25, 2021).

Bordwell, D. (2008), *Poetics of Cinema*, New York: Routledge.

Boroditsky, L. (2000), "Metaphoric Structuring: Understanding Time through Spatial Metaphors," *Cognition* 75 (1): 1–28.

Boulous Walker, M. (2017), *Slow Philosophy: Reading against the Institution*, London: Bloomsbury.

Bourdieu, P. (1990), *The Logic of Practice*, trans. R. Nice, Stanford, CA: Stanford University Press.

Bracke, A. (2018), *Climate Crisis and the 21st-Century British Novel*, London: Bloomsbury.

Bradley, R., and M. Drechsler (2014), "Types of Uncertainty," *Erkenntnis* 79 (6): 1225–48.

Brassard, G. (2020), "Review of *Weather*, by Jenny Offill," Goodreads website. https://www.goodreads.com/review/show/3170366011 (accessed June 25, 2021).

Brooks, P. (1984), *Reading for the Plot: Design and Intention in Narrative*, New York: Knopf.

Brooks, P. (2008), "The Ethics of Reading," *Chronicle of Higher Education* website. https://www.chronicle.com/article/The-Ethics-of-Reading/20323 (accessed June 25, 2021).

Buell, L. (2005), *The Future of Environmental Criticism: Environmental Crisis and Literary Imagination*, Malden, MA: Blackwell.

Bunzl, M. (2015), *Uncertainty and the Philosophy of Climate Change*, New York: Routledge.

Butler, J. (2016), *Frames of War: When Is Life Grievable?*, London: Verso.

Calarco, M. (2008), *Zoographies: The Question of the Animal from Heidegger to Derrida*, New York: Columbia University Press.

Calvino, I. (1981), *If on a Winter's Night a Traveler*, trans. William Weaver, New York: Houghton Mifflin Harcourt.

Canavan, G., and P. Wald (2011), "Preface," *American Literature* 83 (2): 237–49.

Caracciolo, M. (2013), "Phenomenological Metaphors in Readers' Engagement with Characters: The Case of Ian McEwan's *Saturday*," *Language and Literature* 22 (1): 60–76.

Caracciolo, M. (2015), "Playing *Home*: Video Game Experiences between Narrative and Ludic Interests," *Narrative* 23 (3): 231–51.

Caracciolo, M. (2016a), "'The Bagatelle of Particle Waves': Facing the Hard Problem of Consciousness in Houellebecq's *Les Particules elémentaires* and Mitchell's *Ghostwritten*," *Critique: Studies in Contemporary Fiction* 57 (5): 487–501.

Caracciolo, M. (2016b), "Cognitive Literary Studies and the Status of Interpretation: An Attempt at Conceptual Mapping," *New Literary History* 47 (3): 187–208.

Caracciolo, M. (2016c), *Strange Narrators in Contemporary Fiction: Explorations in Readers' Engagement with Characters*, Lincoln: University of Nebraska Press.

Caracciolo, M. (2018), "Posthuman Narration as a Test Bed for Experientiality: The Case of Kurt Vonnegut's *Galápagos*," *Partial Answers* 16 (2): 303–14.

Caracciolo, M. (2019), "Ungrounding Fictional Worlds: An Enactivist Perspective on the 'Worldlikeness' of Fiction," in A. Bell and M.-L. Ryan (eds.), *Possible Worlds Theory and Contemporary Narratology*, 113–31, Lincoln: University of Nebraska Press.

Caracciolo, M. (2020a), "Flocking Together: Collective Animal Minds in Contemporary Fiction," *PMLA* 135 (2): 239–53.

Caracciolo, M. (2020b), "Negotiating Stories in the Anthropocene: The Case of Nathaniel Rich's *Losing Earth*," *DIEGESIS* 9 (2). https://www.diegesis.uni-wuppertal.de/index.php/diegesis/article/view/394 (accessed June 25, 2021).

Caracciolo, M. (2020c), "Object-Oriented Plotting and Nonhuman Realities in DeLillo's *Underworld* and Iñárritu's *Babel*," in E. James and E. Morel (eds.), *Environment and Narrative: New Directions in Econarratology*, 45–64, Columbus: Ohio State University Press.

Caracciolo, M. (2021), *Narrating the Mesh: Form and Story in the Anthropocene*, Charlottesville: University of Virginia Press.

Caracciolo, M. (2022), *Slow Narrative and Nonhuman Materialities*, Lincoln: University of Nebraska Press.

Caracciolo, M., and G. Ulstein (2022), "The Weird and the Meta in Jeff VanderMeer's *Dead Astronauts*," *Configurations* 30 (1).

Cardboard Computer (2020), *Kentucky Route Zero*, Microsoft Windows.

Chakrabarty, D. (2014), "Climate and Capital: On Conjoined Histories," *Critical Inquiry* 41 (1): 1–23.

Chalmers, D. J. (1995), "Facing Up to the Problem of Consciousness," *Journal of Consciousness Studies* 2 (3): 200–19.

Clark, A., and D. J. Chalmers (1998), "The Extended Mind," *Analysis* 58 (1): 7–19.

Clark, T. (2015), *Ecocriticism on the Edge: The Anthropocene as a Threshold Concept*, London: Bloomsbury.
Coetzee, J. M. (1999), *The Lives of Animals*, Princeton, NJ: Princeton University Press.
Coetzee, J. M. (2008), *Diary of a Bad Year*, London: Vintage.
Connolly, W. E. (2017), *Facing the Planetary: Entangled Humanism and the Politics of Swarming*, Durham, NC: Duke University Press.
Cooper, M. (2010), "Turbulent Worlds," *Theory, Culture and Society* 27 (2–3): 167–90.
Coplan, A. (2004), "Empathic Engagement with Narrative Fictions," *Journal of Aesthetics and Art Criticism* 62 (2): 141–52.
Costikyan, G. (2013), *Uncertainty in Games*, Cambridge, MA: MIT Press.
Crist, E. (2013), "On the Poverty of Our Nomenclature," *Environmental Humanities* 3 (1): 129–47.
Crownshaw, R. (2017), "Climate Change Fiction and the Future of Memory: Speculating on Nathaniel Rich's *Odds against Tomorrow*," *Resilience* 4 (2): 127–46.
Crutzen, P. J. (2002), "Geology of Mankind," *Nature* 415 (6867): 23.
Csicsery-Ronay, I. (2008), *The Seven Beauties of Science Fiction*, Middletown, CT: Wesleyan University Press.
Currie, M. (2007), *About Time: Narrative, Fiction and the Philosophy of Time*, Edinburgh: Edinburgh University Press.
Danielewski, M. Z. (2000), *House of Leaves*, New York: Pantheon Books.
Dannenberg, H. P. (2008), *Coincidence and Counterfactuality: Plotting Time and Space in Narrative Fiction*, Lincoln: University of Nebraska Press.
De Bruyn, B. (2010), "Borrowed Time, Borrowed World and Borrowed Eyes: Care, Ruin and Vision in McCarthy's *The Road* and Harrison's Ecocriticism," *English Studies* 91 (7): 776–89.
Deedee (2020), "Review of *Weather*, by Jenny Offill," Goodreads website. https://www.goodreads.com/review/show/3230801375 (accessed June 25, 2021).
Demaria, F., F. Schneider, F. Sekulova, and J. Martinez-Alier (2013), "What Is Degrowth? From an Activist Slogan to a Social Movement," *Environmental Values* 22 (2): 191–215.
Deudney, D., and G. J. Ikenberry (1999), "The Nature and Sources of Liberal International Order," *Review of International Studies* 25 (2): 179–96.
Di Paolo, E. A., M. Rohde, and H. De Jaegher (2010), "Horizons for the Enactive Mind: Values, Social Interaction, and Play," in J. Stewart, O. Gapenne, and E. A. Di Paolo (eds.), *Enaction: Toward a New Paradigm for Cognitive Science*, 33–87, Cambridge, MA: MIT Press.
Diamond, C. (2003), "The Difficulty of Reality and the Difficulty of Philosophy," *Partial Answers* 1 (2): 1–26.
Dix, H. (ed.) (2018), *Autofiction in English*, Basingstoke: Palgrave Macmillan.
Doležel, L. (1998), *Heterocosmica: Fiction and Possible Worlds*, Baltimore, MD: Johns Hopkins University Press.

Dunlap, R. E., and A. M. McCright (2016), "Challenging Climate Change: The Denial Countermovement," in R. E. Dunlap and R. J. Brulle (eds.), *Climate Change and Society: Sociological Perspectives*, 300–32, Oxford: Oxford University Press.

Egan, J. (2012), "Black Box," *New Yorker* website. https://www.newyorker.com/magazine/2012/06/04/black-box-2 (accessed June 25, 2021).

Ehrenreich, B. (2020), *Desert Notebooks: A Road Map for the End of Time*, Berkeley, CA: Counterpoint.

Ensslin, A. (2014), *Literary Gaming*, Cambridge, MA: MIT Press.

Eskelinen, M. (2001), "The Gaming Situation," *Game Studies* 1 (1). http://www.gamestudies.org/0101/eskelinen/ (accessed June 25, 2021).

Evans, B., and J. Reid (2014), *Resilient Life: The Art of Living Dangerously*, Cambridge: Polity Press.

Evans, R. (2017), "Fantastic Futures? Cli-Fi, Climate Justice, and Queer Futurity," *Resilience* 4 (2–3): 94–110.

Faber, M. (2014), *The Book of Strange New Things*, London: Hogarth.

Festinger, L. (1957), *A Theory of Cognitive Dissonance*, Stanford, CA: Stanford University Press.

Finn, E. (2017), *What Algorithms Want: Imagination in the Age of Computing*, Cambridge, MA: MIT Press.

Fludernik, M. (2003), "Scene Shift, Metalepsis, and the Metaleptic Mode," *Style* 37 (4): 382–400.

Fludernik, M. (2005), "Time in Narrative," in D. Herman, M. Jahn, and M.-L. Ryan (eds.), *Routledge Encyclopedia of Narrative Theory*, 608–12, London: Routledge.

Fludernik, M. (2009), *An Introduction to Narratology*, London: Routledge.

Fludernik, M. (2012a), "How Natural Is 'Unnatural Narratology'; or, What Is Unnatural about Unnatural Narratology?," *Narrative* 20 (3): 357–70.

Fludernik, M. (2012b), "Narratology and Literary Linguistics," in R. I. Binnick (ed.), *The Oxford Handbook of Tense and Aspect*, 75–101, New York: Oxford University Press.

Forster, P. M., H. I. Forster, M. J. Evans, M. J. Gidden, C. D. Jones, C. A. Keller, R. D. Lamboll, C. L. Quéré, J. Rogelj, D. Rosen, C.-F. Schleussner, T. B. Richardson, C. J. Smith, and S. T. Turnock (2020), "Current and Future Global Climate Impacts Resulting from COVID-19," *Nature Climate Change* 10 (10): 913–19.

Frasca, G. (2003), "Simulation versus Narrative: Introduction to Ludology," in M. J. P. Wolf and B. Perron (eds.), *The Video Game Theory Reader*, 221–35, New York: Routledge.

Freud, S. (2003), *The Uncanny*, trans. D. McLintock, London: Penguin Books.

Gagliano, M., J. C. Ryan, and P. Vieira (eds.) (2017), *The Language of Plants: Science, Philosophy, Literature*, Minneapolis: University of Minnesota Press.

Gardner, M. (1970), "Mathematical Games: The Fantastic Combinations of John Conway's New Solitaire Game 'Life,'" *Scientific American* 223 (4): 120–3.

Garland, A. (2018), *Annihilation*, Paramount Pictures.

Garrard, G. (2004), *Ecocriticism*, New York: Routledge.

Gell, A. (1992), "The Technology of Enchantment and the Enchantment of Technology," in J. Coote and A. Shelton (eds.), *Anthropology, Art and Aesthetics*, 40–63, Oxford: Clarendon Press.

Genette, G. (1980), *Narrative Discourse: An Essay in Method*, trans. J. E. Lewin, Ithaca, NY: Cornell University Press.

Gerrig, R. J. (1993), *Experiencing Narrative Worlds: On the Psychological Activities of Reading*, New Haven, CT: Yale University Press.

Ghosh, A. (2016), *The Great Derangement: Climate Change and the Unthinkable*, Chicago: University of Chicago Press.

Giddens, A. (1990), *The Consequences of Modernity*, Stanford, CA: Stanford University Press.

Golumbia, D. (2009), *The Cultural Logic of Computation*, Cambridge, MA: Harvard University Press.

Goodbody, A., and A. Johns-Putra (2019), "Introduction," in A. Goodbody and A. Johns-Putra (eds.), *Cli-Fi: A Companion*, 1–19, Oxford: Peter Lang.

Gould, S. J. (1987), *Time's Arrow, Time's Cycle: Myth and Metaphor in the Discovery of Geological Time*, Cambridge, MA: Harvard University Press.

Greenblatt, S. (1988), *Shakespearean Negotiations: The Circulation of Social Energy in Renaissance England*, Berkeley: University of California Press.

Groff, L. (2018), *Boca Raton*, Seattle: Amazon Original Stories.

Grove, R. H. (1995), *Green Imperialism: Colonial Expansion, Tropical Island Edens and the Origins of Environmentalism, 1600–1860*, Cambridge: Cambridge University Press.

Grusin, R. (ed.) (2015), *The Nonhuman Turn*, Minneapolis: University of Minnesota Press.

Gumbrecht, H. U. (2014), *Our Broad Present: Time and Contemporary Culture*, New York: Columbia University Press.

Hacking, I. (2006), *The Emergence of Probability: A Philosophical Study of Early Ideas About Probability Induction and Statistical Inference*, Cambridge: Cambridge University Press.

Hampe, B., and J. E. Grady (eds.) (2005), *From Perception to Meaning: Image Schemas in Cognitive Linguistics*, Berlin: De Gruyter.

Haraway, D. (2016), *Staying with the Trouble: Making Kin in the Chthulucene*, Durham, NC: Duke University Press.

Harrington, A. (2008), *The Cure Within: A History of Mind-Body Medicine*, New York: Norton.

Harris-Birtill, R. (2019), *David Mitchell's Post-Secular World: Buddhism, Belief and the Urgency of Compassion*, London: Bloomsbury.

Hayles, N. K. (1999), *How We Became Posthuman: Virtual Bodies in Cybernetics, Literature, and Informatics*, Chicago: University of Chicago Press.

Hayles, N. K. (2017), *Unthought: The Power of the Cognitive Nonconscious*, Chicago: University of Chicago Press.

Hegglund, J. (2019), "A Home for the Anthropocene: Planetary Time and Domestic Space in Richard McGuire's *Here*," *Literary Geographies* 5 (2): 185–99.

Hegglund, J. (2020), "Unnatural Narratology and Weird Realism in Jeff VanderMeer's *Annihilation*," in E. James and E. Morel (eds.), *Environment and Narrative: New Directions in Econarratology*, 27–44, Columbus: Ohio State University Press.

Hegglund, J. (2021), "Drawing (on) the Future: Narration, Animation, and the Partially Human," in J. Alber (ed.), *The Apocalyptic Dimensions of Climate Change*, 109–24, Berlin: De Gruyter.

Heise, U. K. (1997), *Chronoschisms: Time, Narrative, and Postmodernism*, Cambridge: Cambridge University Press.

Heise, U. K. (2008), *Sense of Place and Sense of Planet: The Environmental Imagination of the Global*, Oxford: Oxford University Press.

Herman, D. (1997), "Scripts, Sequences, and Stories: Elements of a Postclassical Narratology," *PMLA* 112 (5): 1046–59.

Herman, D. (2002), *Story Logic: Problems and Possibilities of Narrative*, Lincoln: University of Nebraska Press.

Herman, D. (2003), "Stories as a Tool for Thinking," in D. Herman (ed.), *Narrative Theory and the Cognitive Sciences*, 163–92, Stanford, CA: CSLI.

Herman, D. (2008), "Narrative Theory and the Intentional Stance," *Partial Answers* 6 (2): 233–60.

Herman, D. (2009), *Basic Elements of Narrative*, Chichester: Wiley-Blackwell.

Herman, D. (2018), *Narratology Beyond the Human: Storytelling and Animal Life*, Oxford: Oxford University Press.

Herman, L., and B. Vervaeck (2005), *Handbook of Narrative Analysis*, Lincoln: University of Nebraska Press.

Herman, L., and B. Vervaeck (2017), "A Theory of Narrative in Culture," *Poetics Today* 38 (4): 605–34.

Heywood, P. (2017), "The Ontological Turn," *Cambridge Encyclopedia of Anthropology*. http://www.anthroencyclopedia.com/entry/ontological-turn (accessed June 25, 2021).

Hicks, H. J. (2016), *The Post-Apocalyptic Novel in the Twenty-First Century: Modernity Beyond Salvage*, Basingstoke: Palgrave Macmillan.

Holgate, B. (2015), "Unsettling Narratives: Re-Evaluating Magical Realism as Postcolonial Discourse through Alexis Wright's *Carpentaria* and *The Swan Book*," *Journal of Postcolonial Writing* 51 (6): 634–47.

Honoré, C. (2004), *In Praise of Slowness: Challenging the Cult of Speed*, New York: HarperCollins.

Horn, E. (2018), *The Future as Catastrophe: Imagining Disaster in the Modern Age*, trans. V. Pakis, New York: Columbia University Press.

Horst, S. (2011), "The Computational Theory of Mind," in E. N. Zalta (ed.), *The Stanford Encyclopedia of Philosophy*. http://plato.stanford.edu/entries/computational-mind/ (accessed June 25, 2021).

Horti, S. (2019), "*Heaven's Vault* Review: A Stunning Setting, but the Story Fails to Find Its Voice," Gamesradar website. https://www.gamesradar.com/heavens-vault-review/ (accessed June 25, 2021).

Hutcheon, L. (1988), *A Poetics of Postmodernism: History, Theory, Fiction*, New York: Routledge.

Hutcheon, L. (1994), *Irony's Edge: The Theory and Politics of Irony*, London: Routledge.

Hutchins, E. (1995), *Cognition in the Wild*, Cambridge, MA: MIT Press.

Hutto, D. D. (2008), *Folk Psychological Narratives: The Sociocultural Basis of Understanding Reasons*, Cambridge, MA: MIT Press.

Ingarden, R. (1973), *The Literary Work of Art*, trans. G. G. Grabowicz, Evanston, IL: Northwestern University Press.

Inkle (2019), *Heaven's Vault*, Microsoft Windows.

Jagoda, P. (2016), *Network Aesthetics*, Chicago: University of Chicago Press.

James, E. (2015), *The Storyworld Accord: Econarratology and Postcolonial Narratives*, Lincoln: University of Nebraska Press.

James, E. (2019), "Nonhuman Fictional Characters and the Empathy-Altruism Hypothesis," *Poetics Today* 40 (3): 579–96.

James, E. (2020), "Narrative in the Anthropocene," in E. James and E. Morel (eds.), *Environment and Narrative: New Directions in Econarratology*, 183–202, Columbus: Ohio State University Press.

James, E., and E. Morel (2018), "Ecocriticism and Narrative Theory: An Introduction," *English Studies* 99 (4): 355–65.

James, E., and E. Morel (eds.) (2020), *Environment and Narrative: New Directions in Econarratology*, Columbus: Ohio State University Press.

Jameson, F. (1972), *The Prison-House of Language*, Princeton, NJ: Princeton University Press.

Jamieson, D. (2014), *Reason in a Dark Time: Why the Struggle against Climate Change Failed—and What It Means for Our Future*, Oxford: Oxford University Press.

Jamison, L. (2020), "Jenny Offill's *Weather* Is Emotional, Planetary and Very Turbulent," *New York Times* website. https://www.nytimes.com/2020/02/07/books/review/weather-jenny-offill.html (accessed June 25, 2021).

Jenkins, H. (2004), "Game Design as Narrative Architecture," in N. Wardrip-Fruin and P. Harrigan (eds.), *First Person: New Media as Story, Performance, and Game*, 118–30, Cambridge, MA: MIT Press.

Jenna (2020), "Review of *Weather*, by Jenny Offill," Goodreads website. https://www.goodreads.com/review/show/3242209283 (accessed June 25, 2021).

Johnson, M. (1987), *The Body in the Mind*, Chicago: University of Chicago Press.

Johns-Putra, A. (2019), *Climate Change and the Contemporary Novel*, Cambridge: Cambridge University Press.

Kahn, P. H. (1999), *The Human Relationship with Nature: Development and Culture*, Cambridge, MA: MIT Press.

Keen, S. (2007), *Empathy and the Novel*, Oxford: Oxford University Press.

Kellerman, J. (2018), *Controller*, Seattle: Amazon Original Stories.
Kemp, L. (2018), "A Systems Critique of the 2015 Paris Agreement on Climate," in M. Hossain, R. Hales, and T. Sarker (eds.), *Pathways to a Sustainable Economy: Bridging the Gap between Paris Climate Change Commitments and Net Zero Emissions*, 25–41, Cham: Springer.
Kermode, F. (2000), *The Sense of an Ending: Studies in the Theory of Fiction*, New York: Oxford University Press.
Kidd, D. C., and E. Castano (2013), "Reading Literary Fiction Improves Theory of Mind," *Science* 342 (6156): 377–80.
Kohlmann, B. (2014), "What Is It Like to Be a Rat? Early Cold War Glimpses of the Post-Human," *Textual Practice* 28 (4): 655–75.
Kohn, E. (2013), *How Forests Think: Toward an Anthropology beyond the Human*, Berkeley: University of California Press.
Kukkonen, K. (2014), "Presence and Prediction: The Embodied Reader's Cascades of Cognition," *Style* 48 (3): 367–84.
Lakoff, G. (1987), *Women, Fire, and Dangerous Things: What Our Categories Reveal about the Mind*, Chicago: University of Chicago Press.
Lakoff, G., and M. Johnson (1980), *Metaphors We Live By*, Chicago: University of Chicago Press.
Lambert, S. (2021a), "'Mycorrhizal Multiplicities': Mapping Collective Agency in Powers' *The Overstory*." In Y. Liebermann, J. Rahn, and B. Burger (eds.), *Nonhuman Agencies in the Twenty-First-Century Anglophone Novel*, 187–209, Basingstoke: Palgrave Macmillan.
Lambert, S. (2021b), *Bodies of Knowledge: Experimenting with Science and Affect in Contemporary Literature*. PhD dissertation, Ghent, Belgium: Ghent University.
Landy, J. (2012), *How to Do Things with Fictions*, New York: Oxford University Press.
Latour, B. (2005), *Reassembling the Social: An Introduction to Actor-Network-Theory*, Oxford: Oxford University Press.
Lethem, J. (1995), *Amnesia Moon*, Orlando: Harcourt.
Levinas, E. (1979), *Totality and Infinity: An Essay on Interiority*, trans. A. Lingis, Leiden: Martinus Nijhoff.
Levine, C. (2015), *Forms: Whole, Rhythm, Hierarchy, Network*, Princeton, NJ: Princeton University Press.
Levine, J. (1983), "Materialism and Qualia: The Explanatory Gap," *Pacific Philosophical Quarterly* 64 (4): 354–61.
Lewandowsky, S., J. S. Risbey, M. Smithson, B. R. Newell, and J. Hunter (2014), "Scientific Uncertainty and Climate Change: Part I. Uncertainty and Unabated Emissions," *Climatic Change* 124 (1): 21–37.
Lotman, J. (1977), *The Structure of the Artistic Text*, trans. G. Lenhoff and R. Vroon, Ann Arbor: University of Michigan Press.
Lovejoy, A. O. (2001), *The Great Chain of Being: A Study of the History of an Idea*, Cambridge, MA: Harvard University Press.

Lovelock, J. (2000), *Gaia: A New Look at Life on Earth*, Oxford: Oxford University Press.
Luckhurst, R. (2017), "The Weird: A Dis/Orientation," *Textual Practice* 31 (6): 1041–61.
Lyotard, J.-F. (1984), *The Postmodern Condition: A Report on Knowledge*, trans. G. Bennington and B. Massumi, Minneapolis: University of Minnesota Press.
Mandel, E. St. J. (2014), *Station Eleven*, New York: Vintage.
Mar, R. A., and K. Oatley (2008), "The Function of Fiction Is the Abstraction and Simulation of Social Experience," *Perspectives on Psychological Science* 3 (3): 173–92.
Maria (2020), "Review of *Weather*, by Jenny Offill," Goodreads website. https://www.goodreads.com/review/show/3184177406 (accessed June 25, 2021).
Marlon, J. R., B. Bloodhart, M. T. Ballew, J. Rolfe-Redding, C. Roser-Renouf, A Leiserowitz, and E. Maibach (2019), "How Hope and Doubt Affect Climate Change Mobilization," *Frontiers in Communication* 4 (20): 1–15.
McDonald, P. D. (2010), "The Ethics of Reading and the Question of the Novel: The Challenge of J. M. Coetzee's *Diary of a Bad Year*," *Novel: A Forum on Fiction* 43 (3): 483–99.
McGuire, R. (2014), *Here*, New York: Pantheon Books.
McGurl, M. (2011), "The New Cultural Geology," *Twentieth-Century Literature* 57 (3–4): 380–90.
McGurl, M. (2012), "The Posthuman Comedy," *Critical Inquiry* 38 (3): 533–53.
McHale, B. (1987), *Postmodernist Fiction*, London: Routledge.
McLaughlin, R. L. (2004), "Post-Postmodern Discontent: Contemporary Fiction and the Social World," *Symploke* 12 (1): 53–68.
Mellmann, K. (2010), "Objects of 'Empathy': Characters (and Other Such Things) as Psycho-Poetic Effects," in J. Eder, F. Jannidis, and R. Schneider (eds.), *Characters in Fictional Worlds: Understanding Imaginary Beings in Literature, Film, and Other Media*, 416–41, Berlin: De Gruyter.
Miall, D. S., and D. Kuiken (1994), "Foregrounding, Defamiliarization, and Affect: Response to Literary Stories," *Poetics* 22 (5): 389–407.
Miéville, C. (2009), *The City & the City*, London: Pan Macmillan.
Miller, D. A. (1981), *Narrative and Its Discontents: Problems of Closure in the Traditional Novel*, Princeton, NJ: Princeton University Press.
Mitchell, D. (2001), *Ghostwritten*, London: Vintage.
Mitchell, D. (2004), *Cloud Atlas*, New York: Random House.
Mobius Digital (2019), *Outer Wilds*, Microsoft Windows.
Morreall, J. (2016), "Philosophy of Humor," in E. N. Zalta (ed.), *The Stanford Encyclopedia of Philosophy*. https://plato.stanford.edu/archives/win2016/entries/humor/ (accessed June 25, 2021).
Morton, T. (2010), *The Ecological Thought*, Cambridge, MA: Harvard University Press.
Mukařovský, J. (2014), "Standard Language and Poetic Language," in J. Chovanec (ed.), *Chapters from the History of Czech Functional Linguistics*, 41–53, Brno: Masaryk University. http://hdl.handle.net/11222.digilib/131565 (accessed June 25, 2021).

Myers, S. L. (2020), "China's Omnivorous Markets Are in the Eye of a Lethal Outbreak Once Again," *New York Times* website. https://www.nytimes.com/2020/01/25/world/asia/china-markets-coronavirus-sars.html (accessed June 25, 2021).

Nagel, T. (1974), "What Is It Like to Be a Bat?," *Philosophical Review* 83 (4): 435–50.

Nagel, T. (2012), *Mind and Cosmos: Why the Materialist Neo-Darwinian Conception of Nature Is Almost Certainly False*, New York: Oxford University Press.

Napolitano, J. D. (2010), "'Mr Melancholy and Mr Magpie': The Lives of Animals in J. M. Coetzee's *Diary of a Bad Year*," *Safundi* 11 (1–2): 49–66.

National Science Foundation (2016), "Computers Play a Crucial Role in Preserving the Earth," ScienceDaily website. https://www.sciencedaily.com/releases/2016/04/160420111133.htm (accessed June 25, 2021).

Nersessian, A. (2013), "Two Gardens: An Experiment in Calamity Form," *Modern Language Quarterly* 74 (3): 307–29.

Nixon, R. (2011), *Slow Violence and the Environmentalism of the Poor*, Cambridge, MA: Harvard University Press.

Norwood, G. (2013), *Essays on Euripidean Drama*, Cambridge: Cambridge University Press.

Nowotny, H. (1989), "Mind, Technologies, and Collective Time Consciousness: From the Future to the Extended Present," in J. T. Fraser (ed.), *Time and Mind: Interdisciplinary Issues*, 197–216, Madison, CT: International Universities Press.

Nussbaum, M. C. (2001), *Upheavals of Thought: The Intelligence of Emotions*, Cambridge: Cambridge University Press.

O'Brien, S., and C. Lousley (2017), "A History of Environmental Futurity: Special Issue Introduction," *Resilience* 4 (2–3): 1–20.

Offill, J. (2020), *Weather*, New York: Knopf.

Ogden, B. H. (2010), "The Coming into Being of Literature: How J. M. Coetzee's *Diary of a Bad Year* Thinks through the Novel," *Novel: A Forum on Fiction* 43 (3): 466–82.

Oziewicz, M. (2017), "Speculative Fiction," *Oxford Research Encyclopedia of Literature*. 10.1093/acrefore/9780190201098.013.78.

Pavel, T. (1986), *Fictional Worlds*, Cambridge, MA: Harvard University Press.

Pendell, D. (2010), *The Great Bay: Chronicles of the Collapse*, Berkeley, CA: North Atlantic Books.

Pick, A. (2011), *Creaturely Poetics: Animality and Vulnerability in Literature and Film*, New York: Columbia University Press.

Pier, J. (2010), "Metalepsis," in P. Hühn (ed.), *The Living Handbook of Narratology*. https://www.lhn.uni-hamburg.de/node/51.html (accessed June 25, 2021).

Pier, J. (2014), "Narrative Levels," in P. Hühn (ed.), *The Living Handbook of Narratology*. https://www.lhn.uni-hamburg.de/node/32.html (accessed June 25, 2021).

Porter, T. M. (1986), *The Rise of Statistical Thinking, 1820–1900*, Princeton, NJ: Princeton University Press.

Povinelli, E. A. (2016), *Geontologies: A Requiem to Late Liberalism*, Durham, NC: Duke University Press.
Powers, R. (2006), *The Echo Maker*, New York: Farrar, Straus and Giroux.
Powers, R. (2018), *The Overstory*, New York: Norton.
Richardson, B. (2015), *Unnatural Narrative: Theory, History, and Practice*, Columbus: Ohio State University Press.
Ricoeur, P. (1984), *Time and Narrative: Volume 1*, trans. K. McLaughlin and D. Pellauer, Chicago: University of Chicago Press.
Ricoeur, P. (1985), *Time and Narrative: Volume 2*, trans. K. McLaughlin and D. Pellauer, Chicago: University of Chicago Press.
Ricoeur, P. (1988), *Time and Narrative: Volume 3*, trans. K. McLaughlin and D. Pellauer, Chicago: University of Chicago Press.
Robertson, B. J. (2018), *None of This Is Normal: The Fiction of Jeff VanderMeer*, Minneapolis: University of Minnesota Press.
Rose, D. B. (2011), *Wild Dog Dreaming: Love and Extinction*, Charlottesville: University of Virginia Press.
Ruppel, C. D. (2011), "Methane Hydrates and Contemporary Climate Change," *Nature Education Knowledge* 3 (10): 29. https://www.nature.com/scitable/knowledge/libr ary/methane-hydrates-and-contemporary-climate-change-24314790/ (accessed June 25, 2021).
Ryan, M.-L. (1991), *Possible Worlds, Artificial Intelligence, and Narrative Theory*, Bloomington: Indiana University Press.
Ryan, M.-L. (2006a), *Avatars of Story*, Minneapolis: University of Minnesota Press.
Ryan, M.-L. (2006b), "From Parallel Universes to Possible Worlds: Ontological Pluralism in Physics, Narratology, and Narrative," *Poetics Today* 27 (4): 633–74.
Ryan, M.-L. (2014), "Space," in P. Hühn (ed.), *The Living Handbook of Narratology*. https://www.lhn.uni-hamburg.de/node/55/revisions/282/view.html (accessed June 25, 2021).
Ryan, M.-L. (2019), "From Possible Worlds to Storyworlds: On the Worldness of Narrative Representation," in A. Bell and M.-L. Ryan (eds.), *Possible Worlds Theory and Contemporary Narratology*, 62–87, Lincoln: University of Nebraska Press.
Salen, K., and E. Zimmerman (2004), *Rules of Play: Game Design Fundamentals*, Cambridge, MA: MIT Press.
Saussure, F. de (1959), *Course in General Linguistics*, trans. W. Baskin, New York: Philosophical Library.
Scalise Sugiyama, M. (2001), "Food, Foragers, and Folklore: The Role of Narrative in Human Subsistence," *Evolution and Human Behavior* 22 (4): 221–40.
Schmitt, A. (2014), "Knots, Story Lines, and Hermeneutical Lines: A Case Study," *Storyworlds* 6 (2): 75–91.
Schneider-Mayerson, M. (2018), "The Influence of Climate Fiction: An Empirical Survey of Readers," *Environmental Humanities* 10 (2): 473–500.

Serpell, C. N. (2014), *Seven Modes of Uncertainty*, Cambridge, MA: Harvard University Press.

Seymour, N. (2013), *Strange Natures: Futurity, Empathy, and the Queer Ecological Imagination*, Champaign: University of Illinois Press.

Smethurst, T., and S. Craps (2015), "Playing with Trauma: Interreactivity, Empathy, and Complicity in *The Walking Dead* Video Game," *Games and Culture* 10 (3): 269–90.

Smith, A. (2015), *How to Be Both*, London: Penguin Books.

Smith, I. (2018), "Review of *The Strange Bird*," Goodreads website. https://www.goodreads.com/review/show/2452235862 (accessed June 25, 2021).

Sperber, D., and D. Wilson (1995), *Relevance: Communication and Cognition*, Malden, MA: Wiley-Blackwell.

Stanzel, F. K. (1984), *A Theory of Narrative*, Cambridge: Cambridge University Press.

Sternberg, M. (1982), "Proteus in Quotation-Land: Mimesis and Forms of Reported Discourse," *Poetics Today* 3 (2): 107–56.

Sternberg, M. (2001), "How Narrativity Makes a Difference," *Narrative* 9 (2): 115–22.

Stevenson, A. (ed.) (2010), *Oxford Dictionary of English*, Oxford: Oxford University Press.

Stinson, E., and B. Driscoll (2020), "Difficult Literature on Goodreads: Reading Alexis Wright's *The Swan Book*," *Textual Practice*. 10.1080/0950236X.2020.1786718.

Suvin, D. (1979), *Metamorphoses of Science Fiction: On the Poetics and History of a Literary Genre*, New Haven, CT: Yale University Press.

Talmy, L. (1988), "Force Dynamics in Language and Cognition," *Cognitive Science* 12 (1): 49–100.

Telltale Games (2012), *The Walking Dead*, Microsoft Windows.

Thatamanil, J. J. (2020), "The Butterfly Effect and the Coronavirus: The Truth of Interrelatedness," Counterpoint website. https://www.counterpointknowledge.org/the-butterfly-effect-and-the-corona-virus-the-truth-of-interrelatedness/ (accessed June 25, 2021).

Thoss, J. (2015), *When Storyworlds Collide: Metalepsis in Popular Fiction*, Leiden: Brill.

Todorov, T. (1969), *Grammaire du Décaméron*, The Hague: Mouton.

Todorov, T. (1975), *The Fantastic: A Structural Approach to a Literary Genre*, trans. R. Howard, Ithaca, NY: Cornell University Press.

Trexler, A. (2015), *Anthropocene Fictions: The Novel in a Time of Climate Change*, Charlottesville: University of Virginia Press.

Trexler, A., and A. Johns-Putra (2011), "Climate Change in Literature and Literary Criticism," *Wiley Interdisciplinary Reviews: Climate Change* 2 (2): 185–200.

Tsing, A. L. (2015), *The Mushroom at the End of the World: On the Possibility of Life in Capitalist Ruins*, Princeton, NJ: Princeton University Press.

Turner, M. (1996), *The Literary Mind: The Origins of Thought and Language*, New York: Oxford University Press.

Uexküll, J. von (1957), "A Stroll through the Worlds of Animals and Men: A Picture Book of Invisible Worlds," in C. H. Schiller (ed.), *Instinctive Behavior: The Development of a Modern Concept*, 5–80, New York: International Press.

Ullrich, J. K. (2015), "Climate Fiction: Can Popular Books About Environmental Disaster Save the Planet?," *The Atlantic* website. https://www.theatlantic.com/entertainment/archive/2015/08/climate-fiction-margaret-atwood-literature/400112/ (accessed June 25, 2021).

Ulstein, G. (2017), "Brave New Weird: Anthropocene Monsters in Jeff VanderMeer's 'The Southern Reach,'" *Concentric: Literary and Cultural Studies* 43 (1): 71–96.

Ulstein, G. (2021), *Weird Fiction in a Warming World: A Reading Strategy for the Anthropocene*. PhD dissertation, Ghent, Belgium: Ghent University.

VanderMeer, J. (2014), *Annihilation*, New York: Farrar, Straus and Giroux.

VanderMeer, J. (2017), *The Strange Bird: A Borne Story*, New York: Farrar, Straus and Giroux.

VanderMeer, J. (2019), *Dead Astronauts*, New York: Farrar, Straus and Giroux.

VanderMeer, J., and A. VanderMeer (eds.) (2012), *The Weird: A Compendium of Strange and Dark Stories*, New York: Tor Books.

Varela, F. J., E. Thompson, and E. Rosch (1991), *The Embodied Mind: Cognitive Science and Human Experience*, Cambridge, MA: MIT Press.

Vella, D. (2013), "'It's A-Me/Mario': Playing as a Ludic Character," *Foundations of Digital Games Conference Proceedings*. http://www.fdg2013.org/program/papers/paper05_vella.pdf (accessed June 25, 2021).

Velleman, J. D. (2003), "Narrative Explanation," *Philosophical Review* 112 (1): 1–25.

Vermeulen, P. (2020), *Literature and the Anthropocene*, New York: Routledge.

Vidal, J. (2020), "'Tip of the Iceberg': Is Our Destruction of Nature Responsible for Covid-19?," *The Guardian* website. https://www.theguardian.com/environment/2020/mar/18/tip-of-the-iceberg-is-our-destruction-of-nature-responsible-for-covid-19-aoe (accessed June 25, 2021).

Viveiros de Castro, E. (2004), "Exchanging Perspectives: The Transformation of Objects into Subjects in Amerindian Ontologies," *Common Knowledge* 10 (3): 463–84.

Von Stuckrad, K. (2019), *Die Seele im 20. Jahrhundert: Eine Kulturgeschichte*, Paderborn: Wilhelm Fink.

Wallace-Wells, D. (2018), "Parenting the Climate Change Generation," *New York Magazine* website. https://nymag.com/intelligencer/2018/12/parenting-children-generation-of-climate-change.html (accessed June 25, 2021).

Walsh, R. (2007), *The Rhetoric of Fictionality: Narrative Theory and the Idea of Fiction*, Columbus: Ohio State University Press.

Walsh, R. (2017), "Beyond Fictional Worlds: Narrative and Spatial Cognition," in P. K. Hansen, J. Pier, P. Roussin, and W. Schmid (eds.), *Emerging Vectors of Narratology*, 461–78, Berlin: De Gruyter.

Walton, K. (1990), *Mimesis as Make-Believe: On the Foundations of the Representational Arts*, Cambridge, MA: Harvard University Press.

Warkentin, T. (2012), "Thinking Like a Whale: Interdisciplinary Methods for the Study of Human-Animal Interactions," in J. A. Smith and R. W. Mitchell (eds.), *Experiencing Animal Minds: An Anthology of Animal-Human Encounters*, 129–41, New York: Columbia University Press.

Watson-Sproat, T. K. (2019), "Why Native Hawaiians Are Fighting to Protect a Mountain from a Telescope," Vox website. https://www.vox.com/identit ies/2019/7/24/20706930/mauna-kea-hawaii (accessed June 25, 2021).

Watt, I. (1957), *The Rise of the Novel*, Berkeley: University of California Press.

Waugh, P. (1984), *Metafiction: The Theory and Practice of Self-Conscious Fiction*, London: Routledge.

Weik von Mossner, A. (2014), "Science Fiction and the Risks of the Anthropocene: Anticipated Transformations in Dale Pendell's *The Great Bay*," *Environmental Humanities* 5 (1): 203–16.

Weik von Mossner, A. (2017), *Affective Ecologies: Empathy, Emotion, and Environmental Narrative*, Columbus: Ohio State University Press.

White, L. (1967), "The Historical Roots of Our Ecologic Crisis," *Science* 155 (3767): 1203–7.

Woelert, P. (2011), "Human Cognition, Space, and the Sedimentation of Meaning," *Phenomenology and the Cognitive Sciences* 10 (1): 113–37.

Wohlleben, P. (2017), *The Hidden Life of Trees: What They Feel, How They Communicate*, trans. J. Billinghurst, London: William Collins.

Wolf, W. (2004), "Aesthetic Illusion as an Effect of Fiction," *Style* 38 (3): 325–51.

Wolfe, C. (2010), *What Is Posthumanism?*, Minneapolis: University of Minnesota Press.

Woloch, A. (2003), *The One vs. the Many: Minor Characters and the Space of the Protagonist in the Novel*, Princeton, NJ: Princeton University Press.

Woods, D. (2014), "Scale Critique for the Anthropocene," *Minnesota Review* 83: 133–42.

Wright, A. (2016), *The Swan Book*, New York: Atria Books.

Yanagihara, H. (2013), *The People in the Trees*, New York: Doubleday.

Zapf, H. (2001), "Literature as Cultural Ecology: Notes towards a Functional Theory of Imaginative Texts, with Examples from American Literature," *REAL: Yearbook of Research in English and American Literature* 17: 85–100.

Zapf, H. (2017), *Literature as Cultural Ecology: Sustainable Texts*, London: Bloomsbury.

Zolli, A., and A. M. Healy (2012), *Resilience: Why Things Bounce Back*, New York: Simon and Schuster.

Zunshine, L. (2006), *Why We Read Fiction: Theory of Mind and the Novel*, Columbus: Ohio State University Press.

Index

Aarseth, Espen 180n.5
Abbott, Porter 37, 93
   Real Mysteries 15, 37, 92, 163
Aboriginal culture. *See* Indigenous culture
About Time (Currie) 31
acceptance of uncertainty. *See* embracing uncertainty
Actor-Network Theory 9
aesthetic illusion 130n.5
affect/affective
   ambivalence 141
   awareness 94
   body and its 44
   climate-related uncertainty 16
   distance 17
   environmental narrative 105n.8
   experience 19, 188
   future-oriented 53
   imagination of 73, 84
   individualized 98
   instability 21, 71
   of literary narrative 184
   nuances of 27
   perspectives on uncertainty 144
   reality of ecological interconnection 129
   resonance 90, 105n.3, 179
   resources 18, 40, 47
   responses 56n.23
   shared 104, 128
   tensions 51
   traumatic 44
   turn 40, 54
Alber, Jan 56n.26, 66–7, 86n.10, 108–10, 123
algorithm/algorithmic 147, 177
   complexity 161–2, 171, 173, 176
   denouement 56n.19, 134, 143, 145
   intelligence 135, 143, 150
   intervention 130, 144
   machine-learning 21
   magic 135–8, 141, 144, 166
   quasi-magical power of 20, 155
   as quasi-religious 134, 148
   strategies 151
   strategies of global surveillance 133
   technology 138, 140
allegory 49–50, 91
Amalgamemnon (Brooke-Rose) 41
Amazon 48, 112, 136
Ameel, Lieven 23n.20, 56n.22
American Psycho (Ellis) 15
Amnesia Moon (Lethem) 19, 63, 75, 77
Andersen, Hans Christian 100
Animal Farm (Orwell) 91
animals 89–104, 142, 170, 186
   desert 94–8
   empathy 90–4
   human beings and 128, 143
   literary 129
   nonhuman 85, 105n.10, 111, 124, 126–7, 129, 143
   pervasive 127
   position toward 105n.6
   superiority of human over 8
   Umwelt 105n.4
   uncertainty 90–4
   unethical treatment of 3
   unknowability and 104
Annihilation (VanderMeer) 63, 69, 72
anomalous suspense 33, 55n.15
Anthropocene 22n.12, 29, 49, 55n.5, 61, 83, 107
   disorder 50
   fictions 10
   (mis)reading of 152n.12
   narrative 144
   narrative theory 64
Anthropocene Fictions (Trexler) 11
anthropological machine 124
anthropomorphism 91–2
Area X 69–70, 72, 164
Armstrong, Nancy 40

artificial intelligence (AI) 9, 133, 137, 142, 176. *See also* algorithm
assemblages 51, 103, 105n.13, 139, 146, 179
Atterton, Peter 105n.6
Atwood, Margaret
  Oryx and Crake 10
Australia 4, 60, 98, 121
autofiction 124, 132n.24

"Babysitter, The" (Coover) 47, 68
Ballard, James Graham 38
Barad, Karen
  Meeting the Universe Halfway 139
Barnard, Rita 152n.9
Barth, John 38
"Bartleby the Scrivener" (Melville) 92
Bayer, Gerd 131n.18
Beck, Ulrich 9, 28
Bell, Alice 108–10, 123
Bellamy, Brent 25
Bendell, Jem 23n.23, 184
Bennett, Jane 57n.34
Bernaerts, Lars 91, 92
Bethesda 79
big data 136
biological diversity 78
"Black Box" (Egan) 19, 27, 42, 44
Bladow, Kyle 56n.23
blood relationship 55n.10
Bloom, Dan 10
Bloom, Leopold 66
Boca Raton (Groff) 35–7, 48, 54
Bogost, Ian 134, 148
  Unit Operations 180n.3
Book of Strange New Things, The (Faber) 19, 63, 81, 84, 87n.22
Bordwell, David 131n.13, 141
Borne (VanderMeer) 51–2, 57n.33, 94–5
Bourdieu, Pierre 6
Bracke, Astrid 116, 118, 119
Bradley, Richard 15–16, 161
Brooke-Rose, Christine
  Amalgamemnon 41
Brooks, Peter
  Chronicle of Higher Education 124
Buddhism 143
Buell, Lawrence 9
Bunzl, Martin 54–5n.2

Butler, Judith
  Frames of War 86–7n.20

calamity form 14–15, 138–41, 144, 151, 156. *See also* form
Calarco, Matthew 124
California 4, 76, 77, 115
Calvino, Italo 39
  If on a Winter's Night a Traveler 107–8
Canavan, Gerry 56n.18
Caracciolo, Marco 56n.22, 56n.31, 85n.5, 85n.8, 86n.17, 105n.1, 105n.3, 105n.11, 105n.13, 130n.3, 131n.9, 153n.17–18
  Narrating the Mesh 8–9, 23n.16
carbon emissions 4
Carpentaria (Wright) 98–9
castaway narrative 6, 118. *See also* narrative(s)
Castle, The (Kafka) 75
catastrophe 76–7, 156
  anthropogenic 94, 139
  climate 26, 47, 184
  conventional understanding of 76
  ecological 36, 51–2, 62, 118, 140
  environmental 14, 53, 60, 81–2, 87n.24, 137, 178, 183
  ethical 81
  human mind and 78
  species-threatening 2
  temporality 63, 163
  unspecified 94
causation 45, 60–1, 115
Central America 171
Central Valley 77
Chakrabarty, Dipesh 29
Chalmers, David 152n.6, 176–7
Chronoschisms (Heise) 38
circulation. *See* narrative circulation
City & the City, The (Miéville) 19, 63, 68, 70–3, 164
Clark, Timothy 50
  Ecocriticism on the Edge 10–11, 61
cli-fi 10–11, 22n.11, 105n.2
climate change 10, 25, 94, 104, 131n.7, 146, 163, 190n.1
  addressing 47
  anthropogenic 22n.11, 163
  bushfires and 61

challenges 4, 27, 54n.1, 55n.2
consequences of 2, 140
Covid-19 pandemic and 3–4
devastation wrought by 100
dystopia and 99
effects of 2, 4, 87n.20
fiction 22n.14, 185
futurity 17, 27, 33, 59, 163, 186
intangibility 72
mitigation 2, 49, 53, 84
multifaceted phenomenon 139
negotiations 14
and pro-environmental behavior 11
real-world threat 37
repercussions 2
societal implications of 11
temporality 32
threat of 184, 189
uncertainty 9, 12, 26, 30, 64, 66
Climate Change and the Contemporary Novel (Johns-Putra) 12
climate crisis 10–13, 89, 116. *See also* climate change
climate uncertainty 13–19, 85, 163. *See also* uncertainty
closure 35–8, 56n.19–20, 181n.20
  argumentative 122
  deny 54
  emotional 16
  expectation of 27, 52
  explicit 46
  formal 20, 138, 150
  immediate 179
  perfect 45
  to planetary crisis 136
  possibility of 20, 34
  resisting 36
  straightforward 144
  teleology and 77
Cloud Atlas (Mitchell) 20, 109, 113–20, 123, 129–30, 131n.13
Coetzee, J. M.
  Diary of a Bad Year 11, 20, 109, 113, 121–5, 127–8
  Lives of Animals 124, 132n.20, 132n.23, 132n.28
cognition 34, 52, 74, 137–8, 143, 147, 150, 152n.4, 152n.14
cognitive dissonance 50, 56n.31, 79, 87n.23

cognitive estrangement 56n.18
cognitive linguistics 59–60, 83, 85n.3
Cold War 30, 38
Coleridge, Samuel Taylor
  Kubla Khan 166
colonialism 30, 38, 40
community(ies) 17, 73, 170–1
  Aboriginal 98–9
  human 2, 5, 14–15, 25, 63, 68, 77, 82–3, 87n.20, 93, 113, 127, 169, 189
  isolated 77
  nonhuman 127
  scientific 146
  small-scale 139
  smart 145–6
complexity(ies)
  algorithmic 161–2, 166, 171, 173, 176
  of the Earth system 13
  ecological crisis 10, 23n.16, 26
  ecology 111
  formal 148–9, 151, 185
  of human societies 2
  imaginative 54
  inscrutable 183
  of life 147
  multilinearity 157
  nonlinearity 177
  science 135, 139
  self-organizing 140, 147
  sociopolitical 29
  unprecedented 13
computational algorithms 135. *See also* algorithm
computational intelligence 134, 156
Connolly, William 60
constructive doubt 190n.1
constructive hope 190n.1
continuous anticipation 33
Controller (Kellerman) 11, 19, 27, 47, 49–50, 60
Conway, John Horton 150, 152n.3
Cooper, Melinda 25–6, 54n.1
Coover, Robert 38, 41, 56n.27
  "Babysitter, The" 47, 68
Coplan, Amy 105n.5
coral bleaching 4
Costikyan, Greg 161
Covid-19 1–3, 21, 189
  crisis 14

effects 4
pandemic 1, 3–4, 185, 188–9
Creaturely Poetics (Pick) 180n.15
Crist, Eileen 55n.5
critical thinking 3
Crownshaw, Rick 54n.1
Crutzen, Paul 29, 55n.5
cultural diversity 78
Currie, Mark 32–3, 55n.16
   About Time 31
cyborgs 41–7
Cygnus atratus 99

Danielewski, Mark 75
   House of Leaves 19, 63, 66, 68, 74
Dannenberg, Hilary 110, 130n.6
Darwin, Charles 28
Dead Astronauts (VanderMeer) 19, 27, 47, 51, 57n.32, 94
Death of Artemio Cruz, The (Fuentes) 41
de Castro, Eduardo Viveiros 63, 112–13, 121
Dedalus, Stephen 66
deep adaptation 184. *See also* resilience
deep time 28, 55n.4, 63, 85n.6. *See also* temporality
defamiliarization 73, 91–2, 96–8, 108
Defoe, Daniel
   Robinson Crusoe 78, 118
del Cossa, Francesco 45–7
dematerialization 40
de Saussure, Ferdinand 112
desert 94–8
destabilizing storyworlds. *See* storyworld
deus ex algorithmo 133–51, 177
   algorithmic magic 135–8
   calamity form 138–41
   narrative form 138–41
   uncertainty 141–5
deus ex machina 8, 20–1, 134, 139–40, 150. *See also* algorithm
developing countries 4
Diamond, Cora 132n.28
Diary of a Bad Year (Coetzee) 20, 109, 113, 121–5, 127–8
Dickens, Charles
   Oliver Twist 109–10
Dillard, Annie 9
Doležel, Lubomír 41
   Heterocosmica 75

domestication 59, 63
Drechsler, Mareile 15–16, 161
dualism 7, 126. *See also* hard problem of consciousness
Dublin 65–6

earnest ontologies 56n.22
Earth
   atmosphere 15
   climate 15
   ecosystems 2, 63
   resources 8
Echo Maker, The (Powers) 89, 93, 105n.1
ecocriticism 9–11, 18
Ecocriticism on the Edge (Clark) 10, 61
ecological crisis 2–4, 11, 17–18, 22n.14, 23n.15, 27–8, 37, 47, 53, 73, 111, 114, 120–1, 135, 147, 149, 151, 152n.9–10, 183, 185–6, 190. *See also* climate change
   apt metaphor 60
   complexity 10, 23n.16, 157
   Covid-19 pandemic and 21
   material and ethical stakes of 107
   negotiation 19
   nonlinearity 63
   planetary scale 61
   profound uncertainty 7
   sociopolitical complexity 29
   spatiotemporal scale 26
   uncertainty 64, 103, 109
econarratology 9
economic growth 8, 14, 28, 34, 183
effective computability 137
Egan, Jennifer 47, 53–4, 56n.24
   "Black Box" 19, 27, 42, 44
egregious gap 37, 162
Ehrenreich, Ben 55n.6
Ellis, Bret Easton
   American Psycho 15
Embodied Mind, The (Varela, Thompson and Rosch) 137
embracing uncertainty 5, 17–18, 54, 151, 183–4, 186
empathy 90–4
   anthropomorphism 92
   cognitive 90, 95–6, 98, 104, 105n.8
   narrative 190n.3
   for nonhuman 98, 103

transspecies 91
unknowability 103
empirical uncertainty 15, 162, 174
enchantment 80–1, 83, 104, 136, 179. *See also* magic; mystery
enmeshment 103–4. *See also* human–nonhuman relations
Ensslin, Astrid 157
entanglement 2, 4, 9, 21, 29, 31, 40, 47, 94, 102, 111, 127, 149, 152n.9, 179, 186. *See also* human–nonhuman relations
enumeration 73–4, 131n.9. *See also* lists
environmental risks 28
environmental storytelling 155–6, 159, 173. *See also* narrative(s)
Environment and Narrative: New Directions in Econarratology (James and Morel) 9
epistolary novel 114
erasure 19, 63, 64, 66–7, 73–5, 81, 84–5, 86n.14
Eskelinen, Markku 158
ethical uncertainty 15, 78, 129, 161–2, 177
ethics 12–13, 21, 41, 56n.29, 92, 179, 180n.15
Europe 4, 99
Evans, Brad 17
Evans, Rebecca 55n.8
exploratory interactivity 159–60, 162, 165, 172–3
extended present 39
extrinsic futurity 34, 37, 47, 49, 54, 55n.16

Faber, Michel
  Book of Strange New Things, The 19, 63, 81, 84, 87n.22
fatalism 2, 190n.1
Ferdinand, Archduke Franz 61
Festinger, Leon 56n.31
Finn, Edward 56n.24, 138
  What Algorithms Want 135–6
first-person narrative 32. *See also* narrative(s)
First World War 61
Flight Behavior (Kingsolver) 10
floating 64, 67, 78–85, 87n.22
Florida 35

Fludernik, Monika 41
Flush: A Biography (Woolf) 91
force dynamics 60–1
form 90
  algorithms 136
  biological 97
  calamity 14–15, 138–41, 144, 151, 156
  collective 125
  essayistic 128
  fragmented and rambling 123
  of human–nonhuman relations 151
  literary 22n.7, 38, 64
  material 66
  metafictional 128
  narrative 5–10, 14, 17, 27, 50, 54, 93, 113, 120, 130, 138–41, 146, 163, 184
  negotiation 5–10
  novelistic 51
  oscillation 72
  productive aesthetic 152n.9
  representation and 23n.22, 37
  science 138–41
  spatial (typographical) 8, 84
  stylistic 101
  uncertainty 72
  unrecognizable 126
formalism 7. *See also* New Formalism; Russian Formalism
formative fictions 184–5
form-content dualism 7
fragmentation 19, 27, 38, 40, 51, 63–4, 66–7, 75–8, 84. *See also* parallel storyworlds
Frames of War (Butler) 86–7n.20
France 42
Frankenstein (Shelley) 117, 133
Frankenstein, Victor 117
Frasca, Gonzalo 158
Freud, Sigmund 85n.1
Fuentes, Carlos
  Death of Artemio Cruz, The 41
future 2
  assumptions 13
  climate 4, 12, 16, 18, 20, 26–7, 37, 48, 93, 100, 111, 113, 118, 185
  collective 78, 134, 145, 163
  destabilizing 28–31, 133
  extrinsic and intrinsic 31–5, 46, 53, 177
  fragmentation of 27

generations 16, 30
indeterminate 83
orientation 32–4, 39
planetary 102
postapocalyptic 20, 129
posthuman 125
shared 89
temporality 53
uncertainty 12, 27, 35, 39, 46, 53, 73, 76, 90, 98, 104, 170, 188
unknowable 4, 14, 140
unstable 18
Western societies 39
future-oriented thinking 25
future-tense narration/narrative 19, 27–8, 35, 38, 40–7, 54. *See also* future; narration

Gaia hypothesis 138–9
gameplay 157–60, 163, 174, 179. *See also* video game
Garland, Alex 69
Gell, Alfred 136
Genette, Gérard 108, 116
Gerrig, Richard 55n.15
Ghosh, Amitav 131n.7
  Great Derangement, The 139
Ghostwritten (Mitchell) 21, 130, 131n.13
Giddens, Anthony 1
globalization 3, 33, 140, 152n.9
Global North 1, 3
global warming 2, 50. *See also* climate change
Golumbia, David 151n.2
Gould, Stephen Jay 55n.4
Great Bay: Chronicles of the Collapse, The (Pendell) 19, 63, 76–7, 86n.19
Great Britain 82
Great Derangement, The (Ghosh) 139
Greenblatt, Stephen 6
grief 40, 141
Groff, Lauren
  Boca Raton 35–7, 48, 54
Grove, Richard H. 78–9

Haraway, Donna 18, 55n.10
hard problem of consciousness 131n.16, 153n.17, 177
Harrington, Anne 22n.3

Harris-Birtill, Rose 131n.17
Hayles, Katherine 9, 138
  How We Became Posthuman 139
  Unthought 137
Heaven's Vault (video game) 21, 157
Hegglund, Jon 61, 85n.9, 181n.16
Heise, Ursula 9, 39–40
  Chronoschisms 38
Here (McGuire) 61–3, 181n.16
Herman, David 22n.2, 22n.5, 36, 55n.12, 56n.21, 65, 68, 87n.21, 190n.5
  Narratology Beyond the Human 90
  Story Logic 63
Herman, Luc 6–7
Hertzfeldt, Don
  World of Tomorrow 181n.16
Heterocosmica (Doležel) 75
Heywood, Paolo 131n.8
Hicks, Heather 116
historiographic metafiction 39
Holocaust 30
Homo sapiens 143–4
Hong Kong 142
hope 4, 8, 43, 45–6, 48, 52, 90, 92, 95, 98, 133, 157, 163, 174–5, 183, 187–90
Horti, Samuel 181n.20
House of Leaves (Danielewski) 19, 63, 66, 68, 74
How to Be Both (Smith) 11, 19, 45–6, 178
How We Became Posthuman (Hayles) 139
human exceptionalism 133, 138, 183
human extinction 12, 133, 140, 156, 180n.1
humanity 2, 10, 144
  climate predicament 156, 183
  collective future 134, 145
  environmental impact 30
  extrinsic future 44, 50
  fate of 20–1, 147
  future temporality 53
  geological record 10
  heroic conception 149
  indeterminacy 135
  intellectual and moral superiority of 8
  involvement in nonhuman processes 102
  metafiction 120
  participation 151

predicament 40, 140
resilient 171
responsibilities toward nonhuman 150
role in novelistic story and planetary
    futures 139
uncertainty 53–4, 104
unstable future 151
human–nonhuman relations 8–9, 15,
    105n.9, 107, 109, 112, 129, 144, 151,
    157, 163, 169, 171, 179, 185
Hutcheon, Linda 39, 107
Hutton, James 28
hyperobjects 29

If on a Winter's Night a Traveler
    (Calvino) 107–8
image schema 85n.3
incredulity 28, 39
indeterminacy 46, 63, 72, 80, 82–3,
    135–8, 140, 143, 147, 167,
    169, 187
Indigenous culture 98, 100, 103
industrialization 139, 169
Ingarden, Roman
    Literary Work of Art, The 68
Inkle 21
In Search of Lost Time (Proust) 41
instability 36, 120–1. *See also* ontology
    acceptance 109
    affective 21, 71
    appreciation of 18
    chromatic 68
    climate future 18
    climate-related 19
    embracing change 66
    mystery and 45
    ontological 85n.9, 118
    projected 2
    semantic 69
    sensory 71
    spatial 19
    symbolic 102
    tangible and vivid 64
    temporal 63
interactive narrative 155–79. *See also*
    narrative(s); video game
    uncertainty types 161–3
    video game narrative and its
        compromises 158–60

interactivity 155, 157–60, 163, 178. *See
    also* environmental storytelling;
    video game
    exploratory 159–60, 162, 165, 172–3
    ontological 159–60, 162, 165, 175
internet reviews 21, 103
intrinsic futurity 34–7, 46, 54, 55n.16
Ireland 142

James, Erin 64, 87n.21, 91
    *Environment and Narrative: New
        Directions in Econarratology* 9
    Storyworld Accord, The 105n.12
Jamieson, Dale 134
Jamison, Leslie 186
Jenkins, Henry 155
Johnson, Mark 59
Johns-Putra, Adeline 13, 55n.9,
    56n.29, 105n.9
    *Climate Change and the Contemporary
        Novel* 12
Joyce, James 66
    Ulysses 65
Judeo-Christian 143

Kafka, Franz
    Castle, The 75
Keen, Suzanne 190n.3
Kellerman, Jesse 53–4
    Controller 11, 19, 27, 47–50, 60
Kentucky Route Zero (video
    game) 21, 157
Kermode, Frank
    Sense of an Ending, The 55n.16
Kidd, David Comer 23n.24
Kiernan, Caitlin Rebekah 22n.15
Kingsolver, Barbara
    Flight Behavior 10
kinship 55n.10
Kohlmann, Benjamin 55n.7
Kohn, Eduardo 112–13
Kubla Khan (Coleridge) 166
Kukkonen, Karin 34

Ladino, Jennifer 56n.23
Lakoff, George 59
Lambert, Shannon 152n.13
Landy, Joshua 23n.24, 184
Latour, Bruno 9

Lethem, Jonathan
  Amnesia Moon 19, 63, 75, 77
Levinas, Emmanuel 92, 105n.6
Levine, Caroline 7
Levine, Joseph 181n.19
Lewandowsky, Stephan 2
lists 73–4, 131n.9, 143
literary criticism 7, 9, 132n.24
literary fiction 5–6, 23n.24, 109, 157
literary games 157
literary imagination 10–11, 26
literary narrative 5, 8, 10, 18, 26, 31, 60, 184
literary realism 66, 108
literary storytelling 183
Literary Work of Art, The (Ingarden) 68
literary world-making 12
Literature and the Anthropocene (Vermeulen) 12
Lives of Animals (Coetzee) 124, 132n.20, 132n.23, 132n.28
Lolita (Nabokov) 79
London 142
loops 155–7, 159, 178, 181n.17. See also nonlinearity
Lopez, Barry 9
Lotman, Jurij
  Structure of the Artistic Text, The 87n.22
Lousley, Cheryl 30, 38, 55n.8
Lovecraft, H. P. 22n.15
Lovelock, James 138
Luckhurst, Roger 94, 164
Lyell, Charles 28
Lyotard, Jean-François 28, 39, 190n.2

magic 171. See also enchantment
  algorithmic 135–8, 141, 144, 150, 166
  computational 139
  of formal complexity 149
  and indeterminacy 80
  and mystery 78
  and "productive indeterminacy" 147
Mandel, Emily St. John 74
  Station Eleven 19, 63, 73, 75
Mar, Raymond A. 22n.2
Marlon, Jennifer R. 190n.1
mastery 8, 37, 90, 129, 146–7, 189

materiality 40, 54, 72, 74–5, 90, 109, 137
Mauna Kea 119, 131n.15
Maus (Spiegelman) 91
McCarthy, Cormac
  Road, The 11
McDonald, Peter 124
McEwan, Ian
  Solar 10
McGuire, Richard
  Here 61–3, 181n.16
McGurl, Mark 85n.6, 143
McHale, Brian 84, 107–8
  Postmodernist Fiction 68, 86n.17
McLaughlin, Robert 39
Meeting the Universe Halfway (Barad) 139
Melville, Herman
  "Bartleby the Scrivener" 92
mesh 4, 8, 83, 181n.19. See also human–nonhuman relations
metafiction 20, 39, 107–14, 120, 123–4, 129, 130n.3, 183
metalepsis 8, 67, 86n.11, 108, 110, 117, 123–4, 130n.2
metanarratives 28, 183, 190n.2
metanovel 128
metaphor 1, 4, 16, 20, 29, 39, 59–61, 64–5, 68, 85n.2, 89, 96, 105n.7, 105n.11, 110, 117–18, 125–7, 137, 143
metempsychosis 126, 130, 131n.18
metonymic mystery 93
metonymy 89, 102
Miéville, China 22n.15, 64
  City & the City, The 19, 63, 68, 70–3, 164
Miller, D. A.
  Narrative and Its Discontents 56n.20
Mind and Cosmos (Nagel) 131n.19
Mitchell, David 12, 131n.10
  Cloud Atlas 20, 109, 113–20, 123, 129–30, 131n.13
  Ghostwritten 21, 130, 131n.13
mold computers 163–71
Mongolia 142
Morel, Eric
  Environment and Narrative: New Directions in Econarratology 9
Morton, Timothy 4, 8, 29
Mukařovský, Jan 132n.32

Mushroom at the End of the World, The
   (Tsing) 169
mystery 21, 27, 35, 167–8, 178. *See also*
   enchantment
   acceptance 83, 189
   ambiguity and 45
   enchantment and 80, 179
   generative 103
   instability and 45
   magic and 78
   metaphysical 104, 169
   metonymic 93
   nonhuman 90, 103
   souls' transmigration 120
   teleology 46
   uncertainty and 46, 81, 121, 170

Nabokov, Vladimir
   Lolita 79
Nagel, Thomas 93
   Mind and Cosmos 131n.19
Napolitano, Joseph 124, 127
Narrating the Mesh (Caracciolo) 8–9,
   23n.16
narration 86n.17
   first-person 6
   future-tense 27–8, 38, 40, 41–7, 54
narrative(s) 1, 133
   empathy 190n.3
   future-tense 19, 27–8, 35, 38,
      40–7, 54
   literary 5, 8, 10, 18, 26, 31, 60, 184
   negotiation in 5–10, 18
   space 59
   storyworld 16
   universals 34, 162
   unnatural 56n.26
   video game 158–60
   visual 63
Narrative and Its Discontents
   (Miller) 56n.20
narrative circulation 6
narrative form 5–10, 14, 17, 27, 50, 54, 93,
   113, 120, 130, 138–41, 146, 163, 184.
   See also form
narrative levels 108, 120, 131n.14
narrative negotiation 5–11, 14–18,
   20, 67, 134. *See also* spectrum of
   negotiation

narrative theory 7, 20, 22n.6, 23n.16,
   31–2, 64–7, 83, 87n.21, 91, 109–11,
   130n.2. *See also* narratology
narratology 7, 22n.5, 56n.27, 64,
   66–7, 85n.9, 91, 111. *See also*
   econarratology; unnatural
   narratology
Narratology Beyond the Human
   (Herman) 90
Native Hawaiians 119
nebula 172–9
negation 39, 67, 73
negative enumeration 73, 74
negotiations. *See also* narrative negotiation
   climate change 14
   ecological crisis 19
   form 5–10
   interpretation and 18
   in narratives 5–10, 18
   of uncertainty 4–5
Nelson, Ted 166
Nersessian, Anahid 14, 140
nescience 14–15, 140, 169
network narrative 141
New Formalism 22n.7. *See also*
   formalism
New York 4
New Yorker, The 42
Nixon, Rob 22n.1
nonlinearity 61, 63, 85n.5, 119, 123, 151,
   160, 165, 177
normalcy 3
North America 4, 79
Northern Australia 98
Northern California 76
North Pole 117
Norwood, Gilbert 134
Nowotny, Helga 39
Nussbaum, Martha 12

Oatley, Keith 22n.2
O'Brien, Susie 30, 38, 55n.8
Odds against Tomorrow (Rich) 54n.1
Offill, Jenny 21
   Weather 21, 185–9
Oliver Twist (Dickens) 109–10
ontology/ontological
   animistic 112
   anthropocentric 63

in anthropology 20
boundaries 8, 16, 20, 108, 112, 164
epistemology and 86n.13
fiction 109–10, 113, 129
human–nonhuman relations 112
Indigenous 113
interactivity 159–60
linear 117
of literature 13
metalepsis 67, 86n.11, 108, 110, 130n.2
mythical uncertainty 81
of narrative in nonlinear terms 112
non-Western 119
perspectival 112
pluralism 47, 107
of scientific modernity 80
security 1, 4, 14, 23n.20
turns 109–14, 129
twists 109–14
Western 20, 118–21, 124, 128–30
Orwell, George
  Animal Farm 91
Oryx and Crake (Atwood) 10
oscillation 19, 41, 63–4, 67, 68–73, 84, 86n.13, 86n.16, 164
Outer Wilds (video game) 155–6
Overstory, The (Powers) 21, 85n.7, 133, 135, 138–9, 145–7, 149–51, 152n.13–14
Oziewicz, Marek 55n.3

Palazzo Schifanoia 45
parallel storyworlds 19, 27–8, 38, 40, 47–54, 60, 150. See also storyworld
Paris Agreement 13
Pendell, Dale
  Great Bay: Chronicles of the Collapse, The 19, 63, 76–7, 86n.19
People in the Trees, The (Yanagihara) 19, 63, 79, 81–2, 84, 87n.22
Perina, Norton 79–81
permafrost 13, 15
phenomenology 16, 32
Philosophical Investigations (Wittgenstein) 71
Pick, Anat
  Creaturely Poetics 180n.15
postapocalyptic fiction 6

posthuman 21, 52, 55n.7, 125, 138–9, 141, 143, 150
postmodernism 28, 38, 40, 107
Postmodernist Fiction (McHale) 68, 86n.17
Povinelli, Elizabeth 112–13
Powers, Richard
  Echo Maker, The 89, 93, 105n.1
  Overstory, The 21, 85n.7, 133, 135, 138–9, 145–7, 149–51, 152n.13–14
prediction 14, 25–6, 29–30, 34–7, 43, 53
probability 25–6, 140
productive indeterminacy 143
pro-environmental behavior 11
pro-environmental beliefs 18
"Proteus principle" 22n.6, 23n.22
Proust, Marcel
  In Search of Lost Time 41
psychological effects of engaging with narrative 16. See also formative fictions
public health 2
Pynchon, Thomas 39

quantum physics 139

Reading for the Plot (Brooks) 32
realism. See literary realism
Real Mysteries (Abbott) 15, 37, 92, 163
Reid, Julian 17
resilience 3, 17–18, 23n.23, 82, 184
Resilience (journal) 30
Rich, Nathaniel
  Odds against Tomorrow 54n.1
Richardson, Brian 56n.27, 86n.10
Ricoeur, Paul 19
  Time and Narrative 31
Road, The (McCarthy) 11
road to freedom 59
Robinson Crusoe (Defoe) 78, 118
Rosch, Eleanor
  Embodied Mind, The 137
Rose, Deborah Bird 105n.7
Rules of Play (Salen and Zimmerman) 158
Ruppel, Carolyn 13
Russian Formalism 108. See also formalism
Ryan, Marie-Laure 47, 65, 109, 117, 158

Salen, Katie
  Rules of Play 158
San Francisco 76, 115
Santa Clara County 146
Saville, Margaret Walton 117
scale 11, 167, 169. *See also* globalization
  cosmic 175
  cultural 6
  geological 52
  human 49, 59, 62, 104, 135
  large-scale destabilization 185
  large-scale urbanization 10
  more-than-human 17, 104, 149
  planetary 49–50, 98, 137, 151, 178
  quotidian 50
  society-wide 184
  spatiotemporal 26
  temporal 28, 30, 63, 139
  unthinkable 140
  variance 49, 60–1
Scalise Sugiyama, Michelle 22n.2
Schmitt, Arnaud 116, 152n.8
Schneider-Mayerson, Matthew 22n.14
science fiction 12, 21, 26, 34, 55n.3, 81, 94, 114, 133, 140, 149, 164, 172, 179
scientific knowledge 2, 38, 121
Second World War 3, 28, 38
self-projection 105n.5
self-reflexivity. *See* metafiction
Sense of an Ending, The (Kermode) 55n.16
Serpell, Namwali 15, 86n.13
Seven Modes of Uncertainty (Serpell) 15
Seymour, Nicole
  Strange Natures 30
Shelley, Mary
  Frankenstein 117, 133
Smith, Ali 47, 53–4
  How to Be Both 11, 19, 45–6, 178
Solar (McEwan) 10
Soviet Union 30
space 61, 63, 85n.1. *See also* unstable spatiality
  antimimetic 66
  blank 52
  conceptual 139
  cultural 31
  destabilizing 67
  domestic 60
  dual 72

  enigmatic 72
  erasure of 75
  floating 64, 78–85, 87n.22
  human-scale 59, 104, 139
  immaterial 72
  interstitial 71, 97
  magical 136
  mental 189
  narrative 59
  nonhuman 74
  physical 66, 169
  points to time 33
  for reality 111
  in real-world 65, 67
  shift 62
  stability 62
  storyworld 20
  structure 59
  temporality and 72
  for uncertainty 110, 161–3, 165, 167
  unnatural 67, 74
spectrum of negotiation 16, 27, 37, 128
speculative fiction 26
Sperber, Dan 56n.17
Spiegelman, Art
  Maus 91
Stanzel, Franz Karl 55n.14
state space uncertainty 15, 174, 177. *See also* uncertainty
Station Eleven (Mandel) 19, 63, 73, 75
Sternberg, Meir 23n.22, 34, 162
Story Logic (Herman) 63
storytellers 1, 19, 36
storytelling. *See* narrative(s)
storyworld. *See also* parallel storyworlds
  destabilizing 64–8, 84
  domain 87n.22
  fragmentation of 75, 77
  interstitial spaces 97
  narratives 16
  oscillating 71
  parallel 19, 27–8, 38, 40, 47–54, 60, 150
  postapocalyptic 73
  relative equilibrium 36
  space 20
  spatial layout 79
  strictures 108
  unstable 83–4
  visual experience 70

Storyworld Accord, The (James) 105n.12
Strange Bird, The (VanderMeer) 20, 57n.33, 90, 93–4, 102–3
Strange Narrators in Contemporary Fiction (Caracciolo) 87n.23
Strange Natures (Seymour) 30
structuralism 16, 27, 38, 46, 50, 52, 54, 56n.20, 64, 73, 86n.12, 109, 111–12, 134–5, 150, 176
Structure of the Artistic Text, The (Lotman) 87n.22
subjectivity 112, 121, 134, 137–8, 144, 149, 153n.17, 187
superorganism 139
Suvin, Darko 56n.18
Swan Book, The (Wright) 11, 20, 90, 93, 98, 103
Swan Lake (Tchaikovsky) 100
Switzerland 142
Sydney 115
symbolic reading 20, 90, 101, 103–4
Szeman, Imre 25

Talmy, Leonard 85n.4
Tchaikovsky, Pyotr Ilyich
  Swan Lake (Tchaikovsky) 100
technology
  advancement 30
  algorithmic 137–8
  augmented body 43
  challenges 133
  computational 130, 136, 138, 166
  control 44
  development 14
  device 149
  digital 33
  of enchantment 136
  human 140
  innovations 38, 44
  mobile 133
  progress 28–9, 38, 146, 149, 183
  protean 136
  science and 27, 53
  solutions 29
  unrestricted progress 8
temporality 27, 59, 77, 83–4, 87n.21. *See also* deep time; future
  alternative models 31
  of climate change 32

  in contemporary fiction 40
  experience of 40
  futurity 19, 53
  linear 55n.6
  looping 157
  metaphors of 59, 118
  as metaphysical concept 38
  more-than-human 63
  narrative's entanglement with 31
  scientific models 29
Thatamanil, John 4
Thirty Meter Telescope 131n.15
Thompson, Evan
  Embodied Mind, The 137
Thoreau, Henry David 148
Thoss, Jeff
  When Storyworlds Collide 130n.2
Time and Narrative (Ricoeur) 31
Todorov, Tzvetan 56n.21, 86n.12
transspecies 3, 91
Trexler, Adam 10
  Anthropocene Fictions 11
Tsing, Anna
  Mushroom at the End of the World, The 169
typography 46, 53, 74, 84, 121–3, 128, 132n.22

Ulstein, Gry 130n.3
Ulysses (Joyce) 65
Umwelt 105n.4
uncertainty 2, 25–54, 90–4, 141–5. *See also* embracing uncertainty
  beyond postmodernist time 38–41
  of the climate crisis 13–19
  cyborgs 41–7
  destabilizing the future 28–31
  elimination of 3
  extrinsic 31–5, 37, 48, 163
  fractures 47–54
  future-tense narration 41–7
  intrinsic 31–5
  lack of closure 35–8
  narrative between extrinsic and intrinsic futures 31–5
  parallel storyworlds 47–54
  phenomenology of 16
  reduction of 14
  rise of 35–8

types 161–3
unconscious cognition 138
Unit Operations (Bogost) 180n.3
unknowable minds 90
unnatural narratology 56n.27, 66–7, 85n.9. *See also* narratology
unreadable characters.
   See unknowable minds
unspatialization 64
unstable spatiality 59–85
   destabilizing storyworlds 64–8
   erasure 73–5
   floating 78–85
   fragmentation 75–8
   oscillation 68–73
Unthought (Hayles) 137

VanderMeer, Ann 56n.28, 85n.9
VanderMeer, Jeff 12, 22n.15, 53–4, 56n.28, 57n.34, 64, 96, 98–9, 101–2, 104, 105n.2
   Annihilation 63, 69, 72
   Borne 51–2, 57n.33, 94–5
   Dead Astronauts 19, 27, 47, 51, 57n.32, 94
   Strange Bird, The 20, 57n.33, 90, 93–4, 102–3
Varela, Francisco
   Embodied Mind, The 137
Velleman, David 23n.19
Vermeulen, Pieter 13, 22n.4, 55n.5
   Literature and the Anthropocene 12
Vervaeck, Bart 6–7
video game 1, 16, 21, 146, 155, 157, 158–63, 178–9. *See also* interactive narrative; interactivity
virus 125–126. *See also* Covid-19
visual narrative 63. *See also* narrative(s)
von Mossner, Alexa Weik 9, 77, 91, 105n.8
von Uexküll, Jakob 105n.4

Wald, Priscilla 56n.18
Walker, Boulous 132n.20
Walking Dead, The (video game) 159–60
Walsh, Richard 22n.4, 27, 56n.17
Walton, Kendall 161
Waugh, Patricia 107
Weather (Offill) 21, 185–9
weird fiction 12, 19, 23n.15, 51, 56n.28, 64, 69, 70, 85n.9, 90, 94, 130n.3, 163–4
weird realism 85n.9
What Algorithms Want (Finn) 135–6
When Storyworlds Collide (Thoss) 130n.2
White, Lynn 8, 152n.10
Wilson, Deirdre 56n.17
Wittgenstein, Ludwig
   Philosophical Investigations 71
Woelert, Peter 59
Wolf, Werner 130n.5
Woods, Derek 49, 60
Woolf, Virginia
   Flush: A Biography 91
world disruption 36
World Health Organization 3, 186
World of Tomorrow (Hertzfeldt) 181n.16
Wright, Alexis 102, 104, 105n.2
   Carpentaria 98–9
   Swan Book, The 11, 20, 90, 93, 98–9, 103
Wyoming 75, 76

Yanagihara, Hanya
   People in the Trees, The 19, 63, 79, 81–2, 84, 87n.22
Yeats, William Butler 100

Zapf, Hubert 5
Zimmerman, Eric
   Rules of Play 158
Zunshine, Lisa 92

www.ingramcontent.com/pod-product-compliance
Lightning Source LLC
Chambersburg PA
CBHW062221300426
44115CB00012BA/2166